B LIPPA
Lippa, Katherine, 1973-,
Hiding in water

Hiding in Water

Hiding in Water:
A Memoir Based Mostly in Reality

Katherine Lippa

Brain Trust Books
Portland, Maine

BRAIN TRUST BOOKS EDITION 2013

HIDING IN WATER. Copyright © 2013 by Katherine Lippa.

All rights reserved. No part of this book may be reproduced or transmitted in any form or by any means, including electronic, mechanical, or storage and retrieval system, without permission from the publisher.
Brain Trust Books
P.O. Box 330
Portland, Maine 04112
www.braintrustbooks.com

PRINTED IN THE UNITED STATES OF AMERICA

Grateful acknowledgment is made for use of the following:
"Snapping Turtle's All Wrong Day." Words by Peggy Parish, pictures by John E. Johnson.
"How the West Was Really Won." Words and music by Grace Hawthorne and John F. Wilson.
"The Diary of a Young Girl." Anne Frank.
1982 letter from Samantha Smith to Yuri Andropov.
1982 letters (two) from Yuri Andropov.
1982 letter from Samantha Smith to U.S. Soviet Ambassador.
1983 speech by Samantha Smith at the Children's International Symposium held in Kobe, Japan.
"Now I Lay Me Down to Sleep." 18th century bedtime prayer.
1802 letter from Thomas Jefferson to Danbury Baptist Assoc.
1985 condolence letter from Mikhail Gorbachev.
1985 condolence letter from Ronald Reagan.
"The Vatican Rag." Words and music by Tom Lehrer.
"The Star-Spangled Banner." Words by Francis Scott Key, music by John Stafford Smith.
"Miracle on 34th Street." 20th Century Fox, 1947.
"Mother." Words and music by John Lennon.
"Sybil." Lorimar Productions, 1976.

ISBN 978-0-9887882-0-6
LCCN: 2013930998
10 9 8 7 6 5 4 3 1 2

Contents

Introduction
Prologue 1
Why He Killed the Mouse 9
Why the Grass Isn't Always Greener 19
Why Living in a Dugout Is Hard 27
Why the Hostages Were Released 34
Why She Wanted to Be Her 39
Why She Tried to Jump Off the Bridge 44
Why She Wrote to the Evil Empire 57
Why She Couldn't Swim 61
Why the Hostages Really Were Released 69
Why Santa Didn't Visit 73
Why Spiders Don't Make Good Magnets 87
Why She Wanted a Buick 95
Why She Wanted a Stalker 102
Why He Threw the Knife 105
Why the Curtains Had to Be Closed 111
Why You Can't Step in the River Once 116
Why the Glass Needs to Be Tipped Degrees 122
Why the Harris Tweed Got Ruined 137
Why Their Birthdates Were So Close 149
Why She Wished Her Dead 155
Why She Knew She Would Be Punished 159

Why He Destroyed Her Treasured Thing   163
Why She Gave Her the Bolt Lock   168
Why it's Okay If You Do It   173
Why God Is a Mafia Kingpin   182
Why She Was a Spoiled Brat   189
Why He Called Himself God   196
Why She Picked Up the Hitchhiker   200
Why the Hostages Really, Really Were Released   203
Why She Screamed   208
Why Her Body Was a Punchbowl   214
Why She Didn't Kill Herself   224
Why Anne Frank Saved Her   226
Why He No Longer Frightened Her   231
Why There Should Be Three   234
Why They Shouldn't Die Alone   239
Why Permanent Marker Is Not for Declarations   243
Why She Was Braver   251
Why It Pays to Be Poor   257
Why She Let Him Go   269
Why the Water Was Invisible   274
Acknowledgements
About the Author

Introduction

The memoir has replaced the first novel. One might even say that I had a literary imperative to share this story. ...I don't say that. In fact, before writing *Hiding in Water* I had to ask myself: am I really so self-absorbed to think anyone would be interested in my life as a kid growing up in Maine in the '80s, whose father claimed to be a prophet from another planet, and who believed that she had psychic powers? The answer, I must admit, is yes I am indeed that self-absorbed. The purpose of *Hiding in Water*, however, is to use that unique platform to share discoveries about our world and who we are in it.

Once I decided the story was of value, I was faced with the technical issues of telling it. There is something inherently fallible in the craft of memoir. After all, how am I to remember the exact words spoken in conversations that took place between two and three decades ago? So to begin the process of writing this book, I spent three years asking questions of those with whom I had the conversations or who, at the very least, were present for them; I looked through legal and medical documents; I confirmed my memory of the weather on any given day with meteorology reports. Overall, I was relieved to find that my recollections matched up with the facts as well as the remembrances of others. And then there was that journal...kept in pristine condition save for the odor of a book that has been tucked away in a box, in a basement, in a house for many years; the rose printed cloth cover still as clean as the day I first wrote on its pages. This journal, that I began at age ten and finished at age fourteen, forms much of the basis for *Hiding in Water*.

The subtitle of the book, *A Memoir Based Mostly in Reality*, has a double meaning. It is my acknowledgment that even with all my keen research, there may be times when I remember events in a way that is different from the memories of others involved. I have done my best to remain objective; still there may be moments when others would disagree with my interpretation. The second meaning of the subtitle has to do with a main theme of the book, reconciling belief with reality: belief in ourselves, in others, in our chosen religions, and even in those who lead our countries.

Prologue

According to my father, my parents met in "some religious organization." According to my mother, they met in a cult. The Holy Order of MANS (plural) was founded in San Francisco in the late 1960's. MANS was an acronym, which at the time was known only to the inner circle of the group. The members of the outer circle must have been left to guess its meaning. *Maybe it's "mastering the art of nothingness."* No that can't be it. *How about "mandatory abdication of normal society?"* Probably not. In fact, it stood for 'Mysterion, Agape, Nous, Sophia,' Greek for mystery, love, mind, and wisdom.

My father, Matthew, was one of the group's founding members. He had been raised in a Jewish household, and though religious law decreed that he was Jewish no matter what, he had displayed an early defiance of tradition. His Bar Mitzvah, the ceremony in which boys participate when they reach age thirteen and become accountable for their actions, lasted only a few minutes. Matthew refused to read aloud from the Torah and walked out. Instead, he entered the fold of adulthood by exploring multiple religions. Inasmuch as Matthew was a spiritual student, he also served a practical purpose for the Holy Order of MANS, building structures like the altar by which lessons were taught and prayers were prayed.

The leader was a man named Earl Blighton, a cult

entrepreneur and former social worker and engineer who had served as an apprentice in other successful groups and then began his own movement. Blighton ordained himself a Science of Man minister and called himself alternately 'Father' Blighton and 'Master Paul,' a name chosen because of the group's adoption of certain apostolic Catholic, or Pauline Catholic, rituals and hierarchy. The Father/Master taught his brand of mysticism to those who had grown weary of the hippie lifestyle and who were searching for a new path to enlightenment. Telepathic training was considered the norm. Spiritual illumination had as much to do with understanding the Universe as it did the belief that with practice one could levitate, become temporarily invisible, and develop the power to move objects with one's mind.

My mother was avoiding her cloistered East Coast family and seeking out individuals she considered to be more open-minded. San Francisco was a whole new world to her. The counterculture explosion there was exciting and liberating. Young people bucked authority and re-imagined the American Dream. Artists created huge papier-mâché animals and attached them to buildings. My mother, an artist herself, dropped acid and watched a crocodile crawl down the exterior of an apartment. When she ran out of money, she found the Holy Order of MANS, or HOOM as it was called by insiders. For my father, HOOM was a true avocation. For my mother, it seemed to be a good place to stay, among intellectuals and the spiritual elite.

The group did some good as well. It purchased houses and filled them with homeless kids from the area. Each young person had to get a job, and the proceeds from that job would go to the organization, which would in turn provide food, shelter and spiritual teachings. In July of 1968, Matthew became the first student to be ordained to mastery. He was appointed to house leader and, encouraged by Blighton and his wife, 'Mother' Blighton, my parents married shortly thereafter. He proposed to my mother with a beautiful ring inscribed, *I love you Elizabeth, for always*. My mother's name is Martha.

In 1969, Blighton announced his intention to revise the order's vow ceremony so that a member's commitment would be for life. Prior to that, commitment was until a person had reached "spiritual maturity." As Matthew intended to start a movement of his own, this would not do. He argued against the revision, and when Blighton refused to reconsider, Matthew led his household in a revolt against the measure.

Blighton did not tolerate any challenges to his authority and removed Matthew from his position as house leader and sent him on a mission to Hawaii to purchase a new property. Martha, who had grown to dislike other aspects of the order (such as how the homeless kids could never get a leg up because all of their money went to HOOM) left with her new husband. In Hawaii, once they called to check in, they were told that they had been expelled from the order and added to the 'banned' list. For HOOM members, this was akin to a sentence of spiritual death.

My parents didn't have enough money to leave Hawaii, so they stayed. My brother, Michael, was born later that year. Most of the locals thought Michael was a Hawaiian baby girl. His lashes were long and thick, and his skin was dark and smooth. In fact, he was simply a combination of Martha's Italian side and Matthew's Russian and Polish lineage.

My parents lived in Hawaii for three years and then moved to Martha's home state of Maine where I was born on June 10th, 1973. It is often said by visitors that Maine feels like its own country. On the one hand, the state has a shockingly limited amount of diversity (in fact, for years it has led the nation in least amount of people of color). On the other hand, only in Maine can you be within one hundred miles of Denmark, Peru and China. That is, Denmark, Peru and China, Maine. Many of the towns are named after countries, including Norway, Sweden, Poland and Mexico. The state also boasts the most stolen and replaced sign in the country, which points to all of these various worldwide namesakes.

Maine is much like other states that rely on the tourist industry, in that we generally dislike tourists. *Come to Maine. Shop at LL Bean. Eat our lobster. But don't talk to us. ...In fact, could you just leave your wallet on the counter and go home? We'll send it back to you after tourist season.* In some ways, Maine was a perfect fit for Matthew, who generally liked to keep his distance from other people unless he was selling them something or teaching them something. Martha designed the house they built in the small country town of Limington. As they were the first residents on the newly bulldozed dirt road, they were given the privilege of naming it. Matthew decided on *Lippaline Lane*.

Together, my parents built a successful business called Dabble Art. Theirs was the start of a popular trend of color-in posters. Martha would draw elaborate black-and-white illustrations of sea adventures, gods and goddesses, forest scenes, and various other-worldly designs. Matthew would package copies of the prints with a set of markers and a clever marketing ploy that reflected the spirit of the times: "Designed for people of all ages, sizes, shapes and colors." Once their products started becoming successful, a larger West Coast company called Doodle Art was formed with the intention of purchasing Dabble Art and expanding. When my parents declined, their new competitor sought to employ a team of artists who could draw similarly to my mother.

Matthew was a natural salesman. He could ask the right questions and be convincing enough so that a prospect would believe they would make a great deal of money by selling Dabble Art posters. If he was unable to persuade a business owner to carry the posters, he would be annoying enough so that they would accept a few just to make him go away. He was dogged in his approach. He went to every store, every craft show, every fair and festival. He even went so far as to travel to New York, where he worked tradeshows.

During one weekend, a gentleman with a Metropolitan Museum of Art badge strolled by the Dabble Art booth more than once. After the third or fourth walk-by, Matthew stopped the man and asked what had brought him there. He told Matthew that the museum was looking for an artist to paint a mural in their lobby. Martha's drawings were exactly the style for which they were looking. Excited, Matthew called Martha to tell her. Her response was absolute. "Matt, I can't go to New York to paint a mural. I've got two little kids to look after." The matter was dropped.

A year later, Martha did ask Matthew to look after her two kids, but it wasn't to paint a mural. She had always had a difficult relationship with her own father, but when he was experiencing a painful and lingering death, she made the three-hour round trip drive every day to spend time with him. She asked Matthew to feed her children and her pet hamster. He agreed. She returned home one night to find that the hamster was dead in its cage and nearly skeletal. Martha asked Matthew if he had fed it at all. He looked up from his newspaper, and spoke with a deliberate tone: "Martha, you never loved your father anyway, so why should I take care of your hamster while you're in a hospital room waiting for him to die?" He resumed reading.

The marriage continued until 1978, when Matthew

had divorce papers served on Martha. She was in her own hospital room having a nervous breakdown when the documents arrived. Before the divorce, my brother Michael and I had been a real team. At seven and four years old respectively, we jumped off of banisters together pretending to be superheroes; we hid dinner peas under the sofa that Martha had built (which had a rise eight inches off the floor); we feigned ignorance together even though those peas were clearly visible to Matthew; when we were upset about minor disappointments, we packed a trunk together and told Martha we were running away; we decided together to stay when she tempted us with molasses cookies, made with our great-grandmother's special recipe. A shift between us began on the night our parents told us they were getting a divorce.

Anyone who has experienced a divorce has a divorce story. Mine goes like this: Michael and I were watching a Dr. Seuss special, though I kept looking over my shoulder, aware of our parents' hushed conversation in the dining area. They approached us, sat down and broke the news, assuring us that it wasn't our fault. Michael turned back to the television and stared silently into the screen. I asked lots of questions and, over the course of the discussion, repeated one question four times to Matthew: "Are you going to stay in Maine?" He answered each time that he would remain until both Michael and I graduated high school, but his eyes became more averted each time he said it. I suspected he was lying. Between questions I looked at Michael, wondering why he wasn't saying anything.

A couple of days later Michael announced to me, "We have to be better so that Mom and Dad will stay together." I couldn't figure out why he would suggest that the problems of these adults were because of something we had done. I thought maybe he had missed some of the conversation because he had turned to the television while I had asked questions. I felt sad for my older brother that he thought this mess was our fault, but I couldn't bring myself to contradict him. "Okay," I said.

Despite our best efforts, the divorce was finalized and Martha moved my brother and me to the suburb of South Portland, Maine. She chose the town because of the superior schools, even though it had been a dream of hers to live in the countryside. Matthew moved to a nearby town.

By the time I started elementary school I was aware that there were many religions and beliefs in my family. Matthew seemed most interested in his own supernatural version of Sufism (which he called "the friendly branch of Islam"). Martha alternated between Agnostic and "spiritual but not religious" (although she had a portrait of the Madonna and Child near her bed and occasionally prayed to rosary beads). Her mother, whom we called Tu-Tu, was a Fundamentalist Christian, which meant she took the Bible literally but did not ascribe to any particular denomination. My Uncle Brian and his wife were Baptists. My Uncle Anthony and his wife were Catholic, although his wife was interested in Transcendental Meditation (or TM), much to Tu-Tu's dismay. My father's family was made up of Reform and Conservative Jews. There was also a Quaker and an Atheist or two in the mix. I didn't understand much of what these beliefs meant. All I knew was that each representative wanted their piece of me. The battle for my spiritual well-being had begun.

Chapter 1
Why He Killed the Mouse

My entire backside was on fire. Just hours earlier, I had left the campsite to pee and now itchy red patches had begun to form between my legs, on my bottom and up my spine. I couldn't stop scratching. "Dad, what's wrong with me?" I screamed out in a panic. I exploded out of the tent that I shared with my brother, Michael, and ran to Matthew's open van, where he was setting up a small wooden and wire contraption the size of an index card.

After inspecting me, he said sympathetically, "Oh Katie. You wiped yourself with a poison ivy leaf."

"I've been poisoned? Am I going to die?" I was six.

"No sweetie. But we're going to need to get you some calamine lotion."

As I lie face down in the tent, Matthew spread the lotion on my back. It soothed but did not alleviate the problem. "I still itch."

"This is the perfect opportunity to use your mind, just like we've talked about before."

"What do you mean?"

"You can use your mind to control the spread of the rash, Katie. You just have to take control of your body and believe that you can do it."

"Do I need the calamine then?"

"For now, yes. Until you're able to train your body to heal itself."

"Would you need the calamine?"

I could hear the smile in his voice. "No. I wouldn't. But I've had a lot of practice."

I squirmed. "It's so itchy, Daddy."

"The sensation of itching is in your mind, Katie," Matthew said as he spread more of the pink salve on me. "You have control over it. You have the choice as to whether or not you feel discomfort. You can choose to concentrate on the sensation your body is giving your brain. Or you can choose to feel something else. What do you want to choose?"

"I want to choose not to feel itchy."

"Good. I want you to breathe in and out slowly. In and out." I followed instructions. "Now as you breathe in and out, I want you to imagine that your whole body is breathing. Every part of your body is taking in oxygen. And as you let out the air, you make the *decision* not to feel itchy, not to feel irritation of any kind." After a few minutes he asked, "Do you feel better?"

As I let out a breath, I nodded that I did. I didn't, but the desire of a child to please a parent far outweighs the most palpable of itches.

When Matthew took us on camping trips or let us visit him at his nearby rental house, his parenting style was based on the premise that all people have a psychic nature and that with special training, a child can harness and build on those abilities. I was a willing participant in the experiment, spending much of my time, energy and emotion in an extreme version of 'magical thinking.'

According to Matthew, being psychic or telepathic or able to speak with people who have died wasn't exactly the goal. It was more like a natural byproduct of the kinds of spiritual principles he told me that he had mastered and that I was on my way to learning. To me, however, the idea of having magical powers was the most interesting part of being enlightened. I saw this as my opportunity to be special, and I very much wanted to be special.

Once the calamine lotion dried, I sat up and asked, "What were you doing when I came up to the van?"

Matthew let out a snort, and his face grew hard. "I was setting up a mousetrap."

My body stiffened. "A mousetrap? Why?"

"There's a mouse in the van."

In a strained voice I asked, "And you're going to kill it?" My palms began to sweat.

"A mouse may not seem like a big deal, Katie, but a little thing can cause a lot of damage."

"But why do you have to kill it? Why can't you just shoo it out?"

His tone was firm. "No."

"Well, can't we get one of those traps that don't kill the mouse?"

"Those traps are expensive. I'm not spending money to save the life of a rodent."

"Well, you can use the allowance money you gave me. I've saved all of it from this summer. That's a dollar a week, and we've been here for five weeks already."

"No."

"Please, Daddy, don't kill it."

"We're not discussing it any further, Katie. Now, go help Michael gather some firewood for tonight."

That night we played the Folded Paper Game, which was really for my benefit as the suffering itchy one, since Michael was never too interested in it. The game was something Matthew had invented. "I'm going to write something down on a piece of paper and then fold it up. Then you're going to close your eyes, and we're going to be quiet for a few minutes. Then you're going to tell me what you see."

The idea was that by being silent and focusing my breath and mind, I could visualize whatever it was that Matthew had written on the paper. Mostly I didn't see anything close to what was written down, but that night I saw a forest. When I told Matthew, he excitedly responded, "The word is *tree*. Look." I gasped as he unfolded the paper and I saw the word "tree" written in black ink. There was no consideration given to the possibility that I might have been influenced by being *in* a forest at the time. There was simply the accolade for my success. I was thrilled.

The next morning when I awoke in the tent, my first thought was about the mouse. My second thought was about the itching. I walked quickly to the van to see that Matthew was already awake and up. He had slept in the back of the vehicle, which he had converted into a sturdy bed. "Did you get the mouse?" I asked, worried.

Matthew responded with a deep, aggravated tone. "No. Not yet."

The next morning was the same. More worry about the mouse, more itching, more annoyance from Matthew.

Then, on the third morning, I awoke with a feeling that was different than worry. It was more like a feeling of inevitable disappointment. There was a lump in my throat, and my chest was tight and achy; it was hard to take deep breaths. I opened the tent and lumbered slowly to the van. As I got closer, Matthew appeared in the doorway, his face bright. In a half-whisper, I asked, "Did you get the mouse?"

"Got 'em," he said with a smile.

After a pause I asked, "Can I bury him?"

Matthew responded in a cheery voice. "I threw him out already."

After a few hours of moping around about the mouse, I decided to look at the bright side. After all, my feeling of dread on that third morning must mean that my psychic trainings were coming along and that, with practice, I could have the same kinds of magical powers Matthew had. Of course, I wanted to be spiritually enlightened too; but the God that I knew was also the one introduced to me by my father. That God could best be described as a sort of genie without a bottle who would give me my world's desires if I only prayed correctly.

...

WHEN MICHAEL AND I returned to Martha's house at the end of the summer, both of us with matted hair and staph infections (and I with dirt-filled scabs) it was not surprising that our mother seemed baffled by our loyalty toward our father. Mine, especially, was fervent and unswerving. Despite the upsets, the poison ivy, the dead mouse, and a few occasions when I had been left alone at the campsite and woke up afraid, I raved with great enthusiasm about the summer. As my mother gave me my first bath in three months and attempted to untangle my hair, I spoke excitedly about how Matthew had taught us to light survival fires in the woods, how he had given me a hatchet for my sixth birthday, and how he had presented me with a plaque he had ordered that read 'World's Best Dishwasher' to thank me for all the dishes I had washed.

A few weeks later, Matthew, Michael and I were playing Frisbee in the park. It was a hot, early September day, and Michael and Matthew both took off their shirts. Perturbed, I said, "It's not fair that girls aren't allowed to take off their shirts but boys and men can."

Matthew flicked the Frisbee smoothly in the air toward

Michael. "So take off your shirt."

I was jarred at the very idea of stripping my top half naked, even though that's precisely the right for which I was arguing. "I don't want to. I just think it's not fair that I can't."

With his eye on the Frisbee zipping his way, Matthew said, "You can do whatever you want to, Katie. You don't have to follow every one of society's rules just because they're rules."

"Well, I think I'll keep it on for now. Thanks though."

Matthew chuckled.

After a while, I had to pee. It seemed I always had to pee. "Dad, I need to use the bathroom."

"There isn't a bathroom anywhere near here. Just go in the bushes."

I looked toward the bushes and saw that there wasn't much coverage from anyone who might pass that way. I imagined poison ivy leaves and got a phantom itch on my bum. I remembered all that itchiness and how angry Martha was when she had to scrub dirt out of my scabs and how they had opened back up and bled. My throat felt constricted. "I don't want to."

"Well, we're not leaving just so you can use a bathroom."

"When are we leaving then?"

Matthew shrugged as he eyed the Frisbee coming toward him. He leapt at it, catching it in his fingertips. "I don't know. Maybe half an hour."

"Just use the bushes, Katie," Michael called from several yards away.

"I don't want to," I retorted. I glanced around to see if anyone else was nearby enough to know that we were talking about my bathroom needs. "And stay out of it. I was talking to Dad, not you."

By the time we got back to Matthew's rental house, my bladder was bursting and I was angry. I stormed into his bathroom, relieved myself and then went directly to his medicine cabinet. I knew that his contact lenses were expensive, and I grabbed the case where they were stored. I studied them for a moment, thinking about what I could do that would upset him. With great indignation, I placed the left contact behind the commode, and I ripped the right one in half. Then I exited the bathroom as if I were just the sweetest little six-year-old in the whole wide world.

Shortly thereafter, Matthew found the contact case with the one ripped lens. He was furious. "Which one of you did this?" he demanded. I hadn't thought so far ahead as to imagine the repercussions of my actions, and I started to regret them immediately. "Well? Which one of you did this?" he asked again.

I bit my lip and looked up at Matthew with wide eyes. Michael glanced up from the television just long enough to say, "I don't even know what you're talking about, Dad."

Matthew turned off the set and then loomed over my brother. "One of my contacts is missing, and the other is ripped in half."

I started feeling even worse as it became obvious that Michael was getting the focus of the inquisition. I didn't feel *so* bad, however, that I was willing to fess up.

Matthew turned in my direction. "Did you do this, Katie?"

"No," I said in a meek, ashamed tone.

"Well who did it? ...One of you better tell me, or neither of you will ever get allowance again."

As soon as money was on the line, I figured I'd better act fast. "I'll go look for your other contact." I went to the bathroom and knelt down by the commode. After a brief search, I found the contact and then began practicing how I would tell him about the discovery and still sound innocent of the charges. Then I carried out the lens to Matthew and with some tentativeness said, "Here's the other one, Daddy."

Matthew looked at me circumspectly. "You just...found this, huh?"

"Yes."

He was clearly still frustrated, but now he also sounded confused and concerned. "Katie, did you do this?"

"No," I said quietly. I looked him directly in the eyes while I lied because I knew that liars look away.

I sat back down next to my brother, and Matthew turned to the both of us, repeating, "One of you better confess, or you won't see another allowance." Michael and I sat in silence. I knew it was wrong of me to destroy Matthew's property and allow him to suspect that Michael could have been the culprit. Even then, however, I was able to come up with a good half-dozen justifications for it. After all, we are all right in our own minds.

...

ON NOVEMBER 8th, 1979, just days after sixty-six Americans were taken hostage in Iran, ABC began airing nightly updates in an 11:30PM show entitled *The Iran Crisis: America Held Hostage*. The show would soon become *Nightline*, hosted by Ted Koppel, and although it aired well after my bedtime, snippets of it also played during the regular evening news program. As a news-watching household, my mother's living room was filled with images of blindfolded hostages and burned-out helicopters after a doomed rescue attempt. It was gripping and frightening. The politics behind it were all very complicated, and I didn't grasp most of it. It seemed that it was somehow connected with the Cold War with the Soviets, but I didn't understand how. What was clear to me was that we were all at risk of being captured and tortured, and at any time the Cold War could get hot, bringing an end to...everything.

Katherine Lippa

The iciness between Martha and Matthew was growing as well. While visions of hostages danced in my head, Matthew told my brother and me that he was leaving Maine for a few months to ride his bike across country and do some camping. Martha said he was leaving because he had put a printer out of business by not paying a twenty-thousand dollar charge. I knew he was leaving for good. Children are smarter than most adults think they are.

By the end of November, thirteen hostages were released, leaving behind a total of fifty-three Americans whom I imagined wanted nothing better than to get back to their families. On Thanksgiving Day, 1979, Matthew arrived at Martha's house in South Portland to say goodbye to his own. After the formalities, Martha and Michael went into the living room, resigned to what was happening. I was angry with both of them for giving up. I stayed in the kitchen with Matthew, sat on his foot and clung to his leg, pleading with him not to leave.

"I have to go," he said. After several minutes of begging and clutching Matthew with all my might, he tugged my arms away from him and patted me on the head. I couldn't bear to look at him as he walked out of the house. Instead, I sat slumped in a pile on the linoleum floor with my face buried in my hands, hoping that he would see my desperation and stay. A moment later I heard his vehicle pull out of the driveway. I decided then that I had better be grateful for what I have on Thanksgiving because I would never know when it would be taken away.

Before Christmas, I asked Santa to return my father and the hostages. When neither happened, I assumed that I hadn't asked in the right way. I had to learn the correct way to ask, the correct way to pray, the correct way to focus my breath in order to have my dreams fulfilled. Grown-ups, it seemed, would be under no obligation to protect me. Grown-ups could hold people hostage in foreign countries. Grown-ups could leave or ask me to leave at any time. I had to figure out a way to be on my own.

On a quiet winter evening, I observed Martha from behind the living room sofa, seeking out any similarities in our appearances. She was full-figured; I was slight. Her eyes were perfectly set, large and brown, like Michael's eyes; mine were downturned in the corners, giving them a droopy appearance. Her heart-shaped face was the ideal size to compliment her Romanesque nose; my face was long and thin. She looked tired; I felt tired.

I leaned over the top of the sofa and told her with great determination, "I don't want to grow up."

"Why not?" she asked with a perplexed look on her face.

"Because I see what you adults do."

Chapter 2
Why the Grass Isn't Always Greener

I managed my schooldays as best I could. I had a crush on a boy who was nice to me in private but unkind whenever anyone else was around. I didn't have many friends, but I did have some peers who allowed me to assist them with projects, and that pleased me. In first grade art class one day, while helping one of my classmates mix paint, a student a few desks away asked another, "Are you going to CCD this afternoon?" I didn't know what CCD was, but the question grabbed my attention.

The other student replied with an enthusiastic, "Yep." Then another said she was going, and then two more said they couldn't make it but were planning to be there the following week.

As soon as Martha got home from work, I ran into the kitchen to greet her. "Mom, I want to go to CCD."

Martha peeled off her jacket with a furrowed brow. "Where did you hear about CCD?"

"At school. Can I go?"

"You're not going to CCD, Katie."

"But a bunch of the kids are going," I whined. I very much wanted to be accepted by the other kids.

"Katie, it's not a party. It's church."

"What do you mean?"

"CCD stands for Confraternity of Christian Doctrine. It's a church program for kids."

"Oh." I was stumped. Martha's mother, Tu-Tu, had taken me to church before, and I had found it so confusing and boring that I couldn't figure out why any kids would willingly go there. "But they seem really excited about going."

Martha opened the refrigerator and took out her two-liter of Diet Pepsi. "I don't know what to tell you, Katie. Maybe they get cookies while they're there. But trust me, it's church."

I didn't want to go to church, and Martha wasn't going to allow it anyway, so I supposed I'd better forget about it.

...

A FEW MONTHS of Matthew being gone turned in to seven months, during which time I grew increasingly anxious for his return as well as the return of the hostages. I viewed the hostages' plight as far more dramatic than my own, but I had made the somewhat anachronous decision that if they were released, my father would come back. I spent my afternoons watching cartoons and trying to *will* the Iranians to release their prisoners.

As Woody Woodpecker antagonized his nemesis, Ms. Meany, my mind got lost in the desert. I took deep breaths, focusing all of my energy on those fifty-three Americans, imagining myself talking directly to their captors: "I command you to release the hostages." I repeated the order in my head over and over until I believed my goal was accomplished, snapping out of my trance only for the pivotal task of going to the refrigerator to look for a snack. It was empty except for some apples and Martha's Diet Pepsi. At first I was annoyed, but that feeling was quickly followed by a sense of guilt. The hostages surely had less to eat than I did; I ought not to complain. I kept an eye on the evening news to ensure the success of my mental mission. When the hostages were not released, I chalked it up to not being focused enough, and I began the process again.

Matthew returned for a brief visit in the summer of 1980. During this time, one hostage was released from Iran, bringing the number down to fifty-two. I took this as a sign to mean that I could guiltlessly forget about those left behind as Matthew took Michael and me around to some Maine campsites. Every road trip with Matthew began with him leading us in a long, drawn out "Weeee're off." Michael and I watched him with great admiration as he read the newspaper while simultaneously maneuvering the steering wheel and stroking his dark, bushy beard. Whenever we traveled Interstate-95, he would ask if we wanted to take off on an impromptu trip to Florida. Michael and I laughed at what sounded like an impossible invitation.

Our travels included a visit to Acadia National Park, which Matthew dubbed 'Katie's National Park' and where my favorite activity was lying in beds of moss and staring up at the sky. I pictured myself walking atop the clouds and then traveling into space on a shuttle, heading to the edges of the Universe. Matthew had told me that the Universe was infinite, and that infinite meant "it goes on forever." I had memorized the planets from a *Life Magazine* special edition Martha had given me, and I imagined myself zooming past them. First, the fiery sun, then cratered Mercury, golden Venus, and then our blue-green Earth. I would take a long time to travel the moon in my mind, sometimes stepping on it as the astronauts had done the year Michael was born. I would fly past the rest of the planets, making a stop to dance on Saturn's rings. Then I would head farther into space, traveling into a darkness speckled by stars and planets that had never been seen by any explorer before me. I would reach an edge of the picture in my mind and think, 'No, the Universe is bigger than that.' I would expand the image. Again, I would hit an edge. 'It's bigger than *that*.' On and on until the dreaminess grew into a frustration over not being able to understand just how the Universe could exist as something that did not have a beginning or an end. My mind wanted to wrap around the concept, but it was always out of reach.

Lying on the moss with Matthew, I asked him the kinds of questions that children ask: Why is the sky blue? What makes a cloud? Why do we see the sun in the day and not the night? And then I asked other questions: Why can't I picture the whole Universe? Why is it that I haven't been able to move an object with my mind yet? Am I really psychic?

"Yes, you are, Katie," Matthew responded. "You just have to give it time. You can't expect to be able to levitate or move things with your mind so early on. It takes practice." He explained that people only use a small percentage of their brains and that was why I couldn't imagine the whole Universe. "When you're able to develop the use of more of your brain, like I have, you'll be able to do those things." I wanted to use *all* of my brain.

Michael pulled me aside one afternoon to tell me, "I know you took Dad's contacts last year." I looked down at the ground and kicked the dirt at my feet. "You have to tell him, or he's never going to give us allowance again." Michael and I were both very concerned about money, so I agreed it would be best to tell the truth and get our allowance back. Matthew was very nice about it. It was obvious he already knew; it seemed that he was just glad I had finally confessed. Best of all, he gave us each a dollar for the week. Michael got a few extra dollars for some of the weeks he had lost, which made me feel better about not having said something sooner.

By the end of the visit, Matthew had gathered some new

followers who came to our campsite several times to hear him speak. They wore raggedy clothes and smelled of stale sweat, but then, so did Matthew. Although Michael and I were instructed to keep quiet during these visits, it seemed to me that just by being his daughter my rank was elevated. Those looking on seemed to agree. "How does it feel to be the daughter of a prophet?" one of them asked me at the end of a meeting.

I didn't know what a prophet was, but I could tell by the man's inflection that he thought it was something good. "I like it," I said with a smile.

Matthew called our guests "students" and "disciples." I had heard Martha's mother, Tu-Tu, use the word disciples when talking about the people who followed Jesus, so it didn't surprise me when Matthew spoke of seeing his disciples "through Christ's eyes." I felt proud and excited to be a part of something so important.

Matthew told of how everyone on the planet was once psychic and had powers but that "as the world became more solid this was lost by the inhabitants." He said that because people like him and the people following him were evolving, they were able to "get back" some of their magical talents. Then he said something particularly exciting to me: "We can see this more readily in the young child. There is more vision and hearing of adjacent planes." Planes, he had told me, were the different levels of being. A lower plane was the stuff that happened on the earth, the day-to-day tasks like grocery shopping and going to school. The higher planes were about magical powers and what made the Universe infinite.

As I looked on with my smile beaming, he told the group, "It is easier for the younger person, especially before the age of seven to be aware intuitively." This, I thought, must be why I was so special to him, why I was getting trained. It also affirmed my desire not to ever become a grown-up. After all, the closer I could stay to being a child, the more powers I could grow and maintain.

I looked at Michael, who was listening but seemed not to be enjoying himself as much as I was. He was three and a half years older than I, and to my knowledge had not developed any psychic abilities. I wondered if he had ever tried, or if he had tried and failed. I wondered if he felt disappointed that our father focused his teachings more on me. I was watching Michael as Matthew continued on to tell the group, "Parents never allow their relationship with a child to be broken, even if the child happens to prove unworthy." I watched as Michael's jaw hardened and his eyes became dark slits.

After the disciples left and Michael was off filling water containers, I asked Matthew, "Daddy, what's a prophet?"

He looked at me and gave a half smile. Then after a pause, he said, "It's someone chosen by God to receive a special message, and who then brings that message to other people." It was exhilarating information: *my* father had been chosen, and *I* was the daughter of the chosen.

Before the summer was over, there was one more adventure to be had. Matthew took us to a multi-day rock concert in a big field. Michael and I both enjoyed being left unattended and spent much time running around and meeting new people. After being off by ourselves for too long, however, Matthew grew irritated and put us in his vehicle to "cool out."

While in the front seats, Michael began poking his finger in the dashboard ashtray. He picked up a small, rolled cigarette and said with a serious tone, "Katie, this is grass."

I thought he was referring to the kind of grass on which we had just been running around. "So?"

Michael smiled impishly. "Dad smokes grass."

"Why would he *smoke* grass?"

"It's not that kind of grass, Katie. It's marijuana."

I knew that marijuana was a drug. When I had tagged along to Martha's alcohol recovery support-group meetings, people talked about it being something that could lead to a lot of bad things. To me, being drunk or high meant being out of control, angry, foolish and irresponsible. I became defensive on behalf of Matthew and tried to turn the tables, "Well, how do *you* know it's marijuana, Michael? Do you smoke it?"

Michael thrust the cigarette back into the ashtray. "Shut up, Katie."

Matthew had already dropped us off for the year to Martha's house when Michael told her about the marijuana. She was not pleased. "He can pay for grass, but he can't pay child support?" She stormed around the kitchen raising her voice about all the groceries she couldn't afford on food stamps alone. "He leaves us on Welfare and then goes off to party in the woods."

To be clear, we were not poor. We were *American* poor. And in some ways, we weren't even that. This meant that while we couldn't get everything we wanted on our birthday wish lists, our refrigerator was not always well stocked, and we didn't have the latest clothes, we also had a lovely home in a lovely neighborhood in a lovely state. The down payment had been courtesy of a small inheritance Martha had received when her father died, that she had been able to keep secure from Matthew during the divorce. We even had HBO for a while, until the twelve-dollar per month charge went up to eighteen dollars. It seemed to be the absence of any consistent financial contribution from Matthew that caused such frustration in Martha and, consequently, made me feel that we lacked in a way we shouldn't have.

Martha started working a second job to make ends meet.

She hired a sixteen year-old female sitter to watch us in the afternoons and evenings, and she returned well after Michael and I went to bed. I liked our new companion very much. It was nice to have company that seemed to enjoy spending time with me. Between Michael and me, however, there was somewhat of a tug-of-war for her attention. Arguments would often turn physical, with Michael and me ending up in kicking matches. Our new dog, Molly, a black Pekepoo, would inevitably opt to protect Michael and nip at my legs. I was deeply offended by her alliance with him.

  The sitter warned us that she would tell Martha if we continued our fights, so to win the battle, Michael began setting small fires in the backyard. This got the sitter's attention, but she didn't quite know how to handle it. After a week of trying to restrain Michael from lighting the edge of the house afire, she quit. Martha left the second job so she would be home by the evening instead of late at night.

Chapter 3
Why Living in a Dugout Is Hard

The strain of two difficult children along with single parenthood, particularly during a time when divorce carried a great deal of stigma, wore on Martha. "Why don't you go live with your father?" was an oft repeated question. As I no longer knew where my father was, that seemed a frightening proposition.

    Martha's frustration could only be eased by Dominic, a man she started dating when I was seven, and even then it wasn't eased much. Martha and Dominic met when she worked as a sitter for troubled youth, a fact I found odd since it appeared that both children in her own home were troubled, and it didn't seem like she had a lot of time to be helping other kids. Her charge was a young boy named Mark, a year older than I, whose parents had divorced. At age eight, Mark threatened to kill his mother and locked himself in his bedroom with a knife; it took three days to get him out. Although he tested Martha often, she managed to gain the boy's trust and help him to heal some of the damage done. Commonality of circumstance led her to begin dating Mark's father, Dominic, who then moved in with us.

    Dominic was a kind, portly man with a soft tone. When he gave me a copy of a book entitled *Snapping Turtle's All Wrong Day*, I felt an immediate kinship. It seemed to me that *all* my days were all-wrong ones. My magical powers weren't working as my father said they should, the hostages still hadn't been returned, I had a hard time relating to kids my own age, and I couldn't articulate many of my thoughts and feelings to the adults in my life. I just didn't seem to fit in anywhere, and when I saw the book's title I came to believe that Dominic understood that. It also gave me a bit of inspiration that Snapping Turtle's day eventually righted itself. I read the book countless times.

Later, Dominic gave me a government-issued Woodstock typewriter, which I planned to use to one day write a book. It was a wonderful piece; black and shiny, and almost too heavy for me to lift. I spent long afternoons typing away on it and then un-spooling the cartridge to see my words as a negative against the black ribbon. I mainly used it to write out my God-genie wishes for the world and for myself: "Bring back my Daddy... Make people stop hurting... Give Mom enough money to buy everything she wants." If a wish seemed too personal or unusual, like wishing for the ability to fly, I would tear up the page afterward so that no one would ever see it.

When Dominic's son, Mark, visited, I showed him the *Snapping Turtle* book and the typewriter, and he said, "Yeah, my Dad's really nice." Mark and I got along well and even spent two or three visits "playing doctor." The relative busyness of both of our parents left us time alone to explore. We pulled down our pants, showed off what we had, touched our respective parts together, and that was that. It was the secret of it that we enjoyed more than anything else. Most of our time, though, was spent laughing and talking in ways neither of us seemed to be able to do with others our own age. As much affection as I had for the boy, Michael had the opposite response. They butted heads at every turn, competing and arguing over board games, cartoons and the affections of Dominic and Martha.

...

MARTHA TAUGHT ME to be careful when using the words 'love' and 'hate' because, as she said, "They're overused words in the English language." It did seem that lots of people "loved" things that weren't very loveable. Loving ice cream or the shuffleboard-style board game Rebound, for instance, did seem a bit peculiar. I loved my parents. I loved my teachers, whom I treated as surrogate parents. And I loved being an American child. I thought our flag was the most beautiful of all the flags I had seen, and as far as I was concerned, it was the greatest of honors to be allowed to help fold it after school. As a good American, I also watched the Lone Ranger and Tonto movies whenever they were on television. And, even though I rarely went to baseball games, whenever I did, I always rooted for the home team. Having American pride seemed to help solidify my status as teacher's pet. After all, what teacher doesn't like a little girl who loves her country? I didn't mind that this position seemed to distance me further from the other kids, as they didn't seem too fond of me anyway.

As a second-grader, I was fascinated by the story of the American frontier and viewed it not as a myth of creation but as a factual representation of American know-how and, more importantly, the possibility of striking it rich. When I got a role in the school musical, *How the West Was Really Won*, I practiced my one line ad nauseam. Every spare minute was spent trying out different ways to say, "You think sod houses are bad, you should try living in a dugout in the side of a hill. We don't just have dirt falling through the ceiling, we have cows and wagons and anything else that happens to wander onto the roof." I practiced my dialogue with a Mainer's version of a Southern accent, which I learned from watching reruns of *The Andy Griffith Show*. I spent hours walking up and down our driveway practicing. "You think sod *houses* are bad... You think sod houses are *bad*... You think *sod* houses are bad." It struck me interesting that the same words could be spoken in different ways to achieve an entirely dissimilar effect.

Dominic and Martha came to the play, along with Mark and my brother, who I was told later, kicked one another throughout the first part of the performance and eventually had to be separated. After the show, I became the toast of the school, albeit a very temporary position. Students and even a few teachers and parents asked me to repeat my line over and over. One classmate even came up to me after school, asking me to say it into her clunky tape recorder, which I gladly did.

Afterwards, she announced, "I'm going to keep this for when you're famous." Then she ran off. Suddenly, I recalled a story I had heard about Native Americans who didn't want to be photographed because they believed the camera would steal their soul. I wanted to get the tape back, but I knew it was only a matter of time before the show was forgotten and the kids started calling me "weird" again, so I didn't want to end my popularity early by chasing after the girl and demanding she hand back my soul. I put it out of my mind and dwelled instead on the idea of becoming famous. That idea I liked.

...

MARK AND MICHAEL were playing kickball in the street, using a ball that Dominic had just gifted Mark. I hung monkey-style from a tree in the front yard, having been disallowed from playing due to the fact that I kicked "like a girl." My defense that I *was* a girl and, therefore, it made sense that I kicked like one, had been met with rolled eyes and headshakes.

A car turned the corner and headed up the street, so the boys scooted over to the lawn, with Michael gripping onto the ball. We all watched as the car made its way closer. Just as it was about to pass, however, Michael winged the ball into the middle of the street. The car hit and flattened it under the tires. The driver screeched to a halt and looked in our direction with wide eyes. Mark yelled at Michael, "What did you do that for?" Michael laughed, and the driver shook his head and started up again.

Mark ran into the house and Michael followed after. I closed my eyes and took a deep breath. Then I let go of the tree limb and ambled up the driveway. I was tired of all the arguing and raised voices, even my own. By the time I arrived in the house, Martha and her son were on one side of the kitchen table and Dominic and his son were on the other.

"Michael threw the ball in the street on purpose," Mark yelled.

"No I didn't."

Martha deflected back at Mark. "I doubt it was on purpose, Mark. It had to be an accident"

"I wouldn't be so sure," Dominic said.

I knew it might raise Michael's ire toward me, but Mark was my friend, so I made the decision to speak up. "Mom, I saw what happened."

She spat out her words. "Katie, stay out of this."

Dominic and Martha continued arguing, and I looked at Mark with apologetic eyes. He sighed at me and offered an understanding look. Neither parent budged, and the issue went unresolved.

Later that evening, Michael seemed unusually pleasant, and he invited Mark to play Rebound in his room. I was surprised that Mark said yes, but I thought it was a good sign for our general household relations that he had let bygones be bygones. I followed after them, as I often did, and stood in Michael's open doorway as the boys set up the game on the floor.

Mark had just placed the pieces on the board when, in an instant, Michael grabbed him around the throat with both hands. He slammed Mark against the side of the bed, choking him with all his might. Mark grabbed at Michael's hands but couldn't remove them from his neck.

"Michael, stop," I yelled, petrified and frozen in place.

Michael kept choking. Mark's face turned red and sweaty, and he started making gurgling noises.

I said the only thing I could think of. "Michael, if you don't stop, I'm going to go get Mom."

Michael's hands dropped, and Mark gasped for air and crawled toward me. Michael sat stone-like on the floor and looked at me with dark eyes. "Fucking tattletale. Tell on me, and you'll be next."

That night, Mark stayed in my room. As I set up a sleeping bag on the floor, I apologized for not trying to pull off Michael from him. "I'm sorry. I just didn't know what to do."

"You wouldn't have been able to help. *I* couldn't even get him off me."

"You should show your Dad while you still have the red marks on your neck." He nodded, but I wasn't sure he was going to do it. He seemed scared of what Michael might do if he told. I brought him some toasted white bread with butter, which I knew he liked. It seemed to cheer him up a little.

As soon as I had a moment alone with Martha the next day, I decided to talk with her about what had happened. I wasn't sure I should spill all the beans right away, so I worked my way into it. "Mom, Michael hasn't been very nice to Mark lately."

Her response surprised me. "I don't want you to get too close to Mark."

"Why not?"

"Katie, Mark is a very disturbed boy."

Katherine Lippa

The possibility of not being close with Mark immediately distracted me from my goal of telling her about what Michael had done. "I don't think Mark's disturbed. He's nice to me."

"Katie, I am telling you to be careful around him."

I went into my room alone and closed the door. I wanted Mark to be my friend, but I needed Martha in order to have a place to live and food to eat. It would be hard for me to stop liking Mark, but for Martha's peace of mind, I would try.

Chapter 4
Why the Hostages Were Released

It is fair to say that, in childhood, I was a petty thief. It began shortly after Martha told me to be careful around Mark, and I was looking for options to prepare for what I assumed would be my eventual life on the streets. To ready myself for what I believed would be the time when I was ultimately told to leave, I stole the toiletries from the bathroom closet of Martha's house and hid them under my bed in several tote bags. I focused on items that looked like they might be useful if one was living alone at the age of seven, like Ben Gay, shaving cream, and strange contraptions I later learned were for douching.

At one point, to cover my tracks, I put my hand lightly on my gut and said to Dominic, "Do you know why I have to keep going to the bathroom?"

With a slightly perplexed look on his face, Dominic answered, "No," to which I responded with an overly enthusiastic, "Me neither." Then I went into the bathroom and stole more toiletries. Martha figured it out the next day when she went to the closet looking for toilet paper. There was none. In fact, the closet was empty. With great concern, she asked me, "What happened to everything in the bathroom?" Eventually I confessed, and Martha sent me to therapy. Michael went too, as he had stabbed a classmate of mine with a long needle while she and I were walking home from school. Between this and the fact that I wet the bed, refused to quit sucking my thumb, and spoke in a higher pitched voice than necessary in order to sound younger, Martha was desperate for some help for us.

I didn't mind therapy. There was hot chocolate at the office, and I was always allowed to have some before each session. It also gave me private fits of laughter that the therapist's name was Dr. Fink. Most delightfully, there was a calm, patient adult on the other side of the desk who asked questions and listened to all of my answers. I didn't volunteer any information to Dr. Fink that I deemed secret. I simply answered his inquiries. Some questions probably didn't occur to him to ask, for instance: Does your father claim to be a diviner of God, and do you think you have magical powers? I got the feeling that this wouldn't go over well, so I kept mum.

...

I SPENT MOST weekends with Martha's Fundamentalist Christian mother, Tu-Tu, who liked to take me to church. Although it was by no means my favorite activity, I quickly learned that there was some benefit to being the daughter of a Jew and a Gentile. Upon introducing me to her church friends, Tu-Tu would say, "This is Katie. She's half Jewish, but only on her father's side, so she's not really a Jew." Her friends seemed to find it fascinating that a real, live Jew was before them, even if I was only "half Jewish." They asked me many questions about how my family handled holidays and whether we went to both church and temple.

I, frankly, liked the attention, even if it made me a little uncomfortable about how different I looked from most New Englanders. My hair was frizzier than that of other girls. My nose was larger and my chin was smaller. I had a scrawny build. New Englanders were of heartier stock than I was. They were of Irish and English descent. Even those whose bloodline was from Italy were usually fairer than Martha, and consequently, me.

I also had no clue about Jewish beliefs or practices and therefore couldn't answer most of the churchgoers' questions about the particulars in how we managed a "half Jewish" home. All I knew was that if you wanted to buy something Kosher, you had to look for the 'K' on the box, which to me erroneously meant that Kit Kat bars must be extra Kosher because of the two 'K's in the name; anything made in Kansas must be Kosher, as must any product containing Vitamin K. Other than that, I was at a loss.

Tu-Tu volunteered me to go up on the minister's platform with a couple of other children and answer some questions. I didn't want to go because I suspected the other kids knew a lot more about the Bible than I did; but I liked the idea of being onstage, so I went. The topic was 'color symbolism in the Old Testament.' The minister asked us kids, "What do you think the color red symbolizes?"

I immediately thought of blood, but another child answered before I did. "Fire," he said.

"That's right. Fire," the minister said. "And what does-"

"-Excuse me," I interrupted.

"Yes?"

"Fire's not really red. It's more of an orange. There's also yellow; but not red."

The minister and several members of the congregation laughed. I lost track of what was said after that. My performance had pleased, and that was all I needed. We got off the platform, and I went back to my seat. I was a little worried that Tu-Tu might not have appreciated my interruption, but she put her arm around me and smiled. The rest of the service was like listening to a foreign language that I found neither engaging nor understandable.

My interests were a reflection of my parents' interests. When I was with Matthew, I was interested in enlightenment. When I was with Martha, I was interested in politics. In the 1980 presidential election, Martha wanted Jimmy Carter to win. Tu-Tu wanted Ronald Reagan to win. Martha said that it was more likely for a president to get re-elected than it was for a new person to interrupt someone's presidency. She told me though that one of the complaints about Mr. Carter was that he hadn't yet secured the release of those fifty-two Americans from Iran. What she didn't know was that I had not secured their release either.

Martha explained that if Mr. Carter could get them out within a couple of weeks of the election, he would win, but if he didn't, he would be considered inept and Mr. Reagan would win. Because Martha wanted Mr. Carter to win, I ramped up my mental efforts to obtain the hostages' release, trying to build my mind power in order to command the Iranians to set them free.

It had looked as though the hostages would be released in October, but then suddenly Iran said no. On November 4th, 1980 Ronald Reagan won the presidency. Mr. Carter and I had both failed. On the same day Mr. Reagan was inaugurated, at the very same time as he took the oath of office, the hostages were released. According to Tu-Tu, this was a symbol of how we as a nation had made the right decision. She told me that the election of Mr. Reagan was "part of God's plan."

Sixty-nine days into the presidency of Ronald Reagan, a man named John Hinkley, Jr. attempted to assassinate him. No one was killed during the attack, but John Hinkley, Jr. had shot and wounded the president and three others; one victim was left paralyzed and permanently disabled. The shooter had done the terrible deed to impress the actress, Jodie Foster. Although the whole incident was horrible, I also learned something significant from it. An actress, through her fame and notoriety, had influenced someone to literally try to kill for her. I didn't want anyone to kill for me; I wanted people to be moved to do good things because of me, but I wanted to be that powerful. The idea of becoming famous rose to the realm of obsession for me. John Hinkley, Jr. was found not guilty by reason of insanity.

...

ALONG WITH THE desire to be famous, my fixation on gathering as many *things* as possible grew. By the end of second grade, my stealing cost me my best friend when I pilfered her sticker book and denied it. My culpability, however, was obvious, and even her mother called me to get it back. By then I had cut out all the stickers and couldn't figure out how to make it right, so I maintained my innocence. Martha had no time to get involved with the situation, much to my relief.

I had altered my relationship with my best friend to the category of 'arch-enemies,' and she continued it by persuading several of our classmates to bully me, including one who pushed me up against the brick wall of the school building and threatened to beat me up if I ever stole anything again. One would think that this would be enough to convince me to stop stealing, but it did not. In fact, stealing acted as a release to the pressure I felt. I would begin to feel anxious about my life and the world in general. Then I would take something from someone else, and I would feel better. It was an easy decision for me that, if I could not use my mind power to *will* toys and trinkets and clothes to me, I would take them.

Chapter 5
Why She Wanted to Be Her

I wrote a book. Our third grade class was assigned the task of writing stories to read to the first graders. Each book was laminated and stapled to look more official. Mine was about a pilot who had met his death in a fiery plane crash. His co-pilot, who had survived, went on to struggle with depression and alcoholism because he blamed himself for the accident. In order to come to grips with the death of the pilot, the co-pilot went to the pilot's grave to dig up the body. There was some question as to whether the pilot downed the plane intentionally, but I left that part a mystery.

Writing the book had been fun but left me feeling a bit unsatisfied. I told Martha that I wanted to write a real book, one that would be published and bound and placed on the shelf of a real library. I was pleased with the theme I had chosen, though. It was dark and twisted like the *Twilight Zone* and *Alfred Hitchcock* episodes that Martha let us watch sometimes. The school didn't feel the same way, however, and the book elicited a parent-teacher conference and more therapy with Dr. Fink.

I felt terrible for Martha that she had been pulled in to talk with my teacher. She seemed so sad all the time, and this just added to it. I was much happier when she got good news from my school. When she had come home just weeks prior and told me, "The teacher says you're the only student she's ever met who uses the words 'quite' and 'rather,'" I beamed with pride for her as much as for myself. In my mind, this business with the book erased all the good that previous parent-teacher meeting had done, and now Martha was worried and upset again.

There was also the issue of the stalling of my psychic and magical development and my inability to happily socialize with most kids my own age. I was not the person I wanted to be. I was frustrated and disappointed with myself. I contemplated ending my life, but at eight years old, I didn't know how to do such a thing. While trying to come up with a way, thoughts of Martha's pain flashed in my eyes. I knew she would be devastated if I killed myself. For the time being, it kept me from pursuing it further.

I decided not to share any of this with Dr. Fink for fear that it might get back to Martha and worry her even more than she already was. But it was Dr. Fink who helped me through the disappointment when Dominic and Martha ended their relationship and my new, surrogate father was gone. I was even a little disappointed several months later when we abruptly stopped going to see Dr. Fink. There was no explanation, just Martha telling us, "We're not going to him anymore," and that was the end of that. I hoped it meant that Michael and I were fixed, and Martha could finally be happy.

By late fall, Martha started dating a man named Frank. I didn't have any particular feelings for him one way or the other. Martha had brought Michael and me to Frank's house a couple of times, and he had come to Martha's house several times to renovate half of the basement into a bedroom for her, but they mostly kept to themselves during those visits. Other than that, my one interaction with him was when he gave me a brief ride around our neighborhood on his motorcycle. When he shifted gears, I got startled and let out a scream. He laughed and poked fun at me when we got back to Martha's house, which annoyed me. He seemed good-natured, but I couldn't say I was fond of him.

When Martha and I were pulling into the driveway one evening, though, she asked, "How would you feel if I got married again, Katie?"

I absolutely did not want her to remarry, in part because it would mean there would be no chance of reconciliation between her and my father. But I wanted her to be happy, and if she wanted to get married, I wanted her to feel free to do so. "That would be great, Mom," I said, feigning cheeriness.

...

BY EARLY 1982, it seemed that everyone in school, at home and on the news was abuzz with talk about the Cold War. Lots of people started referring to the president as Ronald 'Ray-gun' behind his back because he seemed to like his weapons an awful lot. Our television was flooded with images of missiles and nuclear bombs.

While America's Cold War against the Soviets grew, so did mine against my arch-enemy. I even went so far as to read *The Diary of Anne Frank* because my arch-enemy had read it. My arch-enemy was very smart, and I didn't like the idea that she had read something I hadn't. Soon into the book, though, I forgot my reason for reading it in the first place. I came to adore Anne. First off, she was Jewish, and although I was only a "half Jew," I liked the comparison. We also both wanted to write books. Anne had hope in the face of fear, which I didn't always, but it was a trait I admired very much. She remained a loving, kind person despite the prejudice that forced her family into hiding, characteristics I also wanted. And she had faults and inner struggles but was still loved by those around her, which I hoped might be true in my life as well. By the end of the book, I wanted to *be* Anne Frank.

It's not that I viewed my life as anything like hers. Maine in the 1980's was far from World War II's Europe, and the disappointment of a child of divorce cannot be compared with the horrors of the Holocaust. It's that I wanted to suffer as she had. I wanted to be in that attic. I wanted to live in fear of being taken to Dachau, or worse Auschwitz, and yet still be able to honestly write words like hers: "In spite of everything I still believe people are good at heart." The only difference was that I wanted to survive and be celebrated for changing hearts and minds. It was a big difference, to be sure. Anne, it seemed, was humble in a way I was not. I wanted people to *think* I was humble, while in fact believing myself to have superior powers and abilities.

I did have, however, a real, concerted interest in the history of the Holocaust. It was important to me to understand just how something so terrible could happen. I worried that if not enough kids and adults understood why things like the Holocaust occurred, then we would all be more at risk of things like nuclear war. In private conversations, I started asking Martha about the Holocaust. She answered everything as best she could. When she didn't know the answers she directed me to our encyclopedia set, where I poured over articles and images of Holocaust survivors and Nazi soldiers. She told me, "I'm proud of you for asking questions like these, Katie." I wondered if, when she was alone with Michael, she told him she was proud of him. I had never heard her say so. It seemed she used a different tone with him, a more abrupt one than she used with me.

Martha told me that when she was a child, teachers made the kids practice hiding under their desks in an effort to prepare for the dropping of the atomic bomb. "It was ridiculous. If an A-bomb dropped on us, no desk would have saved us." She chuckled and shook her head, but her comment made me nervous. The threat we were all facing was no longer just atomic; it was nuclear.

As frightening as the threat of nuclear annihilation was, however, I considered that it might be my opportunity to be like Anne. I imagined myself surviving in the rubble of a nuclear explosion. I would somehow emerge a hero, saving lives and inspiring the world.

Chapter 6
Why She Tried to Jump Off the Bridge

Two days before my ninth birthday, on June 8th, 1982, President Reagan delivered a well-publicized speech in which he warned America that we were on the verge of World War III. He stated, however, that he believed the Cold War to be "winnable." In his estimation, we would lose millions of people, but we would inflict more damage on Russia than they would on us. If they dared to attack us, the "Evil Empire" would be "left on the ash heap of history." My heart raced with fear. I stole twelve sheets of stickers from the local drugstore.

    Before my summer arrival to Matthew's new home in San Francisco, he sent photos of himself to Michael and me. At first, I just focused on his face, which I missed so much. Then I noted that he was wearing a new trucker's hat. He had never been a trucker, but he was keen on wearing the hats. His beard had grown out a great deal, and Martha said, "He looks like a mountain man." I saw that he was seated before some drywall and guessed that he had just put it up. It was Martha who pointed out that he was surrounded by beer bottles and open cans; I hadn't noticed.

    I traveled alone to San Francisco, as Michael's visit was delayed by the need for him to attend summer school. Matthew met me at the gate, and the sight of his wooly beard made me smile with a sense of comfort. As we walked along, I spotted several people wearing orange robes. Their heads were shaved with the exception of ponytails in the back, and they were chanting something that sounded like, "Hairy, hairy, hairy."

As Matthew and I passed by them I asked, "Are those people saying 'hairy' to get their hair back?"

"They're not saying 'hairy.' They're chanting 'Hare, Hare, Hare.'"

"Oh. What does that mean?"

Matthew explained that these were Hare Krishnas, and they followed a branch of Hinduism. "They're chanting their names for God and inviting other people to join in."

"Why?"

"They believe it helps them get closer to God, and by doing that they won't get reincarnated anymore, and they'll be able to return to the kingdom of God." Reincarnation, he explained was "a repetition of life" during which the person has to get re-born on earth to work out certain things they didn't get right the first time around. He explained that the Christians do this by being "born again" in one lifetime and then following God's commandments. By doing this, they believe that when they die they will go to heaven.

"What do you believe?" I asked.

"I believe we are born from the stars and, when we die, we return to the stars."

I wondered if maybe that was why I liked thinking about space so much, because I had been born from there and wanted to get back. I also wondered if maybe I was supposed to be a Hare Krishna, and that was why I kept thinking about ending my own life. "So, the Hare Krishnas want to die?"

"What do you mean?"

"Well, you said they're chanting God's name so that they

don't have to live for more lifetimes, so that they can go back to the kingdom of God. Does that mean they don't want to live?"

"Well, they want to live in enlightenment in this lifetime so that they don't have to come back."

"Oh." As someone who hoped to have an excuse to end my life, I was a little disappointed.

One of the Hare Krishnas reached out to me with a bowl of what looked like mud with vegetables sticking out of it. "No thank you," I said. As we left the airport, I whispered to Matthew, "What was that?"

"Just some food. They're vegetarians."

"They only eat vegetables?"

"They can eat other things, but they don't eat meat. They believe that killing an animal is the same as killing a person."

"Is that what you believe?"

"No," he said flatly.

I thought about the mouse from the campsite three summers before and wondered if it had come back for another lifetime.

San Francisco was not nearly as flat as Maine. As we drove to Matthew's apartment, it sometimes felt like we were completely vertical. At times, I worried the van might flip backwards. When we got to the top of one very high hill and stopped at a red light, Matthew asked, "What do you see down there?"

"Lots of buildings and people and the water."

"You can see far, right?"

"Yes."

"When we look at life from the top of a mountain, there aren't limits. You can see far."

"That's true," I didn't know what he was getting at.

"You can look at things from the point of view of

Krishna or Buddha or Christ, and if you're on top of the mountain it all looks the same. When you start walking down the mountain and get closer, you may find little differences. Some people may eat animals, and some people may not. But if you have the ability to see from the mountain, you just see."

I smiled. All it meant to me was that my father saw from the top of the mountain. "Is that why you have a beard?" His head cocked to one side. "Mom says you look like a mountain man."

He threw back his head and laughed.

A few days into the trip, Matthew introduced me to his friend Howard, a young man who had followed Matthew all the way from the East Coast to be in his classes and learn from him. I felt an immediate kinship with Howard, in part because he was Jewish. While I still didn't have much familiarity with Judaism, I apparently looked like a Jew, and so did Howard.

Howard was a magician, which I found fascinating. I had once read about a magician named Howard Thurston, who was a rival of Harry Houdini. Howard Thurston was considered by many to be an even better magician than Harry Houdini but had never reached his competitor's level of success or fame. "Did you become a magician because of that Howard?" I asked him one day.

"No, it's just a coincidence."

"Dad says there are no coincidences."

A week after my arrival, Martha called wanting to know what I had done with my Aunt Judy's driver's license. Aunt Judy was Matthew's sister, but she and Martha had stayed in touch after the divorce. Although I hadn't taken the license, Martha certainly had reason to think I might have.

"I know you took it, Katie," she said over the phone.

"No I didn't, Mom."

"Look, your Aunt Judy needs her license. Just send it back in the mail today."

I got more irritated. "Mom, I didn't take her license. Did you ask her when she saw it last?"

"Yes, she said she had it a few days ago and now it's gone."

"Well, I've been here for a week, and I haven't seen her for two whole months."

"Katie..."

"I didn't take it Mom. You know I haven't seen her since that Easter-Passover dinner we had at her place. Just ask Aunt Judy."

She was firm in her tone. "Judy called *me*, Katie. She's the one who thinks you took it."

I was at first stunned and then incensed. "How did she even know about my taking things?"

"I told her months ago, Katie."

"Mom, I never took anything from her, so there was no reason to tell her. And she's *my* aunt. You're not even related to her anymore."

"Katie, I'm not going to argue with you about this. Let me talk with your father."

I paused. "That's what this is really about isn't it? You want an excuse to tell Dad that I've been taking things."

"Well, he should know. It's his fault you're doing this, Katie."

"Fine." I stormed into the other room and thrust the phone at Matthew. "Mom wants to talk to you."

I went into the spare bedroom and cried.

A while later Matthew tapped on the open door and asked if he could come in. I nodded. He sat down on the floor, where I was curled up in a ball. We were quiet for a long moment. "I'm going to teach you a technique to help calm yourself down when you get upset." I hoped that maybe Martha hadn't told him about the stealing.

He had me stretch out my legs on the floor and close my eyes. His voice was kind and calm. "Breathe in through your nose and out through your mouth. In through your nose, out through your mouth." After a minute or so of this, he asked, "What's your favorite color, Katie?"

"Electric blue," I said quietly.

Then, he continued, "Take a deep breath." I did so. "Now, I want you to picture an electric blue light coming out of your mouth as you breathe out. It's a pure, blue light, a safe light, and it's there to protect you. As you breathe out more, the light grows until it begins to surround you." I did this for another minute or so, and then he asked, "Are you surrounded by the safe, blue light now, Katie?" I breathed out again and nodded. "Okay, now, I want you to imagine yourself floating up. You're still surrounded by the safe, blue light. And you're in a beautiful field. There's green grass and flowers and trees." I pictured the field in South Portland that I called 'the Dinosaur Lands' because the trees reminded me of the ones depicted on *Land of the Lost*. I felt serene and at peace. "Are you picturing it?" he asked. I nodded slowly. "Good, Katie. Now, you can go to this place any time you feel upset."

He slowly brought me back out of the meditation and asked if I wanted to go visit the Golden Gate Bridge. I smiled with relief, figuring that if Martha had told him about the stealing, he would have brought it up by now. I eagerly said yes.

We left the house, got in his car and drove the hills and valleys to a parking area near the Golden Gate Bridge. Then we got out and started meandering toward it. The first thing I noticed was that the bridge wasn't golden at all, but a burnt orange color. We were quiet as we strolled along. Then, a short time into the walk, Matthew said, "So, I heard you've been taking things."

I cringed. I knew that Martha was right, that he should know, but even though I thought of Matthew every day, I mainly only saw him during summers and occasional spring vacations, and I didn't want to spoil his image of me. More than anything, I was ashamed. "Yes," I said quietly.

"Well, that meditation I taught you earlier is something you can use when you have the urge to take things."

Tears flooded my face. "Okay."

He hugged me. His embrace was gentle and warm. He patted my back and broke free from me. "Okay. Now let's cross that bridge."

"Okay."

As we started across, Matthew said, "It's a big deal to walk across the Golden Gate. Millions of people come each year to see it and make the trek."

As we got to the middle of our walk, I wanted to share something with Matthew. He was so nice about my stealing, that I wanted him to know one of my deepest secrets. "Dad?" I said.

"Yes."

"I want..."

"What?"

"...I want to. I sometimes want to..."

He grew impatient. "What, Katie?"

I stopped in my tracks, and he followed suit. As if asking permission, I said, "I want to kill myself."

There was a pause, and then he said lightheartedly, "Okay."

At that moment, I couldn't tell if he was really okay with my killing myself or if he just didn't believe me. I decided it was the latter, which made me feel like I had to prove it to him. I immediately started to climb up and over the hand rail. He grabbed the back of my pants and ripped me down. "Get off of there," he yelled. "What the hell are you doing?" I was silent for the rest of the walk.

Martha called a few days later to tell me Judy had found her license.

With all the sarcasm my nine-year-old mouth could muster, I responded, "No kidding."

Without missing a beat, Martha continued. "She used it to write a check and left it at the store where she was shopping."

I was crisp in my response. "Yeah, well..."

"So...did your Dad talk with you?"

"Yes."

"Good. Well, honey, that's not the only thing I called to tell you."

"Oh great. What else?"

"I decided not to marry Frank. I decided that if I'm going to remarry, it needs to be for me, not so that you kids can have a father."

"Okay," I said trying to sound let down. I was vaguely disappointed that I wouldn't have a reason to wear the pink chiffon flower girl dress Martha had gotten for me, but my relief far outweighed my desire to don lovely clothes.

Matthew, it seemed, also had someone in his life, though I didn't know her name. One night, the sound of a flute woke me up. On the way to the bathroom, I caught a glimpse of them in the living room. They were both naked, sitting cross-legged on the floor. It didn't seem that either noticed me. Matthew was smiling at the woman and then put the flute up to his lips and began to play. She was gone by the morning, and I decided not to ask him about her. I felt embarrassed about seeing him naked and didn't want him to know the image of him was now stuck in my head. Moreover, asking him who she was would make the woman more real. My parents, it seemed, were moving on from one another.

I went with Matthew to set up for one of his classes because Howard, who had taken on the role of assistant, had to perform at a magic show. I was pleased to be able to help.

The classroom was actually a small, carpeted office he had rented in a downtown San Francisco building. Matthew had me set up the glass money jar and the sign that read, "Suggested donation $100." As the students filtered in, I watched as Matthew nodded to each one. There were eight students in all. It wasn't as many as I had hoped for him, but it would be a total of eight hundred dollars if they all paid. I wished he weren't asking for money at all because I didn't want him to be disappointed if he didn't get the full amount.

The class felt like it lasted a long time, and I got a bit antsy, but overall, it was good to see my father leading the group. His assertion that he was a prophet seemed substantiated by his small group of eager-to-believe disciples. After all, they were adults; how could they be wrong?

The one thing that did strike me as strange was how pretty and flowing the words seemed, compared to all the rules. Even during the relaxation technique, there was a specific positioning of hands and bodies that had to be done at specific times for the relaxation technique to work properly. It didn't seem very relaxing to me.

When the class was over and the last of the disciples had finished thanking Matthew, I immediately walked over to the money jar. It didn't look like the participants had given the full donation, but there was a hefty amount. Matthew closed the door to the classroom and began counting the money. He seemed chagrinned. I didn't like seeing him disappointed. "Maybe you don't have to charge money at all."

He put the money in his wallet. "I'm not charging them. I'm giving them the opportunity to donate. It's an important part of the process."

"What process?"

"By meeting with them, I'm giving them the chance to catch some very important lessons. These lessons can't just be taught. They have to be caught, and only certain people can present them. I'm giving up my time to give others the opportunity to become enlightened."

"Could they go to the library and read a book to get the lessons?"

He chuckled. "There is no one book that offers what I offer. They would have to spend years in the library to get what I can show them if they're willing and able to learn."

...

MATTHEW AND HOWARD took me to a magic convention for Howard to get some new props. We passed by many magicians who were selling the secrets to their tricks. After a while, I noticed that all the magicians were men. "Why aren't there any lady magicians here?"

"There aren't a lot of women who become magicians," Howard said.

"But that doesn't mean you can't," Matthew added. "In fact, it may be a good sales point to set yourself apart from the rest of them."

"Hmmm." I didn't want to be a magician; I wanted to have real magic.

A magician with an empty aquarium tank caught my eye. He was folding up a piece of tinfoil on the table. "What's he doing?"

"Let's watch," Matthew said.

The magician placed his newly constructed tinfoil boat inside the tank. The boat bobbed up and down, afloat on...nothing. "Whoa." Next, the magician produced a plastic cup and began bailing out the tank. It looked like he was miming the whole thing, but the tinfoil boat bobbed and lowered with each cupful. I got up close to confirm that there was no sleight of hand or wires or special effects. The magician had done something to make the water invisible.

"How did he do that?" I asked, as we walked on.

"If you want, I can tell you," Howard said.

"No," I nearly shouted. "Don't tell me."

"But you just asked how he did it."

"I know I did, but I don't really want to know. And besides, I thought magicians aren't supposed to tell people how to do their tricks, unless it's another magician."

"Well, that's not really a magic trick. It's science," he responded.

"Oh. Well still, I don't want to know." I was a curious child who always wanted the answers, as long as they didn't dissolve my belief that there was real magic in the world and that I could be a part of it. If Howard explained how the trick was done, then I couldn't believe it was real.

...

MATTHEW TOOK ME to visit his friend Zaire, who was going to help organize more of Matthew's spiritual workshops. Zaire had a booming personality and flaming red hair. His voice was distinctive; part gravel, part hippie smooth. Upon meeting him, he asked, "Can I have a hug?" I had never hugged a stranger before, and I didn't have any desire to start, but when I looked to Matthew, he nodded at me, so I obliged. The hug lasted longer than I had wanted; but since I hadn't wanted to hug him in the first place, any amount of time probably would have seemed too long.

    That night, back at Matthew's apartment, the phone rang. Matthew was making dinner, so I picked up. "Hello?" I said.

    "Hi." I could tell from the unique voice that it was Zaire, and I anticipated that he would ask to talk with Matthew. But then he said something that made me realize he was calling for me and at the same time hope that it wasn't really him on the other end of the line. He asked me, "Do you touch yourself?"

    "What?"

    "Do you touch yourself between your legs?"

    "I..."

    "Why don't you touch yourself right now?"

    I kept my voice light, as if he was calling with a pleasant how-do-you-do. "I think you want to talk with my Dad."

    I yelled for Matthew, who came to the phone a moment later, wiping his hands on a dish towel. I handed him the receiver, but there was no one on the other end any longer. I didn't tell Matthew what he said, and when he asked who it was, I answered, "I don't know." It bothered me a lot. This was an adult man, and the idea that there were adult men in the world who would talk to little girls this way scared me. Worse, I was certain I knew who this man was, and I didn't like that he was associated in any way with my father and his spiritual teachings. Like many things, though, as much as it troubled me, I couldn't find a way to talk about it.

...

THAT FALL I began fourth grade. In retaliation against my classmates for not liking me as much as I wanted, and because I developed the belief that I deserved to have the good things I thought they all had, I stole many students' pencils and erasers and bookmarks. As classroom discussions took place about who the thief could be, however, I started to worry that I might get caught. Rather than quit stealing altogether, which I was not prepared to do, I decided it was best to switch my efforts to thieving only from family and marketplaces.

A clerk caught me stealing a piece of grape taffy from the local convenience store and told me not to come back. I didn't. Martha caught me filching a $20 bill and some costume jewelry earrings from Tu-Tu, as well as returning from the local drugstore with two tubes of unpaid-for lipstick. As it turned out, I wasn't a particularly good thief; I had gotten caught nearly each time I stole something. For a mother who had multiple distractions, Martha was awfully good at zeroing in when I took something that wasn't mine.

To add insult to injury of a self-inflicted lousy year, my arch-enemy displaced me as teacher's pet. She was called on to answer questions. She was assigned the plum portions of books to read aloud. She was handed the lead in the class comedy play without any auditions being held, while I was given the meager role of "Neighbor #1." I devoted myself to the part, however, and ended up getting some good laughs on my brief lines. It was a secret pleasure that her speeches seemed to fall flat. After the show, my teacher from the year before flung back the stage curtain and said with great animation and surprise, "Katie, you were wonderful. Are you going to be an actress when you grow up?"

The attention solidified my goal of fame and fortune. I knew I wanted to be four things: a writer of books, a famous actress, a good witch with real magical powers, and a savior of the world. Not only had my parentage taught me that all of this was within my grasp, but I had come to believe that if I didn't accomplish all of these birthrights, I was a failure who was better off dead. My very survival was contingent upon my success. Go big or go home.

Chapter 7
Why She Wrote to the Evil Empire

Christmas 1982 was on its way. I would later learn that as I was preparing my detailed list for Santa that year, another little girl from Maine was writing a letter of her own. Ten-year old Samantha Smith reached out to Soviet Premier Yuri Andropov to express her worry about the United States and the USSR getting into a nuclear war.

It started when Samantha Smith asked her mother Jane if there was going to be a World War III. She too had seen all those frightening images of missiles and bombs on television. She had also seen a program during which the scientists contradicted President Reagan and said that a nuclear war would destroy the Earth. According to them, no one would win. She woke up one morning wondering if this was going to be the last day of the Earth.

When Samantha asked her mother who would start a war and why, her mother showed her a newsmagazine story that depicted Yuri Andropov. They read it together. Samantha recognized that the people in America and Russia were similar in that we all worried about war. She asked her mother to write to Mr. Andropov. In turn, her mother suggested that Samantha pen the letter.

Samantha wrote to Mr. Andropov: "I have been

worrying about Russia and the United States getting into a nuclear war. Are you going to vote to have a war or not? If you aren't please tell me how you are going to help to not have a war. This question you do not have to answer, but I would like to know why you want to conquer the world or at least our country. God made the world for us to live together in peace and not to fight."

While Samantha and her mother dropped off her letter to the post office, I prayed to Santa Claus that he would whisk me away for Christmas Eve. When my wish did not happen, I felt disappointed with myself for still not being able to use my mind control skills correctly.

In April of 1983, excerpts from Samantha Smith's letter were published in the Soviet newspaper *Pravda*. In reference to her question about why Mr. Andropov might want to conquer the world, he stated, "We think we can pardon Samantha her misleadings, because the girl is only ten years old."

Samantha was pleased that *Pravda* had printed her letter, but couldn't understand why no attempt was made to answer her questions. She sent a second letter, this time to the Soviet Ambassador to the United States, in which she wrote, "I thought my questions were good ones and it shouldn't matter if I was ten years old." A week later the Soviet Embassy called Samantha at home to say that a reply from Yuri Andropov was on its way.

On April 26th, 1983, Samantha received a response from Yuri Andropov, typed in Russian on cream-colored paper and signed in blue ink. It was accompanied by an English translation, which read in part: "We in the Soviet Union are trying to do everything so that there will not be war on Earth. ...Soviet people well know what a terrible thing war is. Forty-two years ago, Nazi Germany which strove for supremacy over the whole world, attacked our country, burned and destroyed many thousands of our towns and villages, killed millions of Soviet men, women and children. ...Today we want very much to live in peace, to trade and cooperate with all our neighbors on this earth, with those far away and those nearby. ...In America and in our country there are nuclear weapons, terrible weapons that can kill millions of people in an instant. But we do not want them to be ever used. That's precisely why the Soviet Union solemnly declared throughout the entire world that never—never—will it use nuclear weapons first against any country. In general we propose to discontinue further production of them and to proceed to the abolition of all the stockpiles on earth." Mr. Andropov compared Samantha Smith to 'Becky' from *The Adventures of Tom Sawyer*. He called her courageous and honest and invited her to see his country and understand more of his culture.

I stayed up late to watch Samantha Smith interviewed on *Nightline* by Ted Koppel. She was charming and pretty, with a healthy, pink face that matched her fashionable pink turtleneck. She wore a red sweater and delicate earrings; her straight brown hair was pulled back, and her wide blue eyes glinted with liveliness. She was in stark contrast to me, with my skinny face and big nose, my droopy eyes and bushy eyebrows, and my thick glasses and my brother's hand-me-downs.

More than that, she had something I did not. She had real humility. Being interviewed on a national television show didn't seem to throw her at all. She was at ease answering questions and simply explaining why it was that she had decided to write to the leader of the United States' greatest enemy. She had clearly taken this action not to become famous but to make a difference. This made her more like my hero, Anne Frank, than I was, and that made me very jealous.

Even where she lived was special. Although Manchester,

Maine was a full sixty miles north of where I lived in South Portland, and I had never been there, I knew that it was named after a European city. Even that fact annoyed me. Samantha Smith was quickly displacing my arch-enemy.

Chapter 8
Why She Couldn't Swim

I was down, and Martha could tell. She looked at me sympathetically from across the room and asked, "What's the matter, kiddo?"

"Nothing." *Nothing* was Samantha Smith, and my inability to live up to how good she was.

Martha asked me if I had started the book I wanted to write, and I told her I hadn't and didn't feel like working on it right then. She asked me, "Well, do you want to help me get things ready for Rainey?" Rainey was to be Martha's new housemate.

The opportunity to feel useful piqued my interest. Martha asked me to help her clean and move a few things around the house. While doing so, I found some Dabble Art posters buried in the back of a closet. I poured over them, asking my mother questions about what had inspired her to draw this and that.

Martha didn't seem impressed with her own ability to draw something that thousands of people had seen and enjoyed. Instead, she shrugged it off. "That could have been better. ...That was my worst one." She gave most of the credit for what she considered the good drawings to outside influences. "I did my best work when I was drunk."

She had stopped drawing altogether by the time we moved to South Portland. She did, however, praise my habit of going to my room and painting something whenever she and Michael argued. "Katie deals with her upsets in such a constructive way."

Rainey moved in a week or so later, and I welcomed her by making her coffee and presenting her with a picture I had drawn of her, Martha, Michael and me at the house. She smiled, thanked me and patted me on the shoulder. Rainey and Martha had met in their alcohol recovery support-group, where Rainey had gone after her daughter Anna died of cancer and Rainey's drinking got bad. Upon first meeting Rainey, many people thought she was a man. Her silver hair was cropped close; her voice was deep and gravelly from years of chain-smoking; she had several tattoos, including ones on her hands; she wore no makeup and nothing feminine, unless you counted multiple, thick gold chains that could rival those of 'Mr. T' feminine.

Rainey and Martha had several friends who were part of two-woman and two-man couples. They didn't seem any different from couples who were comprised of one woman and one man, except that depending on their heights and weights, they could swap clothes. This seemed to me to be an excellent way to add to one's wardrobe.

It never occurred to me to ask if Martha and Rainey were ever a couple, and it wouldn't have mattered anyway. Rainey quickly became a fixture of stability. We would exchange glances when Martha and Michael argued, and she often took me aside to occupy my time by playing Uno. Whenever I was around her, I felt protected and safe.

...

BY MY TENTH summer I was weary from all of the fighting at home and I didn't really want to travel with Michael to

Matthew's new place in North Carolina. I wanted to see Matthew though, and once I got there I quickly made a friend at the camp that Matthew had gotten a job managing. My new friend was the first black child I had ever officially met. She kindly answered my multiple questions about her hair, which I found fascinating. It was coarse and in little braids with pretty pink, white and baby blue beads strung in it. We compared palms and noted how hers and mine were similar in color though the rest of our skin was not.

Another little girl, who was white, warned me that I shouldn't be talking to my new friend because, "Black people are dirty." Not everyone appeared to feel as she did. In fact, it seemed from how most of the kids got along that she was in the minority. Still, it bothered me, and I spent extra time with my new friend after that just to make a point to the little white girl that I disagreed with her. I didn't tell my new friend what was said about her because even though I believed she had a right to know, I didn't want her feelings to be hurt.

On the last day of camp, one of the older girls, who was in Michael's age group, lost her bottle of Mountain Dew. A great search ensued by all the campers. Finally, near the end of the day, the girl said that whoever found the bottle could have it. It was minutes after that announcement when Michael pulled the bottle from the back of the freezer in Matthew's office. I suspected foul play but kept mum on the subject.

After all the campers left, Michael and I took the bottle to the picnic area. The soda was slushy inside, and Michael leaned back his head while holding the opening of the glass bottle over his mouth and swatting the bottom of it with his open palm. Small drips came out. "Do you want some?" he asked. I did.

He told me to lean back my head, and towering over me, he held the downturned bottle over my open mouth. Then he began hitting the bottom of the bottle. One, two, three, and then... the bottle slipped. The glass smacked my mouth and the bottle crashed onto the ground. Michael and I both stood stunned for a moment, staring at one another. Then I ran screaming and looking for Matthew.

My front tooth was chipped, and Matthew said we would have to go to a dentist. I had never seen him so angry. I sat in the front passenger seat, and Michael sat in the back. The whole way there, Matthew told Michael over and over again what a careless thing he had done and how it was going to cost Matthew money. I peered in the rearview mirror at Michael. He looked small and sad, and I felt awful for him.

The tooth was repaired, and after Matthew's responsibilities with the camp ended, we three traveled together throughout North Carolina. It was hot as we rode in the van down the highways and back roads, picking up hitchhikers along the way. There was an exciting element of living on the edge when we let these young men into the vehicle. They often smelled of sour sweat, and I was a little worried they may be carrying knives or guns. But they always turned out to be harmless post-hippy youths heading toward home or just traveling around trying to "find" themselves. Matthew would get into long conversations with them about mysticism and the Universe and how to develop their innate psychic powers. It was as though he were collecting disciples along the route.

As we headed toward the coast, we stopped at a convenience store. The white clerk's attention was elsewhere as Matthew set down some snacks and sodas on the counter. He peered over Matthew's shoulder to a young black man who was in the aisle behind us. Nodding his head in the direction of the man, he whispered, "I think he stole something." Then he called the man a terrible name that I had never heard spoken aloud before but had seen in Martha's encyclopedia set in a cross-reference to the racism of the Holocaust. I looked at Michael in shock. As I opened my mouth to say something, Michael gave me a quick glance of warning. I stood silent, staring at the man behind the counter as if he were an alien.

Matthew paid for the purchase and as we left, Michael and I pounded him with questions: "How can he get away with saying that?...Do people say that all the time here?...Do you think the black man heard him?...Didn't people stop being racist when the Civil War ended?"

Matthew would only say, "Everyone is entitled to their beliefs, and even if we would say they're wrong, there are some people you just can't change. And, no, racism did not stop when the Civil War ended."

I spent a lot of time thinking about race after that. None of my relatives had ever said anything about the problem of racism, and a lot of them were Christians. Then there was Matthew, who saw everyone through "Christ's eyes" but didn't say anything to the store clerk when he had been so offensive. I didn't get it. It seemed to me that part of being spiritual meant understanding problems like this and doing something about it. I decided that I would start praying to my God-genie and using my powers to fix it so that no one in the world would be a racist.

We spent a lot of time near the ocean, where I preferred to stay on dry land while Michael and Matthew swam and splashed and dunked one another. I had been afraid of water as long as I could remember. Martha had told me that she even had a hard time sponge-bathing me as a newborn. I would shriek and cry until she lifted me from the sink and wrapped me in a towel.

To feel like I was at least a small part of the action, I would step an inch or so into the ocean and wait for the last bit of waves to rid my feet of sand. Then the water on my feet would cause more sand to stick, and I would have to step in the water again. This cycle would occupy me for a long time.

Matthew convinced me to get in the water one day so that he could teach me how to swim. "Come on. It's fun in the water. You'll be glad you learned." Reluctantly, I obliged, more because I wanted to please him than because I wanted to learn to swim. He suggested I take off my glasses, but I told them I had to keep them on so that I could at least see what I was doing.

As I got closer to him, he backed up. "Where are you going?" I asked, starting to panic.

"Don't worry," he laughed. "You're fine. Come towards me."

I made my way to him and wrapped my arms around his chest, pushing myself up out of the water as much as I could.

"Okay, let go and swim toward me again."

"I don't like the water, Dad."

Matthew peeled off my arms and released me back into the ocean like a fisherman with a catch that was too small. Then he backed up a few feet. "Water is very spiritually significant, Katie. It represents higher wisdom. Our bodies are made of two-thirds water. You shouldn't be afraid of it."

I started clumsily treading my feet. "Well I am. There might be sharks. And also I don't want to drown."

"You're not going to drown.

"What about the sharks?"

"They're not going to bother you."

"Oh great. So there *are* sharks in here. Jeezum crow."

He backed up in the water as I dog-paddled toward him. Just as I would get close to him, he would back up again. "Dad, will you please stay put?"

"I'm not going anywhere" he said with a smirk.

The frustration was immense, and I gave up and went back to the sand.

Later, Michael offered to teach me to swim. It was not typical for him to offer to do something nice, and I didn't want to turn him down, especially after the trouble he had gotten into with the Mountain Dew bottle chipping my teeth. So despite the fact that I officially considered the water enemy territory at this point, I went with him.

"Be careful of the riptides," Matthew said as Michael towed me along in the water.

"Riptides?" I called back. To Michael, I said, "I forgot about those. Sharks, drowning, and now riptides? Why does anyone ever go in the ocean?"

We were far away from the shore and up to our necks in the water. When I took off my glasses to wipe off a few drips, Matthew was nothing but a blur. I put my glasses back on and searched out Matthew through the smeared lenses. I found him sitting on the sand but couldn't tell if he was looking at us or not.

Michael stood before me, close. His arms were by his side under the water while mine floated on top of the waves. He smiled. "I want you to do something."

"What?" I asked suspiciously.

"It's nothing bad. I just want you to hold some mud."

"Hold mud? I don't want to."

He rolled his eyes. "Just do it, Katie. You'll like it. It's smooth."

I glanced back at the shore. Matthew was still seated on the sand. Something didn't seem right, but I couldn't figure out what. "What do you want me to do?"

His smile returned. "Just reach your hand down and I'll put the mud on it."

I hesitated. "I don't really want to. I don't like mud."

"Katie," his voice raised a little. "It's no big deal. Just do it."

I slipped my hand under the water and Michael took it in his. Then I felt something.

"Isn't it smooth?"

"I guess."

"Rub it."

"I don't want to." I started feeling very worried that I wasn't touching mud at all. But I couldn't believe that it might be a part of him he was having me touch. It didn't make any sense.

"Hey." It was Matthew's voice yelling to us. I looked up. He was standing on the edge of the water. "Come back in, you two."

I wondered if he knew what had just happened. And then I wondered again if what happened really happened. I decided again that I must be wrong. Back on the sand we were all very quiet.

Chapter 9
Why the Hostages Really Were Released

While my visit with Matthew was finishing up, Samantha Smith was just starting her summer. In July of 1983, Samantha, accompanied by her parents, took up Yuri Andropov on his invitation and went for a two-week trip to the Soviet Union. The news coverage of Samantha was tremendous, and with every story, I cringed a bit more. My jealousy of Samantha as a person and my envy of the attention she was getting grew in leaps and bounds.

I coveted the fancy Russian teapot and lacquered box and clothes Samantha received during the trip. She had also been given Yuri Andropov's personal calling card, which he had sent because he was ill during her visit and could not meet her in person. She looked so happy in the pictures and video. I resented the fact that everything seemed to be going her way, and I hoped that she was at least a little disappointed by the fact that she didn't get to meet her host face-to-face.

By the end of her visit, Samantha Smith had gone to the Kremlin, the Russian Friendship Society, the Pioneer Camp Artek, and the Kirov Ballet in Leningrad. She had been given a gorgeous folk costume with a pearl headdress and had a luncheon with the first woman cosmonaut. More than that,

Samantha Smith had set in motion something huge. Images of Russian children and their parents were all over American televisions. Suddenly, they weren't our enemies. They were more like us than they were different. They were Moms and Dads and sons and daughters, just like us.

...

IN OCTOBER OF 1983, while I was looking for the comics, I spotted a small article in *The Maine Sunday Telegram* about something called the "October Surprise." I liked surprises, so I started to read, but it didn't have anything to do with the kinds of surprises I liked.

The journalist had written about a group of people who thought President Reagan and Vice President Bush had something to do with those fifty-two American hostages in Iran being released on the very day Ronald Reagan officially became President. There was also something in it about a possible agreement they had made to sell weapons to Iran. I didn't understand how one had anything to do with the other. Also, while I didn't have any feeling either way toward Mr. Bush, Mr. Reagan seemed like a nice enough fellow. I pictured him as a friendly grandfather, or what a grandfather would be like if I had one. I couldn't imagine our own president and vice president doing something bad to us, and I figured it must be sour grapes against the winners. I assumed nothing would come of it and went back to looking for the comics.

...

ADVERTISEMENTS FOR A new television movie ran on a daily basis on ABC. The movie was called *The Day After*, and it was marketed with the tagline, "The end of the familiar." It was clear from the commercials that it would be a graphic film about the effects of a nuclear holocaust on a small town in Kansas. I imagined it as a Cold War version of *The Wizard of Oz* and deemed it an important part of my understanding the potential for nuclear war. I nagged Martha for a week to watch. On the night it aired, we had a showdown in the living room. "Katie, you are not going to watch a movie about nuclear holocaust."

"Why not?" I asked in the high pitched child-voice I reserved only for her. "You're always telling me you want me to be more grown up."

"Stop talking in that voice, Katie. You're not four years old; you're ten. And watching *The Day After* is not going to help you grow up. It's going to give you nightmares."

"So what? I already have nightmares." I had been having a recurring nightmare for nearly three years, since I had seen a Woody Woodpecker episode set in a fun-house, followed a few hours afterwards by Michael refusing to change the channel while a horror movie about a murderous clown played on HBO. My dream focused on me trying to help a family escape a violent, twisted amusement park in which I too eventually got caught.

"Katie, you're not watching *The Day After.*"

Rainey walked in from her bedroom. She ruffled my hair and sat down in the chair next to Martha. I was indignant. "So, you're going to be out here watching the movie, while I'm in the room right next to the living room; but I can't watch?"

"That's right," Martha said. I rolled my eyes.

"It's starting," Rainey said to Martha.

Martha glanced up at me. "Go into your room and shut the door."

In a huff, I followed her instructions. For a while, I tried to listen through the door to hear the movie, but Martha had turned the volume too low. I scowled and got into bed. Keyed up and unable to sleep, I made my annual winter wish that Santa would pick me up on Christmas Eve, and we would travel the world together, dropping off presents. We would pick up my elementary school crush, and he would be so impressed with my association with Santa that he would fall in love with me. My mind wandered into space, and I was soon jumping from planet to planet, trying again to imagine the expansiveness of the Universe. When that became too frustrating, I changed focus and started wondering if there really would be a war between America and the U.S.S.R. It worried me that some people still called the Soviet Union "the Evil Empire." It seemed to me that if I were called evil, it would make me pretty upset, and that it wasn't a good idea to upset one's enemies. I wondered if it upset the people and government of the Soviet Union enough to take action against us. I wondered if Yuri Andropov had been honest when he said that Russia would never take up arms first.

It seemed there was always supposed to be a good side and an evil side and never an in-between. Mr. Reagan told us that we were the good side and the U.S.S.R. was the evil side. But Samantha Smith had shown us that the people of the Soviet Union were just regular folks who cared about their families.

And if our president and vice president had anything to do with the delayed release of those fifty-two American hostages in Iran, would that make *them* evil? And if that was the case, could they be trusted not to start a war? It was all starting to feel a little muddy. I wanted it to be like it was in the westerns, where it was easy to tell who the "good guys" were and who the "bad guys" were. Or, in baseball, no matter who played there was always "our team" and the "other" team. Our team was made up of good, honest players, while the other team was filled with "a bunch of lousy cheaters." But it didn't seem like it was as simple as I might hope, even when it came to my own goodness or badness. I so wanted to be good, and yet I knew a lot of my thoughts about Samantha Smith and my arch-enemy were dreadful. It led me to wonder...was I evil?

Chapter 10
Why Santa Didn't Visit

I was ten and a half years old (that 'half' was very important to me). Michael was about to turn fourteen and had been getting in more and more trouble in school. He had joined a group of his friends in building a secret fort in the woods where they drank, smoked marijuana and played Dungeons and Dragons. When the police found and burned down the fort, they informed the parents that the boys had painted the anarchy symbol, an 'A' surrounded by a circle, numerous times on the interior and exterior walls.

This was of particular concern since there had been many news reports at that time regarding satanic worship, and each of these stories had been accompanied by images of the anarchy symbol and the pentagram, which looked similar. Anarchy, the pentagram, and Satanism had all become interchangeable in many minds. The game Dungeons and Dragons had taken on the role of a perceived gateway to Satanism, reinforced by such movies as the Tom Hanks TV movie *Mazes and Monsters*, in which the lead character's mind snaps after playing the game.

Martha was so afraid of what might happen to Michael that she allowed Tu-Tu to come to the house before Christmas, in an effort to try to persuade Michael into the Church. I was in my room for most of the visit, but as Michael and Tu-Tu sat in the living room outside of my door, I could hear how polite my brother was to Tu-Tu and how accurate his use of the English language was. I was surprised. He didn't speak to Martha or me that way, so I had just assumed he didn't know how. It didn't occur to me until then that he was choosing to speak in the crude way he did.

Michael kept assuring Tu-Tu that he was fine and that he didn't think that church was the answer for him. At the end of the visit, he walked Tu-Tu through the kitchen and outside to her car. I came out of my room and was sitting in the living room when I heard Tu-Tu's scream from the driveway. Frozen with fear, I then heard Martha rush outside and return to the kitchen with Tu-Tu. Michael went to his room, and Martha brought Tu-Tu into the living room and sat her down. Tu-Tu was breathing fast, and her palms and knees were bloody. Her nylons had torn and the tops of her shoes were scuffed. Martha left the room, and when I asked Tu-Tu what happened she said, "I was walking down the steps, and I when I looked over my shoulder at Michael, I didn't see him there. I saw the face of Satan. And then I felt a shove on my back, and I fell onto the ice."

"Michael was behind you?" I asked, confused. "Did he...push you?"

"No, no. It was Satan. Satan was there. I saw Satan's face."

Martha brought in a washcloth and some Band-Aids. After cleaning and bandaging up Tu-Tu's cuts, she left and went into Michael's room. I sat silently with Tu-Tu as her breathing calmed.

Christmas came a week later, and Santa had not scooped me up for a trip in his sleigh. This time, I was more surprised than disappointed. I had thought for certain I had focused my breathing correctly and had gotten my prayers down pat.

Something wasn't quite right with my mind-control powers, but I wasn't sure what.

One of the first presents I opened was a book with delicate roses printed on the cloth cover. As I flipped it opened and realized that the pages were blank, I exclaimed, "A diary."

Martha smiled. "Diaries are for little kids, Katie. This is a journal. It's so you can start writing down your thoughts for the book you want to write."

I was thrilled.

The next day, Samantha Smith left for a well-publicized 10-day trip to Japan. In an interview, Samantha remarked on how her vision for peace had been reinforced after watching *The Day After*. The pit of my stomach grew heavy. Samantha Smith was just a year older than I, and she had gotten to see the movie. I didn't know at whom I was more angry, Martha for not letting me watch, or Samantha Smith for being hailed as the end to the threat of World War III.

At the Children's International Symposium held in Kobe, Japan, Samantha Smith delivered a moving speech. She began by talking about her visit to the Soviet Union the summer before. "But, today, we are not here to look back on the summer or to look backward at all. We are here to look ahead. I spent the last several weeks picturing myself in the Year 2001, and thought of all the things that I would like the world to be eighteen years from today."

She proposed a unique solution for world peace that she called an International Granddaughter Exchange. "The International Granddaughter Exchange would have the highest political leaders in nations all over the world sending their granddaughters or nieces [or] grandsons and nephews to live with families of opposite nations. Soviet leaders' granddaughters would spend two weeks in America. American leaders' granddaughters would spend two weeks in the Soviet Union. And, wherever possible, granddaughters of other opposing countries would exchange visits and we would have better understanding all over the world. ...If we start with an International Granddaughter Exchange and keep expanding it and expanding it, then the year 2001 can be the year when all of us can look around and see only friends, no opposite nations, no enemies, and no bombs." It was official. Not only had Samantha Smith become a media darling. Samantha Smith was saving the world.

...

BEFORE I HAD to go back to school, I spent part of the winter vacation with Tu-Tu. We got in a conversation about my father's family, and she told me, "I have no problem with Jewish people." She repeated a story she had already told me about her only interaction with a Jewish girl in elementary school. "When I was young, there was a Jew in my class. You know, with the curly hair."

I refrained from interrupting her and saying, "Um, curly hair like mine?" Instead I listened as though I had never heard the account before.

"Everyone was so cruel to her," she said. "They would say awful things. But I was always very nice to her. I defended her. I don't know whatever became of her. Mother wouldn't let me invite her over because she was, well, a Jew."

Martha's brother, my Uncle Brian, came over to Tu-Tu's house for a visit, and we went for a walk in the brisk cold. I loathed the cold, but I liked visiting with Brian because he was always very calm, and Tu-Tu could get a little high-strung. As we walked, I kept my eyes on the ground so as not to slip on the ice. "You know," Brian said. "God doesn't like it when you look down while you're walking. He wants you to look ahead so that you can see the road before you." When I looked up, I immediately lost my footing. I caught myself and took Brian's hand in mine. For the rest of the walk, I tilted up my chin as if I were looking straight ahead, but I continued to peer down. Whenever he turned his head to look at me, I jerked up my eyes.

That night, Tu-Tu and I prayed together. She held my hands and knelt beside the convertible sofa-bed, which she had gotten specifically for us grandkids. I liked the feel of her soft hands against mine. "Now I lay me down to sleep," she prompted me. "I pray the Lord my soul to keep. If I should die before I wake, I pray the Lord my soul to take. If I should live another day, I pray the Lord to guide my ways. Amen." She kissed me on the forehead, leaving a cool wet spot, and then turned off the lights and went to her bedroom down the short, narrow hall. As soon as she was out of sight, I covered my head with the blankets, silently twisting with fear. 'If I should die?' I repeated over and in my head. Praying could make things happen, and if I prayed about death, I might make myself die. As much as I thought about ending my own life, I still had things I wanted to accomplish. Praying about death seemed like risky business to me. That night I dreamt about the haunted amusement park again.

...

WHEN SCHOOL RESUMED I overheard one of my classmates talking about how his six-year old brother had "finally learned that there's no Santa Claus." At four and a half years the little boy's senior, I had learned no such thing and was very concerned that he had spent Christmas in tears over something that couldn't possibly be true. Then I wondered if it may be true. Maybe Santa was imaginary. Back home that evening, I approached Martha, who was lying down on the sofa. I asked her, "Mom, is Santa real?"

She sat up and looked at me softly. "Katie, Santa Claus is

a feeling. It's a spirit that exists in everyone at Christmastime." I walked away confused. Santa couldn't grant my wishes if he was just a 'feeling.' Then again, it explained why I hadn't been able to use my powers to cajole him into picking me up in his sleigh on Christmas Eve.

But I hadn't mastered my prayers to my God-genie yet, and I hadn't been able to use my own mind-control powers to influence my peers or surroundings. Without Santa, I needed a new magical influence. Enter, Kitty. On January 4th, 1984 I decided that I would call my journal Kitty because that is what Anne Frank called her diary. But Kitty would not just be my sounding board. She would be a real person, with real magical powers, who could bestow those powers onto me. Kitty, I decided, would work in tandem with my God-genie and my own developing powers to help me get all of the things I desired. Together, we would be a holy trinity.

...

I WIPED MY drippy nose on my mitten as the snow crunched under my feet. Walking in the forest near my house was a peaceful getaway from the noise of home. The air was crisp and smelled of pine. I considered for the second time that day how I could get on *Star Search*.

The snap of a twig from several feet away stopped me in my tracks. My heart beat in double-time, and I held my breath. Was it a kidnapper? Was Michael following me? Was it one of the boys from down the street there to beat me up? Or maybe it was a squirrel...or a bear...or a ghost. I snapped my fingers in an effort to protect myself from evil spirits. This was part of my self-imposed set of rules for dealing with monsters and phantoms.

Another few seconds of standing still and I decided that whatever had made the noise was gone or at least had chosen not to attack me. If it was a person, he must have left. If it was some ghoul, I had *willed* it away. And if it was an animal, it would surely sense in my eyes that I meant it no harm. We would bond in a kind, soulful way, and it would become my animal friend in the forest. I would visit and bring it food. It would comfort me when I was sad. We would speak to one another with our minds, or, better yet, it would be able to speak in actual words to me. Just to be on the safe side though, I slowly turned and quietly made my way back out of the woods.

As I reached the edge of where the trees met the lawn of my neighbor's backyard, I matched up my boots so that they were parallel and the tips were completely flush. I could not allow myself to leave the forest until my feet were evened up to the millimeter. A few tries of shuffling my boots slightly and I had accomplished the task. I continued across the street to Martha's house.

Looking down as I approached the driveway, I thought about how Uncle Brian had told me that God doesn't like it when a person looks down while walking. I looked up and continued, stumbling where the driveway had heaved at the last frost. I lifted my head again as I climbed the stairs to the house but banged my knee on one of the steps.

I fumbled with my key and unlocked the front door. Michael was standing a few feet away from the entrance. "Thanks for opening the door for me," I said with sarcasm as I pulled off my scarf.

He had been watching me from the window. "What are you? Drunk?" he asked.

"Ha ha, Michael. That's so funny I forgot to laugh." Our dog, Molly, jumped on my legs. She seemed a little stir crazy from being inside all day. In the springtime, I would occasionally take Molly for walks, but mostly it didn't occur to any of us that she might like to get out of the house. It was also not so unusual to have an indoor dog, particularly in such a cold climate. I petted Molly's head to give her a bit of attention.

"Ma," Michael called out. "Katie's drunk again."

I raised my voice. "You're the druggie. I've never had a drink in my life except when Mom and Dad gave us that sip of wine when we lived in Limington and once when Mom let me take a sip of her beer."

"Geez, you're so freakin' gullible." Michael shook his head. A foot taller than I, he snapped his fist in my direction, just close enough so that I jerked back my head. "Ha," he said triumphantly.

"Quit it," I demanded.

Although this process was customarily followed by two quick punches to the arm and the phrase "two for flinching," Michael had learned that actual physical contact with me would result in a terse conversation with Martha, so he opted instead for getting as close as he possibly could without touching. Occasionally this behavior was accompanied with the lyrical repetition of the statement, "I'm not touching you."

I heard Martha's footsteps coming up from her basement bedroom. She emerged her normal tired-looking but beautiful self.

"Ma," Michael chuckled, "Tell Katie to stop getting drunk and falling in the driveway."

"I'm not drunk," I said in a panicked voice. "Mom, I'm not drunk."

Her tone was worn. "Calm down, Katie. Michael, stop teasing your sister. And, by the way, I would prefer you not make jokes about drinking."

Michael mocked, "Alcoholism is a disease."

"It *is*, Michael."

"I was kidding." Michael crossed his arms and leaned against the counter.

"I know, but it's nothing to laugh at. You don't know what it was like when I was drinking." She poured herself a glass of Diet Pepsi from the two-liter in the fridge.

I pulled off my snow boots and sat down at the kitchen table, hoping Martha would join me. She sat down across from me, pulled out one of her Now 100's discount cigarettes and lit it. I jumped up to empty her ashtray and set it back down in front of her before changing my seat so I could be next to her. She took a drag and said, "I made sure not to get loaded around you kids, but I was a blackout drunk."

"Mom, we've heard all this." Michael rolled his eyes.

"I know, but you need to hear it again. You've got the same genes. Both of you do. And you need to be careful...especially you, Michael. I know you're still drinking."

"Give me a break, Ma." Michael shook his head and stormed off to his bedroom.

For a moment the only sound was the drip of the kitchen faucet. Martha left her cigarette in the ashtray and got up. At first she tried to tighten the faucet head with her fingers, but that didn't work so she got a wrench from the brown, metal tool cabinet she kept in the kitchen. She angled the wrench around the faucet, and her hand slipped. "Fuck a duck," she said. I stifled a chuckle. Then she got the wrench back in place and, with the flick of her wrist, quickly fixed the drip. I liked watching Martha fix things. I was proud of her for doing things on her own that were ordinarily done by men.

By then I knew that Martha knew I hadn't been drinking, but I wanted her opinion on what my Uncle Brian had said. With a quiet voice I tried to find my way into the conversation. "I really wasn't drinking, Mom. It's just that Uncle

Brian told me I shouldn't look down while I walk."

"What? Why?" She sat back down and tapped the long ash of her cigarette into the ashtray.

I treaded carefully. "Well, he kind of said that God doesn't like it."

She raised both her voice and her eyebrows. "What?"

I quickly added: "I'm not going to do what Uncle Brian said though because if I don't look down, I trip."

Martha shook her head and closed her eyes. "Those people are nuts."

That night, I prayed to Kitty and my God-genie for Martha and her relatives to get along better. I prayed for Matthew to come back. I prayed to be like my hero, Anne Frank. I prayed that I would become more famous and do more good things than Samantha Smith was doing. I prayed for an end to racism. I prayed that God would give me all the pain of the world. "I can take it," I pleaded to Him. I believed that I could somehow feel the suffering of millions, and I so badly wanted it to end. "Just make the world stop hurting. Please. Give it to me instead."

I prayed for the ability to become invisible and to fly. I prayed that my closet would turn into a magic porthole to a warehouse filled with every book in the world and people-sized versions of all my Barbie clothes. I prayed that I would one day go on a NASA mission and that school children all over would wait impatiently as TV carts were wheeled into their classrooms. They would watch me with wonder and anticipation as I stepped foot on a newly discovered planet. I prayed that God would give me the ability to use every bit of my brain. I prayed to understand the expansiveness of the Universe. I prayed to be able to count to infinity. I prayed that I would wake up looking pretty.

The next morning I got ready for another day at school.

I had been wearing a retainer, called a palatal expander, which was cemented to my upper molars. After years of thumb sucking, the roof of my mouth had narrowed, and each morning and evening for six months, Martha had to use a small key to widen the expander, which would in turn widen my upper jaw. The process resulted in a six-month headache. On this morning Martha grumbled about my Uncle Brian's comments about God. I opened wide as she inserted the key in its slot, poking the roof of my mouth as she did so. I winced at the discomfort. "Keep still, Katie. ...By the way, if Brian says anything like that to you again, I want you to tell me. Or if Tu-Tu does. The two of them are a pair." I chose not to tell her about the "if I should die" prayer.

The walk to school was easy, since Helena H. Dyer Elementary was on the same street as Martha's house. I could stroll around the curve, passing 'Pig Road,' named so by the teenagers whose parties were broken up regularly by the police, and be at school in less than five minutes. Or I could jump the fence to our neighbor's backyard and be there in less than a minute. I only dared jumped the fence when I was with Michael, and I stopped completely on the day I learned that a friend of his had once caught his stomach on a fencepost. No surgery was needed, but there was a scar to remind him, and everyone he showed, of the imminent and physical dangers of breaking the rules.

As I approached the schoolyard, I slowed down. Much like my rule for leaving the forest, I could not allow myself to enter the yard without evening up my feet. With precision, I brought together my boots, sliding my left foot against the icy ground until it matched my right foot. Success. I entered the schoolhouse with a deep breath and a sigh.

In the classroom, my eye was drawn to the boy I liked,

who was combing his hair with the hot-pink comb that he carried in his pocket every day. I liked that he carried a comb in what was considered to be a girl's color. Anything that fell outside of typical social lines impressed me. It also struck me as a positive thing that for all their meanness to one another and to me, my classmates never teased the boy for having a pink comb.

To get a little sympathy, I complained to a classmate about how my head hurt from turning the key on my retainer. She seemed interested, so I continued to open up the conversation, explaining how Martha had told me to tell her if my Uncle Brian or Tu-Tu said anything religious to me.

"Why do you call your grandmother Tu-Tu?"

"Oh, well, because my parents met in a cult in San Francisco, and the cult leader sent them to Hawaii to buy a house, but that was really a trick to get them out of the cult, and then they were kicked out, but they didn't have enough money to leave Hawaii, so they stayed for three years, and then my brother was born, and Tu-Tu is Hawaiian for Grandmother."

My classmate looked at me with a puzzled expression. "What's a cult?"

When I told her that it was a "fake religion where they brainwash all of the members," she seemed shocked, so I quickly changed the subject and asked how her vacation was. Later that hour, I got to help her with her decimal points, which pleased me. On the walk home, I worried about whether I had said too much when I talked about the cult. It seemed I was always either saying too much or not enough.

Rainey was the only person at home when I arrived. "It's colder than a witch's tit in a brass brazier out there," she said in her thick Maine accent. I laughed. I had started calling Rainey 'Mom Number Two.' She called me 'Twat.' Having never heard the word before, I assumed it was simply a term of endearment. I thought it sounded cute: *Twat.*

"You got some mail, Twat," Rainey said. She handed me a large manila envelope. Inside was the eight by ten autographed glossy photo I had requested of Tom Wopat, A.K.A. 'Luke Duke.'

Rainey and I played Uno together for over an hour. We talked about her children, including her daughter Anna who had died of cancer. She told me that my pinkies, which were both curved slightly inward, were just like Anna's had been. I had never given much thought to my pinkies before, but I liked having any connection with a child of Rainey.

I won two rounds of Uno and then Rainey won two rounds. The perfect stopping point. Rainey set down the cards. "You're too skinny, Twat. I'm going to make you some mashed potatoes."

"From the box?" I asked.

"No. You know I make 'em fresh. That box crap is what your mother uses."

I set the table, guessing at which side of the plates to put the silverware and glasses.

Rainey stirred the pot of boiling potatoes and said, "I saw on the news that Samantha Smith is writing a book."

"I heard," I said. "I bet it has a lot of grammatical mistakes. She's from a back-woodsy part of Maine, you know." I switched the subject. "Do you know that my Dad's Mom, my Grandma Barbara, corrects Michael's and my grammar in our letters and sends them back to us? She has to correct more of Michael's grammar though."

"Why don't you read Samantha Smith's book first before you decide it's not any good?" The words stung. Rainey was mine. I believed I was her favorite child, and I intensely disliked the idea that she admired or was fond of any other children. I wasn't even thrilled when she mentioned her grandkids. Somehow I felt I had proprietary rights on her affection.

"Nah. I've got too many other things to read." As far as I was concerned, Samantha Smith could take a long walk off a short pier. If I couldn't be her, or at least be like her, I didn't want to hear about her.

Martha and Michael returned together a short while later. Michael had mouthed off in school, and Martha had gone to pick him up. This set the tone for an edgy evening. The four of us ate in near silence, with the exception of the occasional request for salt and pepper. After dinner Martha told Michael to wash the dishes, and he refused. The two began arguing, and Rainey and I went off to our respective corners of the house, hers across from the bathroom and mine off of the living room. For the rest of the evening, I played Candy Land and Rebound by myself and admired my picture of Tom Wopat. I prayed again that night for all the pain in the world and to be able to use all of my brain.

Chapter 11
Why Spiders Don't Make Good Magnets

I wet the bed again. It was the third time in as many days, and I feared Martha's response. The day before, she had told me, "I know you're doing this on purpose, Katie."

She had been indifferent to my tears or my claim that, "I swear, I didn't mean to do it."

I bundled the soaked sheets and snuck down the basement stairs, being careful to avoid the steps that creaked so that Martha wouldn't hear me from her bedroom. I hid the sheets in the bottom of the laundry basket, under a pile of dirty clothes to be washed. With a heavy sense of shame, I tiptoed back upstairs.

During the heat of battle the day before, I had been bold enough to at least ask Martha why she thought I was wetting the bed on purpose. "It's all about your father. You're trying to get back at me."

She reminded me that just after the divorce, I had stomped my feet and shouted, "You made my Daddy go away."

"But Mom, I was four years old."

"Well, it still hurt. You don't forget something like that."

I didn't want her to be reminded of my perceived betrayal by showing her that I had wet the bed again, and I didn't want to get in trouble for something I was almost certain I was not doing on purpose. So I made my bed as if there were sheets under the comforter, planning to sleep on the stained, damp bed pad until I would be issued clean sheets that weekend.

Martha's concern that I was trying to get attention by wetting the bed seemed to be exacerbated by the fact that Matthew was due in town the next day for a brief visit. The two of them were planning an intervention of sorts for my brother.

At school that day, I went to the library to see if there was a copy available of Samantha Smith's book, but there were none on the shelf, nor any listed in the card catalog. That surprised me a little. I thought for a brief, happy moment that perhaps Samantha Smith was not as beloved by the Helena H. Dyer Elementary School library as she was by the rest of Maine and the world. I hesitated to ask the librarian about the book because I didn't want any of the grown-ups in my life to know I was interested in Samantha Smith. My fascination with her, however, overpowered my ego. I approached the librarian and quietly asked about the book. The rules of the library were to keep the volume of one's voice low, but also I didn't want anyone else to hear me asking about it. The librarian's face lit up, and she seemed to forget her own rules. "Oh, *that* book. I think it's due out next year. Isn't Samantha Smith wonderful? She's the pride of Maine." I smiled and agreed, gritting my teeth a little as I did so. I didn't want to talk about Samantha Smith or hear about how wonderful she was. I only wanted to read the book because I wanted to imagine doing something even more impressive and helpful than she had done.

In history class we learned about Thomas Jefferson and read the words of his 1802 letter to the Danbury Baptist Association: "...legislature should make no law respecting an establishment of religion, or prohibiting the free exercise thereof, thus building a wall of separation between Church and State." The teacher asked us why this separation was important and several hands shot up, including mine. A girl with freckles and a ponytail answered, "Because not everybody is the same religion, and it's not fair to make some people feel left out because they're different." Being different, it seemed, was the crux of most of the world's problems, not to mention my own.

The house was quiet when I got home. When Martha returned that evening, she told me that Matthew had come to take Michael to dinner and that Rainey was playing BEANO and would be spending the night at the home of one of her kids.

Michael hadn't done his chores, so Martha and I washed the dishes together. While I scrubbed and she rinsed, I told her about reading in school about the "wall of separation" between Church and State. "But why is it that in the pledge, we say 'under God?' And why is it that on money, there's 'In God we trust?'"

"Because there's not really anything separating Church and State."

"But there's supposed to be," I said, placing a plate in the dish drain.

"A lot of things are *supposed* to be, Katie."

"I think I'm going to start saying the pledge without 'under God.' I don't think it's right that we have to say it if school is part of the State." As I figured it, being an American allowed me to keep a wall of separation in my own life.

Martha's voice was tired, but she was clearly trying to sound interested. "Good for you, kiddo," she said. I smiled.

During dinner, I picked at the tough meat on my plate. I was rarely hungry, and eating often left me with a stomachache. I ate more when Rainey cooked, in part because the food was a little better, and in part because I felt like she had gone to a lot of trouble specifically for me, and I didn't want to let her down.

In much the same way that people are sometimes more polite to strangers than family members, when Martha cooked, I didn't feel so much need to make eating a production. I grimaced at the canned string beans and grey-brown steak. Martha noticed. "You know, Katie, there are starving people in the world."

"Where?" I asked.

"In Africa and China and even in America."

"In America?" I asked with genuine concern.

"Yes. There are a lot of kids who don't get to eat at night. You at least get food."

"I didn't know that kids in America are starving."

"Well, now you know. Now eat."

I started to cut the meat, and then I paused. "Okay, but how is my eating going to help? I may even be taking food out of their mouths."

Martha laughed. She sounded impressed when she replied, "That was a good one, Katie."

Pleased with myself, I considered that maybe I could compete in the comedy performance segment of *Star Search*.

"Get me some Pepsi, will you?" Martha said, interrupting my momentary fantasy.

"Okay."

I glanced at the Winston Churchill quote Martha had posted on the refrigerator door years earlier: "If you're not a liberal at twenty, you have no heart. If you're not a conservative at forty, you have no head."

When I pulled out the Pepsi bottle from the refrigerator I accidentally slammed the door and a magnet fell onto the floor. With an anxious tone I said, "I'm sorry. I didn't mean to do that." I snatched up the magnet from the floor and put it back in its place.

I was relieved when she told me, "It's alright Katie." I

poured her Pepsi and sat back down. "That reminds me of when you kids were little," she continued. "I found this huge wolf spider in the kitchen, and I grabbed the nearest spray can. I can't remember what it was, but it shellacked that spider with all its legs sticking out." She spread out her fingers on both hands to demonstrate.

"Awwww, gross," I exclaimed with morbid fascination.

"No. It was so interesting looking, I glued a magnet to the belly and stuck it on the fridge."

"Whoa. It was on the fridge when we were little?"

"Yes. But then one day I got mad and slammed the refrigerator door, and the spider fell and smashed into a bunch of pieces." She made a creepy crawly motion with her hand toward mine and had a sly glimmer in her eye. "Its little legs were all over the linoleum."

"Ewwww. That is wicked neat but also wicked yucky."

...

MARTHA AND MATTHEW talked in raised voices in the kitchen about how their intervention with Michael was failing. He had skipped school and taken off for the afternoon. I hadn't seen much of Matthew during his visit, as the focus was on getting Michael "back on track." I listened from the living room and then went into the kitchen and stood in the entryway watching them. It was strange to see them in the same room. I so badly wanted Matthew back in our lives on a permanent basis; but there in that room, standing on opposite sides of the dining table, they just didn't seem to be a match. It was like they were cut from different cloths with patterns that didn't go together. Martha turned toward me. "Katie, we're talking."

That was my cue to leave, and I didn't take it. I felt a boiling from inside. I may have had some trouble with stealing at one time, but it had been over a year since I'd taken anything, and that business with Matthew's contacts happened when I was six. For years I had been, for the most part, pleasant and agreeable. I respected my elders; I was good in school; I always did my chores and sometimes did Michael's chores. I was even doing my best not to drink any fluids at night so that I wouldn't wet the bed. I hadn't stabbed anyone with a needle, or lit any fires in the backyard, or tried to strangle anyone, or been on drugs, or had to go to summer school, or been foulmouthed. Suddenly, I blurted out, "I'm the good one, and you two spend all your time on Michael."

Matthew was motionless; his face lacked any discernible expression. Martha looked at me with pain in her eyes. "I'm sorry honey. You're right."

"It's okay," I said quietly.

"No, it's not," she said. "We do have to talk, though. Why don't you go draw for a while?"

I went to my room. My brother arrived soon after, and I heard muffled shouts and pleas and cries. Matthew came in to give me a hug and a kiss before leaving for the night and told me that we would "spend some time together" before he left Maine.

The next day Martha took me to our doctor's office for my annual checkup. Dr. Kaz was always friendly and charming and kind to me. When Martha suggested to him during the appointment that I had been wetting the bed on purpose, he replied, "She's not doing it on purpose, Martha. Some kids don't get control of their bladders until they're older." She argued with him to no avail. He was adamant that this was not some subconscious revenge, but in fact a fairly common biological occurrence, even for ten-and-a-half-year-olds. "She's small. Her bladder's small. It fills up, and she has to pee. It's as simple as that."

I looked toward her and, in the silence of my mind, said, "Ha. I told you so."

Matthew wasn't allowed in the house if Martha wasn't home, but he could park his van in front of it, so we played backgammon on the bed he had built in the back of the vehicle. After the final round I asked, "Can we play the Folded Paper Game?" He agreed and blocked my view as he wrote down a word on the paper. Then I focused my breathing and told him what I saw. We played for a while, but I didn't come up with any connections. Finally, he seemed a bit frustrated with me, and we stopped.

After the failed intervention and before Matthew was to leave, he installed a dance bar in front of my closet, and Martha gave me a poster of a ballerina. Under the ballerina's pirouetting feet read a quote from William Arthur Ward: "If you can imagine it, you can achieve it. If you can dream it, you can become it." By the time the poster was hung, Matthew was gone again.

Martha took me to McDonalds and we sat across from one another at a small table, quietly eating hamburgers. I glanced up, and my eyes widened as a man with a full, dark beard walked through the doorway. For a moment, I thought it was Matthew, and when I realized it wasn't, I could feel my face sink. Martha looked toward the door and then back to me. She paused for a moment before gently saying, "You thought that was your father, didn't you?" I nodded. We continued eating our hamburgers in silence.

The next day, things were back to our version of normal. Martha and Michael shouted at one another in the kitchen, and Rainey and I stayed alone in our rooms. The noise was terrible. As the yelling continued, I sat on the mustard yellow carpet, hugging my legs and rocking myself back and forth. I tried to *will* them to stop arguing. I prayed that my God-genie would give me all of their upset and make them be quiet.

Then there was a slam of my brother's door and a final

admonishment from Martha; then a pause. My door opened, and I looked up to see my mother. She stopped short and stared at me. Her brows furrowed and her tone was harsh. "What are you doing?" she asked.

In a flash it occurred to me that if I said that I was rocking back and forth because I couldn't stand listening to the arguing, she might turn her anger toward me. Instead, I said, "I'm upset about Daddy leaving."

She immediately softened and approached me. Out of sheer sadness and exhaustion, I burst out crying. She sat next to me on the carpet and cradled me. As she stroked my hair and held me, she told me, "I know, Katie. I know." The lesson was clear: being comforted is much more pleasant than being scolded.

That night, I practiced moving things with my mind. I tried moving my Barbie dolls, and when I could not accomplish the task I tried moving a piece of paper with no success.

Before bed, I prayed again for all the pain in the world. "If you don't want to give it to me permanently, just give it to me for one minute. I can take it." And then... "If I can't be something great, please let me die."

That night I dreamt that I could *almost* fly. My body lifted up over the pavement and then dropped back down. Up and then down, up and down. I never could quite get the lift I needed to stay in the sky.

Chapter 12
Why She Wanted a Buick

Although, at nearly eleven years old, I still had a hard time talking with most people, I was comfortable enough around Martha to yammer away. I kept talking and talking until finally she said, "Katie, you need to find a creative outlet for your dramatic energy." She was trying to gather all the dirty clothes for the laundry, and I decided to give her a break from my talking for a while. I knew that money was a great stressor for Martha, so, to save on electricity, I had taken it upon myself to turn off the lights after anyone left a room. When she left the living room with the laundry basket in hand I flipped all the switches. "Katie, would you please stop turning off the lights?" she said. "I'm coming right back into the room."

"Oh, sorry. I thought you were done." I immediately forgot about deciding to give her a break and followed her down to the basement, chatting about nothing in particular. Her cat, Kickus, a nasty American Longhair that was feral when she found him the previous year, purred at Martha's leg and then hissed at me as I walked down the stairs. I was convinced the thing had it out for me. Martha headed toward the washing machine and started separating the dirty laundry. I had hidden yet another set of peed-on sheets in a bundle at the bottom of the basket, and she was about to find them. I kept talking in an effort to distract

Hiding in Water

her. It didn't work.

She spotted the sheets and halted with a sigh. "Katie," she said as she shook her head. "You're going to have to start doing your own laundry."

"But Michael doesn't, and he's three and a half years older."

"Well, he doesn't wet the bed." She poured the laundry detergent into the machine.

I became indignant. "That's not fair."

"Life's not fair, Katie."

My mouth dropped open. "You don't have to be so mean about it."

"If you want to think I'm mean, Katie, that's fine. At least I stayed." I was silent. 'At least I stayed' seemed to be the mantra of motherhood.

We passed our dog Molly's bathroom area as we trudged back up the stairs. Molly had a small nook in the basement where we spread out newspapers over a plastic garbage bag for her to do her business. Michael and I were supposed to switch off cleaning it up every other day, but it was obvious that it hadn't been done in some time. Martha asked, "Whose day is it to clean up Molly's papers?"

"Well, I did it last Thursday, and Michael was supposed to do it on Friday, but he didn't. And I didn't think it was fair for me to have to do it yesterday with the extra poop. And today's his day."

"Well somebody's got to do it."

Kickus swatted a claw at me on the way back up the stairs. I spent the rest of the afternoon and evening watching television, dodging the cat, who flicked its tail menacingly at me whenever I passed by, and pouring over the Service Merchandise store guide, wishing each item would magically appear in my closet overnight.

On television there was a news teaser about Samantha Smith. Why did she have to be so...perfect? I changed the channel. Much to Martha's dismay, I watched two *Brady Bunch* reruns in a row. "Katie, I've asked you not to watch that show. I don't want you to grow up believing that's a real family." If she knew my deepest thoughts, she would probably be more concerned with my watching *Bewitched* reruns and trying to figure out how I could wiggle my nose to perform magical tasks.

From the living room, I heard Michael come into the house. I held my breath, preparing to hear another blowup and considering whether I should sneak off into my room.

Martha's voice was strained. "Where have you been, Michael? It's late."

"Out," he responded.

"Let me see your eyes. Jesus, Michael, they're all glassy. And you reek."

"Ma, just leave me alone." A second later his door slammed. My body relaxed. I waited a moment before going to the kitchen and asking Martha if I could help her make dinner.

"No, honey. But will you go downstairs and take care of Molly's food and papers? I can't deal with your brother right now."

"Okay, Mom."

I didn't like going to the basement when no one else was down there, but I had developed a way of dealing with it. It was part of my rule-set for fending off monsters. This included the following: If no one is accompanying you or already down in the basement, snap your fingers on the way down the stairs. At night, when you switch off your bedroom light, you must run and then leap onto the bed (it is a good idea to have the covers already pulled back in preparation). The bedroom closet door must be completely closed by the time the light is turned off, so that any monsters that may be hiding therein can't escape during the night. Even during the hottest, most humid nights of summer only one foot can dangle out from under the sheet, and even then it cannot dangle so low as to be easily grabbed or clawed at from under the bed. It is preferable to wear socks in bed for extra protection. A pillow, sheet or blanket (and, if possible, all three) must be pulled up over your head. You are allowed to peek out only to look at the alarm clock. In the bathroom, when no one is taking a shower, you must keep the shower curtain open so that no monsters can hide behind it; but if your mother likes the curtain closed because it looks tidier, you should never look at the closed curtain when you enter the bathroom. Instead, rush past the opening where the curtain and the wall meet and avert your eyes to look either at the sink, mirror or commode. You should avoid bathing at all costs, but if your mother tells you that you must, it should be a bath and not a shower because monsters can grab and strangle you in the shower. When you absolutely must bathe, whip back the shower curtain as fast as possible so that no monsters hiding behind the curtain can grab you. The faster you open the curtain, the faster the monsters are forced to disappear. Ignoring these rules will have dire consequences.

I spent the rest of the evening writing in my journal. I very much wanted Kitty to be like Anne Frank's Kitty, a confidant to whom I was always honest. I sometimes found being honest a challenge, as the adults in my life had such differing opinions, and I wanted to please them all. Being honest with one, I feared, might upset the other. It was a delicate balance I very much wanted to maintain. Still, I so badly wanted to be good, or at least good enough.

I believed that if I were good, I would one day be rewarded with the right answers. When I imagined heaven it was a place where those who got there would find out...everything.

This did not only include the answers to such grand questions as *the meaning of life*, although that was certainly a part of it. It meant finding out the answers to questions I had previously gotten wrong on any and all quizzes and tests. It meant using my entire brain, so that I would be able to do all the magical tasks I desired. It meant never having anxiety because I would always know what was going to happen from moment to moment until the end of time.

After school the next day, I walked home in the cold, hugging my Holly Hobby lunchbox to my chest. Just before I made it to Pig Road, I saw a Buick swerve to miss some children. They screamed, intimidated by the hulking steel. I smiled to myself and decided that one day I would buy a Buick. The closer I got to the house, the more my cheeriness left me. The air was dry and frigid, and the sky was dark. I could tell it was about to snow, and I began to cry. It wasn't the kind of crying done to get anyone's attention, at which I was also quite skilled; I was just so cold that I couldn't imagine ever being warm again.

We weren't allowed to touch the thermostat when Martha wasn't home, so as soon as she arrived I asked if we could turn up the heat. "We can't right now, honey. It's too expensive."

"How much does it cost to run a house, Mom?"

"Oh, about a thousand dollars a month," she said.

"A thousand dollars?" I exclaimed. I hadn't realized that it cost so much money. "And your job pays you that?"

"Well, not quite. Your father's supposed to help, but he doesn't. That's why we have food stamps."

"Are they stamps like the kind on envelopes?"

She sounded surprised. "I haven't shown you before?

"No. I've never seen them."

"They're in a book. I'll show you." She dug in her purse and showed me a small stapled booklet about the size of a dollar bill. It read 'U.S. Department of Agriculture' on the front. She let me flip through it and showed me how some of the coupons were valued at five dollars and others were ten dollars, for a grand total of sixty-five dollars.

I was impressed. "And you just give these to the cashier instead of money?"

"Yes."

"That's wicked cool."

She pulled the book out of my hand. "There's nothing cool about it, Katie. It's humiliating. The last time I was at the store I pulled out the food stamps and two women behind me started talking about 'Welfare Mothers' living off the state. We wouldn't be in this position if it weren't for your father, Katie."

I didn't want to talk about Matthew. "One day, I'm going to have a lot of money, and I'm going to buy you a house."

Her tone softened. "Oh, honey. You don't have to do that. Every kid wants to buy their mother a house when they grow up. But I have a house. You just try to be the best *you* that you can be and don't worry about buying me a house."

That night, Rainey made chipped beef on toast, which she called by its military name, "shit on a shingle." Martha was walking into the kitchen when Rainey said to me, "Twat, go ahead and set the table."

Stopping short, Martha exclaimed, "Rainey..." Her eyes were wide and her mouth was agape with just the hint of a smile at the corners.

"What?" Rainey responded. "She knows I love her."

There was something in the exchange that I missed, but I decided not to question it.

As we ate, Martha moaned, "Mmmmm." This was not the first time she seemed to derive such pleasure from eating.

"Mom," I said. "Can you stop making those noises? It's embarrassing."

She was smiling and unapologetic. "I enjoy my food."

"Do you have to enjoy it so much? Geesh."

Michael peered at me and in an annoyed tone said, "You eat like a princess." I hadn't noticed that when I held my fork, I stuck out my crooked pinky. I saw his comment as a sign of things to come; one day, I *would* be a princess. I imagined I would be like Princess Grace, a big movie star who marries a prince in a foreign land. In my brief fantasy I left out the part where the princess dies in a horrible car crash.

After dinner, I went with Rainey and Martha to their support group meeting, where we heard lots of people talk about "hitting bottom." Afterwards, Martha announced that she was going to go back to school to get a college degree and get us off of Welfare. I was thrilled and proud.

Chapter 13
Why She Wanted a Stalker

I wrote another book. I had learned from my third-grade experience two years prior, of writing about the downed pilot and the co-pilot who dug up the body, that it was probably better for me to stick with lighter fare. I wrote my book about a lamp named Charlie, who was born in a factory, but is found to be defective and, therefore, gets thrown away by the President of the United States. Charlie is then rescued from the trash by a married couple, named Carrie and Marty, who take Charlie into their home and appreciate him for the wonderful lamp he is. Then, once the president sees what a good lamp Charlie turns out to be, he reconsiders bringing him back to the White House. It might be the end for Charlie's, Carrie's and Marty's friendship, but all ends well. Charlie is brought to the oval office, and not only do Carrie and Marty get to visit him there, but they also gain the ear of the president and get to advise him on social and economic issues pertaining to the lower and middle class. No one died in this book, so I figured I was safe.

After I finished writing, Martha and I ate dinner together and watched the news. There was another story about Samantha Smith. This time it was about how she had become the subject of a stalker. A teenaged boy named Robert John Bardo had taken a bus to Maine in an attempt to meet her but was stopped by the police and sent home. I didn't know what a stalker was, but I decided then that I wanted one.

I sneezed and was annoyed when Martha didn't say, "Bless you," so I got up in a huff and walked to the kitchen. When I opened the refrigerator I saw that it was nearly empty except for Martha's Pepsi and a few carrots. I sighed, walked back into the living room and plunked down on the sofa. "Tu-Tu saves money by cutting open her toothpaste tubes and using the last bits of toothpaste inside. And also she rinses and dries out her paper towels afterward so she can use them again." These seemed to be smart ideas that I thought could be of help in Martha's war with money.

"She's so crazy. She acts like she's still living in the Great Depression."

"What was the Great Depression like?" I asked. We hadn't studied it in school, but my elder relatives referenced it frequently.

"Well, your grandfather used to shoot rats in the street." A glint formed in her eyes. "He told me once, 'Never touch the metal of the gun with your fingers. The acids destroy it, and also, depending on where that gun gets used later, you don't want your prints on it.'"

My eyes widened. "Did he ever shoot anybody?"

She dismissed the statement. "No." And then... "Well, not that I know of. Although I wouldn't be surprised." She nodded toward the book shelf. "If you want to see what the Depression was like, go get that book on the shelf."

I got up and walked toward the books. "Which one?"

"The one with the black-and-white photos. I've seen you looking through it before. It's the one over on the top shelf on the right."

I pulled off the hefty book from the shelf and sat down

on the sofa with it on my lap. As I flipped through the pages I began to get lost in the images. It was hard to believe that the pictures were of America and Americans. There was one with police officers standing guard outside the entrance to New York's closed World Exchange Bank; unemployed men vying for jobs at the American Legion; migrant pea pickers camping in tents and lean-tos; impoverished families living on the edges of highways; and one image called "Migrant Mother," which had a caption about how the woman's family lived on frozen vegetables from the surrounding fields as well as birds that the children killed.

"Why didn't anyone help them?" I asked.

Martha snorted. "Because rich people are selfish and spoiled."

This posed a conundrum for me. I badly wanted to be rich to make our lives better and to have all the things in life that I desired, but I didn't ever want to be selfish and spoiled. According to Martha, they were inextricable concepts.

I put back the book on the Depression and got another one from the shelf. "What's this book?"

Martha peered up. "Let me see. It's an etiquette book."

"What's etiquette?"

"It means 'manners,' like respecting your elders and how to behave at parties.

I opened the book to a page that read, "Never discuss politics, religion, or money in mixed company." I bit my lip. Those were the three main things I thought about. But then, as a general rule, I wasn't invited to parties, so I figured I didn't have to worry. I considered re-writing my book without the political angle but decided I didn't like the fifth-grade teacher enough to worry about it.

Chapter 14
Why He Threw the Knife

The argument started innocently enough. Michael and I were both in the kitchen. He was standing, and I was seated at the dining table. I asked offhandedly, "Have you ever noticed that you, Mom and Dad all have names that start with 'M,' and mine begins with 'K'?"

"That's because you're adopted," he said with a sly grin.

"That would mean we're both adopted because we look exactly alike," I responded in a snide tone.

His amusement turned to disgust. "I don't look like you, you spaz."

"Well, you look enough like me so that people know we're related, jerk."

It was the 'jerk' comment that set him off.

He pulled back his fist as if he was going to punch me and instead kicked me in the shin. I kicked back. He slapped me on the side of the head, and I tried to slap him but missed. "I'm telling," I said. I got up out of the chair and rushed toward the door to the basement. Molly nipped at my heels.

"You'd better not," Michael said with a growl.

Just as I put my hand on the doorknob, I felt a rush of air on the left side of my face. I jerked back my head and saw that the point of one of his knifes had landed in the door, just centimeters from my head. It was a hunting knife with a four-inch blade. I knew he kept knives on him, and he had certainly taunted me with them, flinging small pen knives at my feet outside in the back yard, but never inside, and never at my head. I turned to face him, shocked. In that moment, I expected to see surprise or guilt in his face, something that would have shown me that he realized he had gone too far. But his eyes were cold and dark. We stood for a moment staring at one another, firmly planted in our spots. Then I flung open the basement door and ran downstairs, screaming for Martha.

Kickus hissed at me as I rushed into Martha's room. Martha was sitting atop her bed, surrounded by books, papers, pens and highlighters. She had apparently taken a break from studying and was mending a pair of pants. I talked quickly. "Michael just threw a knife at me."

"Why?"

"Does it matter? Mom, he threw a knife at me."

"Katie, you two are going to have to start dealing with your problems on your own."

"Mom," I cried out.

She sighed. "Go get him."

I got as far as the bottom of the basement stairs and called up, "Michael, Mom wants to see you."

I sat down on Martha's bed. I felt nauseous, so I focused on her sewing basket, which had at one time belonged to my great-grandmother. It was a small rectangular box about six inches wide, made of golden colored woven wicker. I had admired it for as long as I had known it existed, and had even asked twice if I could have it if Martha ever decided she didn't want it anymore.

Michael entered the room. Martha's tone was calm but concerned. "Michael, did you throw a knife at your sister?"

"Yeah."

I looked at her as if to say, 'I told you so.'

"Go get the knife, Michael," she said.

While Michael was gone Martha closed her eyes. "I cannot deal with this fighting. You two *have* to work things out."

Michael returned a moment later with the knife in hand, sheathed in black leather.

"Give it to me," she said.

He looked positively glum as he handed it over.

"I am taking this knife away from you for three months, Michael."

"Three months," I piped up. "That's all?"

"Katie, quit it. Listen, you two. I'm doing the best I can without your father. You need to start handling things in an adult way. Now, I've got things to do, so both of you go back upstairs and don't bother one another."

Michael and I trudged up the stairs silently and went to our rooms.

Within days, Michael had picked the simple lock on Martha's door and taken back his knife. The day after that, I entered his room to look for it, in an effort to hide it from him. I figured that if I found it he couldn't tell Martha on me because he wasn't supposed to have it in the first place. I opened his desk drawers and searched them thoroughly.

In the last one I found a short story he had written for his English class. It was several stapled pages long but torn in half. On the top of the first page was written in red pencil, "A for creativity. F for grammar." I held both halves in my hand. *A for creativity. F for grammar.* He had tried. He had followed through on an assignment and thought he wrote a piece that was worth something, but because he wasn't good with grammar he had failed. He had torn it in half, but he had saved it.

I considered Michael's school path. Before we moved to South Portland, we had been in Country School, which Martha always said was not as good academically. When we moved, I entered first grade and he entered fourth grade. There wasn't much I missed between Country School and Helena H. Dyer Elementary, and my transition had been pretty seamless. It occurred to me that I started learning cursive by second grade, but for as long as he had been in Country School, he hadn't been taught cursive. So that meant that by the time we were in South Portland, he was already two years behind. Then there was his age. As a December-born child, he was on the older side of the kids. "No wonder he's always behind," I said to myself. In that moment, my sadness and compassion for him competed with my resentment and anger.

I left Michael's room without searching further for the hunting knife. He never threw it at me again, only brandished it on occasion to run his thumb down the blade or run it against the grain of the cat's fur while silently glaring at me. He continued to throw the pen knives, but those had become an acceptable part of our interactions.

. . .

MICHAEL AND I were visiting our Great-Uncle Phil for the weekend. Uncle Phil was a gravelly voiced smoker with a thick Maine accent and a bawdy sense of humor. He was also remarkably strong for his age. He and my Uncle Anthony had recently transported a piano up two flights of stairs. Phil was at the top of the piano pulling it, and Anthony was at the bottom pushing it. Then, in amidst the grunting, Phil shouted, "Anthony. Anthony. Stop a second."

"What's the matter, Phil?" Anthony said, out of breath.

"You got a cigarette?"

Like the rest of the family, Uncle Phil was also very

frugal. One day, while grocery shopping, he stopped short at the apple basket. Disapproving of the newly risen cost, he said, "Jesus, you'd think they were giraffe's balls the price is up so high."

Uncle Phil lived with a woman named Skip. Phil had previously been married and divorced, and he and Skip were told by his priest that he couldn't get married again in a Catholic Church. Rather than marry in a Protestant Church, they decided to live "in sin."

Skip, Phil, Michael and I sat at their kitchen table. There were dozens of potted plants in the house. Everywhere I looked, there were leaves and blooms.

"You have a lot of plants," I said to Uncle Phil.

"Those are Skip's," he said.

I turned to Skip. "You have quite a green thumb, Skip."

Skip and Phil chuckled. "Well, yes I do," Skip said. "It's nice of you to notice. So, tell us about school. How is it going?"

I rambled on about my most recent book and how I had to prepare my Valentine's Day cards for the following week. After a minute or so, I noticed Michael getting up from the table and walking away, but I didn't think much about it until he called me into the living room. "Katie, come here a second."

"Why?" I called back.

"I want to show you something."

"I'm talking."

"Just come in here."

I looked at Skip and Phil, shrugged my shoulders and got up from the table. When I entered the living room, Michael grabbed me by the elbow and leaned down to my face. He whispered through gritted teeth. "What do you think you're doing, telling Skip she has a green thumb?"

"But it's a compliment," I tried to explain.

"I know exactly what it means, and it's not a compliment." He pointed his finger in my face and said, "Don't you ever call anyone that again. You need to apologize."

"No I don't need to apologize. Having a 'green thumb' means you're good with plants. It's a saying."

He loosed his grip and stood up straight. "Just don't say it again."

I was both annoyed at my brother and embarrassed for his mistake.

...

VALENTINE'S DAY CAME a week and a half later. Martha stood in the open doorway of my room with one hand behind her back and said, "I have a present for you, Katie." Then she pulled my great-grandmother's sewing basket from behind her.

"Really?" I asked, with a sudden burst of excitement.

"Really." She handed it to me and looked on with a sweet smile as I opened and closed the basket over and over again.

I slid the clasp back into place and looked up at her. "This is wicked awesome, Mom." I threw my arms around her and she held me close. When she let go, I walked over to my dresser and set the basket on top of it. "I'm going to put it right next to her soap dish and under the needlepoint that she did." The soap dish was white porcelain with hand-painted flowers and gold leaf trim around the edge. The needlepoint had an image of Jesus surrounded by children against a crisp white background. Underneath Jesus was embroidered the words "Suffer little children unto me. Matthew 19:14." I had not known that 'suffer' in this instance meant 'bring,' and I thought it meant that suffering children should turn to Jesus. I liked having him watch over me. Martha did not.

"I wish you'd get rid of that old thing. It's so ugly."

"I like it," I said, still smiling at my new treasure.

Chapter 15
Why the Curtains Had to Be Closed

As I lie in bed that Saturday morning, my mind drifted from one thought to another. As was customary, I tried to figure out the expansiveness of the Universe and infinity. I imagined getting kidnapped and then being rescued by 'Faceman' or 'B.A. Baracus' from *The A-Team*. Fantasies about Faceman ended in marriage. Fantasies about B.A. Baracus ended in him tossing my attackers aside while repeating, "I pity the fool." I imagined Samantha Smith being long forgotten and me taking her place as the girl from Maine who was saving the world and writing books.

In an effort to get out of the warm, comfy bed, I tried to move my covers with my mind. Unsuccessful, I finally stretched my arms, let out a big yawn and got up the old fashioned way.

The first stop was the bathroom, where I spotted a note from Michael taped to the toothpaste tube. It read precisely: "Katie, you are a hemroid." I peeled off the note from the tube and ran to Martha.

"Mom, what's a hemorrhoid?" I demanded.

She seemed utterly baffled by my question. "What?"

"Michael left me this note." I thrust it at her. She took it in hand and, upon reading it, began to laugh. Frustrated, I asked again, "What's a hemorrhoid?"

"It's nothing. Don't worry about it. I'll just save this

though." She gently folded the tape onto the paper and tucked the note in her pocket. Switching the subject, she said, "We'd better do your retainer." I peered at her with suspicion as she turned the key in my palatal expander. I was sure that note meant something unpleasant. She was still smiling when she said, "It's good you're getting this thing taken out before you visit your father. He wouldn't know what to do with it."

...

I WAS LYING on the sofa watching television when Martha returned home from her college classes. As she entered the living room, she said of the open curtains, "Katie, would you please close those?" Generally, I would shut them as soon as I heard her car pull up, but on this day I forgot. As I pulled the draw cord for the curtains, I said, "I get why you don't want the curtains open at night, so that no one sees in, but why do we always have to close them when it's still light out?"

"I like it dark."

The rule was that when Martha came home, she got the sofa, so I moved to a nearby chair.

The phone rang. "Katie, will you get that? If it's for me, tell them I'm not here."

"Do I have to? I don't like having to lie." Although I was by no means a purely honest child, I wanted to be more truthful, and having to lie for my mother bothered me in particular. I had begun to get anxious whenever I heard the phone ring.

"Katie, just answer the phone please." I followed instructions and told the person on the other end of the line that my mother wasn't there. Then I went back to watching television.

When dinner was ready, Michael and I hungrily sat down at the kitchen table. It was one of our few mutual favorites, macaroni and cheese with hotdogs. Martha had set two plates, and she walked into the living room leaving us alone in kitchen.

After a confused moment I called to her. "Aren't you going to eat too?"

"I've already eaten," she called back.

I was certain she hadn't.

...

I WAS CONSTIPATED as a child. Throughout the schooldays I often found myself having the urge to use the bathroom but not having much success. One day, I was in the girls' room stall right next to my classmate whom Michael had stabbed with the needle years before. We had remained on good terms despite the incident. As she was becoming more popular, however, we were growing distant. I sat on the commode, trying to hold in what was making its way out. 'Of all the times to finally go,' I thought to myself.

And then, when I couldn't bear holding it any longer, it came out like rabbit pellets. I knew she could hear. Out of embarrassment I sat for an extra long time, until I heard her flush, wash her hands and leave. Eventually, I ambled back into the classroom. My classmate was seated next to two other popular girls, and I averted my eyes as I passed. It was no use. As I walked by, she said slowly, "Plop...plop...plop." The other girls laughed. I cringed and slunk into my chair.

A mention of my latest social blunder to Mom meant another trip to Dr. Kaz. He prescribed a chocolate tasting laxative, which I liked and made sure to take every morning.

My constipation was big news in the family. My Uncle Anthony patted me on the shoulder and chuckled as he joked, "You know what they say about constipated people? They don't give a crap." My Mother's Aunt Madeline told me to bring in a book to read while I was "going," and took to asking me, "Did you have a BM today?" each time I entered her house. I was somewhat distressed that my entire family seemed to know my bathroom issues. On the other hand, it was nice to be the center of attention.

It was Tu-Tu who took a direct, if uncomfortable, approach. Each time I visited for the weekend, she would fill a red rubber bag with warm water and attach a long, thin hose with a nozzle at the end. Then she would instruct me to insert the nozzle into my rectum and squeeze the bag. She would leave the bathroom, and I would sit wondering how I could escape. A few times I tried to follow her directions, but I just couldn't seem to get the hang of it, nor did I particularly want to. It felt like my body wasn't mine, and others could experiment on it at will.

Finally, I got in the habit of waiting for what seemed like an adequate enough time, then quietly uncapping the bag and pouring out the contents into the sink. I would wash my hands the way Tu-Tu had taught me, an over-under motion with the soap for twenty seconds and then rinse under steamy hot water. Then I would emerge with a smile on my face to tell her I had finished.

On a Sunday afternoon, I came out of the bathroom to find Tu-Tu preparing lunch. "Uncle Brian's going to join us," she said. When Brian entered Tu-Tu's apartment, he gave me a big hug. Tu-Tu and I set up three of her folding tray tables as Brian flipped through the enormous Bible that sat atop a pedestal next to the television. Then Tu-Tu presented us with homemade lentil soup. It was delicious, and I swallowed a big bite.

"Chew," Tu-Tu said.

I held the spoon in my hand, confused. "Chew soup?"

"Yes, you should chew everything you eat. Twenty times each bite." She surely liked the number twenty an awful lot. As Tu-Tu counted, I chewed each spoonful of soup twenty times before swallowing.

Then Brian spoke up. "You know, it's important that you

become a Christian, Katie, so that we can still eat together when you get older."

"What do you mean?" I asked.

"Well, we eat together now, but we're really not supposed to. Christians are only supposed to break bread with other Christians."

"Oh," I said. I looked to Tu-Tu for guidance as to how to respond. She had a closed-mouth smile but had her eyes trained on her soup as she silently chewed. It seemed to me that while my mother would not likely appreciate a conversion to Christianity on my behalf, she would still eat meals with me, whereas if I didn't become a Christian there would come a time when the rest of her family might not. I weighed my options carefully but made no immediate decisions.

Chapter 16
Why You Can't Step in the River Once

My two-week spring vacation was coming up. I was to visit Matthew for its entirety, and Michael would be with us for the second week. Matthew had joined a commune on a small parcel of farmland in North Carolina. The commune was very well-organized, with a dozen or so adults sharing possessions and resources. Everyone had chores. There was a large garden to be tended, group meals to be prepared, and rooms to be cleaned. I became the house dishwasher while I was there.

Matthew instructed his housemates on everything from the appropriate way to garden to the appropriate way to travel a spiritual path. Sometimes the other members appeared interested, and sometimes their eyes glazed over. When that happened, I felt embarrassed for my father. He didn't seem to notice when others were indifferent. Or if he did, he didn't seem to care.

Matthew took me to a peaceful stream, where I picked daisies and braided them together to make necklaces. As difficult as it was for me to relate to my peers, it was even harder for me to witness my father not being able to relate to his. I wanted him to understand that some of the people at the commune might not want to hear him talk about his ability to see them through Christ's eyes. I didn't know quite how to bring it up though. I handed him a flower necklace to wear and asked, "What do you do if someone doesn't want to learn from you?"

"I don't get fixated on that."

"But what if they talk behind your back?" I closed my eyes, worried about how he would respond. Then, once I worked up the nerve, I opened them.

He answered with a firm but not unkind tone. "It's important for the pupil to respect the teacher. If a person notices that others are speaking against the teacher, then that person needs to weigh it impartially and look to him or herself to make a correction. It's important not to partake of anyone else's poison by returning the same to them or even by keeping some memory of it in your heart."

I took it to mean that I shouldn't worry about what anyone else thought. As long as I believed in the teachings of my father, nothing else mattered.

When Michael arrived, we worked with Matthew as carpenter's assistants for a dollar an hour. On a day off, he told us he was taking us to a barbeque. "There's going to be a pig on a spit," he said. Having never seen any animal on a spit before, Michael and I were intrigued.

A stop at Matthew's bank left Michael and me in the vehicle while he deposited a check. Our windows were down to allow for a breeze, and as we sat waiting, a police car came up behind us. When it passed by Michael craned his head partway out the window and yelled, "Pig." I gasped. Then the police car stopped.

My heart was in my throat as a tall uniformed officer got out of the car and approached us. He looked down at my brother with coal black eyes that matched his hat and said with a slow drawl, "Did you just yell 'pig' at me?"

Michael didn't miss a beat. "No. We're going to a

barbecue, and I was yelling about the pig that's going to be there."

Then the officer turned to me. "Is that true?"

I could feel my face turn flush. I wasn't about to incur my brother's wrath on this one, and technically we *were* going to a barbecue where there would be a pig so, "Yes," I said meekly.

The officer eyed Michael and me circumspectly and then said, "Alright. Just don't let it happen again."

Once the officer drove away Michael let out a belly laugh. I wiped sweat off my brow. We didn't say a word about it when Matthew came back to the car.

At the barbecue, there was indeed a pig on a spit. It was hideous. Its front and hind legs were bound, and a metal rod was jammed through its mouth and out through its bottom. I quickly turned away. When I did so, I realized that all the white people were on one side of the yard, and all the black people were on the other side. I didn't see them mingle or even talk with one another. It was as if there were two different barbecues happening side by side.

...

WHEN WE RETURNED to Maine, I told Martha about the stream I had visited where I made chain necklaces out of flowers. She chuckled. "Did you step in the same river twice?"

"Huh?" I asked.

"It's a Buddhist saying. 'You can't step in the same river twice.'"

"What does it mean?" I inquired.

"It means that even though things may seem the same from day to day, there are always changes. Just like the river. The river seems like it's the same from moment to moment, but it's really changing all the time. So, you can't step into the same river twice."

An internal light bulb went on. "Oh, I get it."

Martha smiled and patted me on the shoulder. "Good. Now try to figure out: 'You can't step into the same river once.'"

"Uh...I don't know. What does that one mean?"

"It means that the moment you try to figure out something, it changes."

"What do you mean?"

"Think about it. The very act of trying to define something changes what that something is. It goes from something being experienced to something being thought about."

"Oh, I see." I had never considered that there might be a difference from the 'me' who did things and the 'me' who thought about things. It was rare for Martha to have time for these kinds of conversations, and I wanted to hear her thoughts on another topic that had been on my mind. "Mom," I said. "Why is it that the black people stay in the South? The white people hate them there."

Martha sighed. "Katie, there's just as much racism in the North; it may not be as obvious, but it's here. In the South, there might be white people who say awful things about the black people; in the North, the white people may not say anything to their faces, but they won't give them a job either."

"But nobody I know is racist."

"How would you know? We have maybe ten black people in Maine." I hadn't thought of it that way. Martha continued. "I once tried to have a conversation with your great-grandmother about her racism, and she said, 'I'm not a racist. Why, a mammy saved my father in the Civil War.'"

"What's a mammy?" I asked.

"Look it up." If 'at least I stayed' was Martha's mantra on motherhood, 'look it up' was her mantra on education. When the E volume of the encyclopedia set went mysteriously missing there were some problems posed, but mostly it was a sound parenting method. Still, I didn't always want to consult a book when the answer could be arrived at more instantaneously.

"Come on, Mom, just tell me."

"A mammy is an offensive term for a black nursemaid who has to take care of the white children of a family."

"Oh." I was silent. I tried to remind myself that my great-grandmother was from a different time. I already knew that when my uncles Anthony and Brian were in their teens in the early 1970's, she had kicked the two of them out of the house for an afternoon because they were drinking Coca Cola. Even though the soda hadn't contained trace amounts of cocaine since 1929, she was caught in the past and refused to allow "drugs" in her home. Still, this new information about an intolerance born of a time and place in history was hard for me to swallow.

...

MAINE WAS IN the midst of a heat wave so Martha held the family gathering for my eleventh birthday in her basement bedroom. The relatives filed in and Michael opened his present first. We always got one present on the other's birthday, which I thought was a very fair tradition. After opening his gift, he presented me with his gift for me. It was his entire collection of stuffed animals. I was not the only one who was taken aback. The multitude of grown-ups chorused, "Wow," and "That's so nice of you, Michael," and "What a great gift."

I gleefully opened present after present, saving the largest box for last. It was one and a half feet tall, a foot wide and a foot deep. Martha had wrapped it in pink floral paper. I stuck the bow on my head and ripped into it to find a brass desk lamp. I gasped. I didn't see another gift around, and certainly nothing so large as a writing desk, but I bit my bottom lip with hope.

Martha smiled and said, "So, we couldn't get the other

part of this gift here in time, but it's coming soon."

I gasped again. "What is it?" I asked tentatively.

"Well, why don't you guess?" Uncle Brian said.

"Um..." A desk was such a huge expense, and if I was wrong, I didn't want anyone to feel bad, so I said, "...a lamp shade?"

Martha shook her head. "It already has a lamp shade. Take another guess."

"A light bulb?"

There were some distinct groans and chuckles. Brian said with gentle sarcasm, "Yes, we couldn't get a light bulb here in time."

"No," Martha said, batting his hand. "Come on Katie. What goes with a *desk* lamp?"

"A..."

"Come on. You can say it."

I winced. "A...desk?"

Everyone cheered. Relief mixed in with joy, and a few days later my beautiful writing desk arrived. It was perfect: dark wood and brass fixtures, two large drawers for notebooks and papers and one long drawer for pens and pencils. To protect the finish, Martha got me an ink blotter, on top of which I set my Woodstock typewriter that Dominic had given me four years earlier.

Chapter 17
Why the Glass Needs to Be Tipped 45 Degrees

Michael wouldn't be in North Carolina until July of 1984 because he had to attend summer school again and was also reaching an age when he was more interested in being with his friends. My solo arrival marked the start of a practice whereby Matthew would have me empty my luggage and then show me how things could be repacked in a more efficient manner. "But why are we doing this, Dad?" I asked, flummoxed.

"If you get anything this summer, you won't be able to fit it in this bag." The possibility of 'getting things' made me much more interested in the activity.

Matthew had left the commune, so the visit was in Chapel Hill, where he had rented a farmhouse from the family of a recently deceased farmer. There was no farm anymore, just a big garden, but the lawn was vast. After Matthew showed me around the yard, he poured us both glasses of water. "The most important thing to do for your health is to drink plenty of water."

Throughout the summer, I was reminded over and over to keep my water glass filled.

Matthew's magician friend, Howard, was his roommate. He was only there for a few days into my visit before he left without notice. He hadn't said goodbye to me, and Matthew hadn't offered to tell me why he was gone. Two days later, when I asked Matthew about Howard's absence, he told me, "He's going through a rough time. His dog died, his car broke down, and his girlfriend broke up with him. So, I suggested he do some camping for a couple of weeks to clear his head." Matthew then gave me strict instructions that I was not to touch any of Howard's belongings, especially his magician's props. I promised that I wouldn't go into Howard's room, but I made sure to cross my fingers behind my back, in order to justify my intention to sneak in at every opportunity.

Whenever Matthew was gone from the house, I went into Howard's room to try to figure out his magic rings. When I could find no break or hidden cut in them, I wondered if maybe he really did have magical powers. Considering the powers that Matthew told me he had, and considering the fact that Howard was his student, I decided that it wasn't such a farfetched thought. In my mind, Howard became magical.

...

GRANDMA BARBARA HAD sent Matthew a check for me so that I could get my first ten-speed bike. Matthew cashed it but wouldn't tell me how much the check was for, only that it would cover the cost of the bike. I wanted a red one, and when we got to the bike store, I zeroed in on a candy apple Schwinn. "That's the one," I exclaimed.

"Well, let's just look around for a while."

"Please, Dad. This is the one."

He looked at the price tag. I asked, "Do I have enough?"

"Yes," he said. "But let's just keep looking.

He picked out a silver Centurion and looked at the tag. "Try this one, Katie."

I reluctantly sat on it and picked out everything I could

think of that I didn't like. "The bar is bulky... The wheels are too big..." and most of all, "It's not red."

"This one is on sale, Katie."

"Yes, but you said I have the money for the other one."

"This one is silver. Silver is faster than red."

We went back and forth without making any headway and then left the store. Back at his house, he extolled the virtue of the silver bike. "I just don't like it, Dad. I want the red one." He suggested that a silver bike was better than no bike, so I finally gave in and we went back the next day and got the Centurion. He handed over a small stack of crisp bills, and the cashier rang up the purchase. Matthew kept the change.

Two days later, I was riding my new bike around Matthew's neighborhood when I approached a large dog. It began growling at me as I got closer and then barked as I passed by. Then it gave chase. I screamed, surprised that it wasn't on a leash. Rounding the corner, I looked over my shoulder briefly and saw the saliva drooling from its mouth. Panicking, I pedaled as fast as I could. 'Silver is faster than red. Silver is faster than red,' I repeated over and over in my mind. Finally, I zipped onto Matthew's dirt driveway and out of the impending clutches of the dog. At the porch, I ditched the bike and ran into the house, slamming the screen door behind me. The dog barked a few more times and then turned tail and sauntered away. It may not have been red, but I was pretty sure that bike had just saved my life.

Matthew and I watched reruns of *Star Trek* together, and a commercial came on for a new movie called *The Karate Kid*. Every few minutes for the next hour, I interjected, "Wax on. Wax off."

Finally Matthew asked, "Do you want to learn Tai Chi?"

I had seen Matthew practice his Tai Chi movements each

morning, and I was eager to learn. When I was seven, he had sent me a book entitled *A Child's Garden of Yoga* by Baba Hari Dass. I had gotten quite good at the poses, though I spent a lot more time trying to do them the "right" way, rather than to "unite with my highest nature" as the book and Matthew intended.

He had me stand opposite him, while he moved his arms and legs slowly and smoothly into each Tai Chi pose. "So, why do you do Tai Chi anyway?" I asked.

"Three reasons." He raised his heels, breathed in and turned his body slightly at the waist, extending his left arm in the same direction. "Health. Tai Chi helps blood and oxygen flow better in the body." Then he lowered his heels to the floor and turned down his left palm. "Secondly, meditation." I asked him if meditation helped him with levitation, since the words had a similar ring to me. "Somewhat. But it requires years of practice before you can get to the level of being able to levitate." His knees bent slightly and his body sunk down. His mouth was slack as he spoke. "Thirdly, Tai Chi is considered a martial art."

"Martial art? You mean fighting?"

He straightened back up. "The purpose of Tai Chi isn't to fight. It's to yield to an opponent rather than meet him with force." To demonstrate his point, he asked me to try to hit him. At first I hesitated, but when he said, "Don't worry, you won't be able to get me," my hackles were raised and I went for it. He was right. I swatted at him, but his yielding technique worked flawlessly. I was left feeling so frustrated that I really did want to slug him. He laughed and held my forehead at arm's length from his body as I swung wildly. "Okay, settle down, Katie."

I ceased my futile actions, sat down on the sofa, and crossed my arms, annoyed and pouting.

...

MICHAEL WAS TO interrupt my visit for two weeks, and I

wasn't pleased. Matthew said that I should be accepting of Michael since he was going to be there for such a short time and he would be leaving before my departure. "I never get to do what I want when he's around," I said with a cross tone.

Then Matthew told me I could have everything I wanted in life; all I had to do was to say the right chant in the right way. "I feel. I sense. I know." Those were the prompt words. But part of getting the chant right was to believe that it worked. I had to believe. I could finally have the power to fly, to become invisible, to have all the riches I desired, if only I believed. His certainty of this made me certain.

I practiced day and night. I practiced aloud when I was alone. I practiced in my head when I was around other people. I practiced on paper when I wrote to Kitty. I created a list of all the things and experiences I wanted in life, and as I practiced the chant, the list grew and grew. I wanted toys and clothes and books and a smaller nose and a bigger chin and not to have to wear glasses and my parents to get back together and to change lives with Samantha Smith and magical powers and money and houses and more, more, more.

I saw a frilly yellow dress in a shop and muttered under my breath, "I feel that this dress will appear in my closet tonight. I sense that this dress will appear in my closet tonight. I know that this dress will appear in my closet tonight." Matthew took Michael and me to a planetarium, and while Michael seemed terribly bored, I was absorbed. I imagined myself floating in space. "I feel that I will be able to fly. I sense that I will be able to fly. I believe I will be able to fly." Of my elementary school crush with the hot pink comb, I said, "I feel that he loves me. I sense that he loves me. I know that he loves me." Everything was up for grabs, if only I believed that I could grab it.

When the chants didn't seem to work, I asked to play the

Folded Paper Game in order to strengthen my psychic abilities. When I wasn't able to make connections between what was on the paper and what was in my head, I tried harder. I had made the decision: I would not stop until I mastered these skills. I would master them, and then I would have every possession I wanted and I would make Samantha Smith fall from her pedestal, and I would take over as the pride of Maine.

...

AFTER DROPPING OFF Michael to the airport, Matthew asked me to go to the kitchen and get him a beer. I came back with a foam-filled mug; the beer was barely visible at the bottom of the glass. "Oh," he said with a hint of disappointment as I handed it to him. "Let me show you how to do it right."

He got up and I followed him into the kitchen. He put the glass I had poured for him in the refrigerator and then got a new bottle of beer and another mug. He narrated as he poured. "First you hold the glass at a forty-five degree angle. When you pour, you aim for the middle of the slope of the glass. See here?"

I peered down at the glass. "Yup."

"Okay, then, when you're at the halfway point, you bring the glass back up straight and continue to pour right in the middle. This makes the perfect head."

"Head?"

"The foam is called the head. It's good to have some, but you don't want the whole thing to be foam. Got it?"

"I think so."

"Good. Now pour another one."

"But you haven't finished this one." He picked up the mug and downed the beer in seconds.

"Whoa," I said, impressed. Over the course of the next few days I became an expert Cocktail Kid, pouring beers at night and picking up cans and bottles while Matthew slept in during the mornings. His drinking never seemed excessive to me, mainly because I was asleep when most of the heavy lifting took place. I did find it strange that there were so many cans and bottles to be cleaned up in the morning, but he seemed okay, so I guessed he could handle it.

Then one evening, he had a couple of people over. There was a greasy looking man and a woman with long red hair, both of whom I'd never met before. The man went immediately to the refrigerator without asking and got beers for the three of them. I stood nearby in the kitchen doorway, but no one looked in my direction. "Why don't you go play in the other room," Matthew finally glanced at me and said. I walked slowly to the spare room he had set up for me.

I sat on the bed, trying to distract myself by flipping through two issues of *Teen Beat* magazine. When I looked at my clock, it was nearly an hour later. It seemed like whatever was going on might last the whole night. I got progressively more nervous as I heard their conversation get louder and louder. I didn't know who these people were or why Matthew had brought them into the house. I worried that they might be untrustworthy strangers who might hurt us. Why hadn't he introduced me? Who were they? Did he owe them money? I hadn't been around this kind of rowdy drinking before, and I began to fear the worst.

With the combination of my wound up nerves and the racket in the kitchen, I couldn't sleep. I considered that as the only sober person in the house, it was my duty to put an end to the rabblerousing. I took a deep breath, opened my door and walked back into the kitchen. The counters were a mess. There were bottles of beer and liquor and dirty glasses and cut up limes and lemons. The woman dipped her glass into the sink. When she pulled it back out, it was filled with green liquid. Then she took a big gulp. From a few feet away, I pushed up to my tiptoes and saw that there was green liquid on one side of the sink and red liquid on the other. Apparently, the sinks had become makeshift punchbowls.

None of the three noticed me at first. "Excuse me," I said. I raised my voice a bit louder. "Excuse me."

"What do *you* want?" the woman asked.

I tried to be calm. "I-I'm not really comfortable with you all doing this."

The three of them burst out laughing. Then the greasy man said, "Well then why don't you go back into your room?"

I looked to Matthew, who continued to laugh. Then I turned, went back into the spare bedroom and locked the door.

It was two days later when the woman came back. She was officially introduced as Elizabeth, and Matthew told me she would be moving in. I overheard some rumblings that Howard's exit had to do with her arrival.

...

MATTHEW TOOK ME to see his mother, my Grandma Barbara, in Virginia for the last part of my visit with him. My Grandma Barbara's favorite word was the F-word, her best friends were gay men in their twenties, thirties and forties, and she got her Master's Degree in Anthropology when she was seventy-two. For a brief time, she grew marijuana in her backyard. She was also a hypochondriac. She once lifted her arm high above her head and said in her New Jersey twang, "I used to be able to raise my arm this high." Then she lowered it, sticking it straight out in front of her and said, "But now I can only lift it this high."

I supposed that her constant concern about her health stemmed from the fact that as a young woman, she was diagnosed with polio just months before the Salk vaccine had been discovered. Told she would never walk again, she worked with physical therapists over the years so that she could at least be on crutches.

She called her latest ones, which were metal, her "sticks," and she decorated them with stickers. Whenever she needed me to hold them so that she could dig in her purse or get in her car, I pretended the sticks were mine. I enjoyed it when passersby looked at me with pity and I looked back with a sad, downtrodden face.

During this visit, I learned that she now had a brain tumor. Matthew explained that the doctors seemed to think there was a good chance it was benign, and then my Grandma Barbara said, "Of course, it's brain surgery, so I could still die."

My eyes widened. In that moment I realized that my Grandma might be dead before I became an adult. Without thinking, I asked, "Can I start calling you by your first name, Grandma?"

She laughed. "Sure," she said.

Matthew said in a quiet, firm manner, "No."

Then Matthew offered something very uncharacteristic for someone who didn't seem to like to be around his family. He suggested that Grandma Barbara move to North Carolina. "You'll be near me, and the weather will be better for your polio."

She too seemed surprised at the offer but said that she would consider it.

...

BACK IN MAINE, I made the tactical error of telling Martha about my activities as a Cocktail Kid. With a raised voice, she asked, "You learned to pour beer?"

"I didn't drink any."

She asked more questions and I admitted that I cleaned up his empty cans and bottles for a few mornings. After I described the general quantity I would pick up, she concluded, "You need to call your father and tell him he's an alcoholic."

"No," I protested.

"Katie, he shouldn't be drinking around you. And he

absolutely shouldn't be having you pour his beer or pick up his empties."

"But I don't want to call him to say that," I begged.

She got up and brought the phone and address book back to the kitchen table.

"Mom, please..."

She didn't say a word, just looked up his number, dialed the phone and handed me the receiver. She sat across the dining table from me and waited.

"Hi Dad," I said meekly when he picked up.

After some dancing around the topic, Martha snapped her fingers at me. I looked in her direction and she mouthed the words, "Tell him."

I took a deep breath and closed my eyes. "Dad, I think maybe you might be an alcoholic."

"What?"

"I think that, well, maybe that you could be one."

He laughed. "Did your mother tell you say that?"

"Yes. But Dad, what if it's true? You may be an alcoholic."

He laughed even heartier. "Well, thanks for letting me know."

I felt timid. "Okay."

"Bye," he said.

"Bye."

He hung up.

Martha's voice was calm. "You did a good job, Katie."

I nodded, wishing I could disappear.

...

MICHAEL AND I were to spend the weekend with Uncle Brian and his wife and kids. On the way out of the house, I hugged and kissed Martha and Rainey and said goodbye.

"Don't say goodbye," Rainey countered. "Say 'see you.'"

"Why?"

"Goodbye is for when someone dies. 'See you' means you'll be coming back."

I thought of Anna and how much Rainey must miss her. I gave her an extra hug and said, "See you" before heading out the door.

The weekend was non-eventful until Sunday morning when Brian and his wife took Michael and me to church. It was a small sanctuary with tacky floral upholstered chairs that had to be taken off of stacks and lined in rows. Michael and I both helped with the row-making.

During the sermon, the pastor spoke of a man who worked for many years as a train station manager. "This is a true story," he began. He told us of a day when this station manager had brought his small son to work. He showed his son the railroad switch, which was of particular interest to the boy. This switch had large gears, and it was the station manager's job to shift these gears in order to move the trains to the proper tracks. The boy fell into the gears, and by the time his father spotted him, there were two trains heading toward one another. One of them needed to be shifted onto a separate track, or they would collide. "The man was faced with an unbearable decision," the pastor said. "If he left his son in the gears, the child would be crushed when he moved the switch, but the people on the trains would be saved. If he saved his son, the trains would collide, and all the people aboard would perish. This man chose to sacrifice his only son, so that the travelers on the trains could live." There were claps and Amen's from the members of the church. I was horrified.

Michael and I didn't talk of the sermon with one another, but when we returned to Martha's house, he was the first one to speak up. Then Martha brought me into the conversation, and we both told her how upsetting it was that people seemed to be happy that the boy's life was sacrificed. I didn't understand that they saw a parallel to the Biblical lessons of Jesus. To me it was just a story about a man who had let his child be killed in a brutal way.

Martha called Uncle Brian, furious. "Don't you *ever* take my kids to church again." I didn't want there to be a rift in the family, but it felt like she was protecting us, and I liked that.

...

KICKUS BECAME ILL. Martha found the cat one morning on Molly's bed, which was highly unusual since Kickus's only previous interactions with Molly were to torment the poor dog. Now it seemed that Molly had curled up next to Kickus and wouldn't leave the thing's side.

Martha took Kickus to the vet and returned crying and empty handed. "I had to have him put to sleep," she said as soon as she walked through the door. The cat had developed kidney problems and the vet had told her that the most humane thing was to put it down.

Martha remarked on how "sweet Kickus was near the end. When I found him on Molly's bed, it was just such a display of kindness. Animals have true empathy." Then with some disgust in her voice she said, "They're more empathetic than people."

I didn't see how Kickus was the sweet one when it was Molly who had shown the kindness, but I agreed with Martha because it was easier and because it was obvious she was in pain. I was sad for my mother and quite moved by Molly's compassion; but more than anything, I was glad that nasty creature was gone.

She had asked the vet to take care of the body, which

made me wonder, "What will we do when Molly dies?"

Martha wiped her eyes. "That'll be up to Michael."

"Michael? Why?"

"Molly's his dog."

Michael clearly liked Molly a lot more than he seemed to like the rest of us, but I was the one who did most of Molly's feeding and paper clean-up, and Martha was the one who washed and trimmed her hair. "What do you mean? Isn't Molly all of ours?"

"No, I bought her for Michael when your father left."

"Oh. ...What did you buy for me?"

"Katie," she said with an irritated tone as she wiped her tear-streaked face. "It's not a competition."

In my head but not aloud, I said, 'Maybe not to you.'

...

ON THE MONDAY before sixth grade started, Martha and I made another trip to see Dr. Kaz. It was getting so that I saw him more often than my father. Martha was worried about my weight, saying repeatedly that I was "too skinny." She seemed annoyed when Kaz said, "She's normal, Martha. Maybe on the low side of normal, but normal."

On the way back to the house, Martha asked, "So, did your father claim to be from another planet while you were with him?"

I was taken aback. "No. Why?"

"Apparently, this summer he told your brother that he's from another planet."

I felt a mixture of surprise, confusion, and a little left out that Matthew hadn't told me he was from another planet. If it was true, that meant that I was the child of someone from another planet, and that was pretty big news not to share with me. From the way Martha was talking, though, I guessed that she wouldn't have been pleased if he had told me. I shrugged, "Well, he didn't tell *me*."

She breathed heavily through her nose. "It's the same thing he told me on our wedding night."

"Really? He waited until you were married?"

She spat out the words like acid, "Yes, he waited until we were married. He also waited to tell me that he wasn't interested in sleeping with me. He wouldn't even have sex with me that night. He said that sex was 'base.' In the whole ten years we were married, whenever I wanted him to sleep with me, I had to get him drunk. When I found out that I was pregnant with Michael, his first words were, 'We'll deal with it.' We'll deal with it. That's not what a husband tells his wife."

I felt compelled to ask, "He didn't want us?"

"Your father didn't want kids, and he claimed he could control his sperm emissions with his mind so that we wouldn't have any."

I knew that the word *sperm* had to do with what men put in women in order to make a baby, but the whole conversation was getting far more graphic than that with which I was comfortable. I took a deep breath and held it, wishing we could go back to talking about how 'skinny' I was. "Did *you* want us?"

Her tone softened. "Honey, the happiest I ever was, was when I was pregnant." She looked sad. I knew she hadn't bargained on this life for herself.

I wondered if Matthew was wrong; that he wasn't from another planet. I had to admit to myself that it certainly was an unusual thing for a person to say. It made me wonder. Martha had often remarked that Vietnam had driven some of the men of her generation over the edge. "Sleepless nights for six months in the jungle would make anyone crazy," she had said.

I wanted to be sure of Matthew's mental acuity, "Mom,

did Dad go to Vietnam?"

"No," she scoffed. She zoomed through a yellow light, clearly riled up. "He got drafted and went for his physical. And he passed with flying colors, but when he went into the sergeant's office to get his papers signed to go to Vietnam, he sat down and calmly said, 'Well, you can send me to Vietnam, but I'm not going to pick up a gun. And it's not because I'm particularly against the war. It's because I just don't feel like it. And I'm sure when I get there I'll meet lots of other people who just don't feel like it either.' He had this stare-off with the sergeant, and then low-and-behold the guy writes something on your Dad's papers and hands them to him without a word. Your Dad walks out of the guy's office and looks down to see what was written, and it's 'physically unfit for service.' More like mentally unfit. I've got to hand it to him for that one, though. Vietnam was a disaster. No one should have had to go there."

She pulled her car into the driveway and shut off the ignition. We sat there for a moment not saying anything.

"Why did you marry him?" I asked. It wasn't a sarcastic question; I very much wanted to know.

Her eyes took on a faraway look, and her voice was soft, "He used to bring me flowers."

Chapter 18
Why the Harris Tweed Got Ruined

I wrote in my journal, begging Kitty to make me "a good witch." I promised her that I would not harm anyone physically, although I fantasized about making it so that Samantha Smith was forgotten and my arch-enemy became more of a social outcast than I was. On the day before sixth grade began in my new middle school, I asked her to "Please make me a witch from tomorrow morning at 7:26am until I die." If Kitty would just give me magical powers (four minutes before my alarm was set, in case I awoke early) I could change everything. I could go back in time and make it so that all the good things that had happened to Samantha Smith happened to me instead. I could make it so that the Holocaust never happened to Anne. I could make it so that no kids were hungry. I could make it so that my family was whole again. And I could make it so that *he* never touched me.

He hadn't ever invited me into his room before that night. Martha was downstairs studying while we were in the living room watching television. I was lying on the sofa, and he was seated in a chair. His tone was easy. "Do you want to go in my room?" he asked.

It seemed out of left field. "Why?"
"So that we can do stuff."
"I'm watching TV."

"Let's just go lie down."

My confusion was starting to turn into suspicion. "Lie down? Why?"

And then he said it. "So that we can touch each other."

"No," I said resolutely.

"Katie, it's no big deal. Lots of people do it. Haven't you ever thought of it?"

"No."

"Come on."

"No. And stop asking me." I turned back to the television. I wanted to leave the room, but I felt paralyzed. I didn't want him to even look at me getting up and walking away. And I didn't want him to think I was going to tell Martha, because that, I knew, would make him mad. I just wanted to ignore it and pretend he hadn't said what he said.

Then, a few minutes later, he cajoled, "Let's just go in my room for a little while."

I was silent. My arms were tight by my sides, and my legs were stiff and straight, outstretched on the sofa. I stared at the television.

"Come on." And then, "If you do this, I'll be nicer to you."

I could feel my body soften a bit. I still said nothing, but I knew that I was considering it.

"I'll stop teasing you. I won't ever be mean to you again."

I stayed silent.

"Mom will be a lot happier because we won't be fighting."

That was it. My voice trembled. "You promise?" I said, still looking straight ahead at the television.

"I promise."

After a long pause, I got up. Then he stood, and I

followed him into his room.

Once we were there, he closed the door behind me. "Take off your clothes," he said.

I had changed my mind. "I don't really-"

"-You already agreed, Katie. I told you, I'm going to be a lot nicer to you after this. Just be quiet so that Mom doesn't hear us."

I took off my clothes and stood naked, holding my hands over my private parts.

"Now lie down on the bed."

I got on the bed.

"Lie *face* down."

I turned over. My face was angled toward the door. I stared at the doorknob.

"Put your head face down so that I can't see you."

I turned my face so that my nose was pressed into the mattress, adjusting myself so that I could breathe.

Then I heard him take off his clothes, and I felt him get on top of me, straddling my legs. He sat atop me for a while touching himself and then told me to put on my clothes and go to my room. I did.

...

I AVOIDED HIM for two days. Then when he was alone in the living room, I walked in and sat down. I needed to talk. "The thing that happened the other day-"

He interrupted me and said, "-I'm sorry about that. I was high. It won't happen again."

I knew we were broken and needed help. "Maybe we should tell Mom."

Then he looked at me with piercing, angry eyes and very quietly, very deliberately said, "You tell Mom, Katie, and I *will* kill you."

...

IT WASN'T LONG before I started wearing only my baggiest shirts. I didn't want anyone to be able to identify my shape as female. My palms would sweat and my throat would tighten if any male glanced at me. Any attention on my body brought on the sense of being exposed, as if a boy or man could see through my shirt. My bathing became even less frequent than it had been. I didn't like seeing my own skin. In the tub, I would pretend that my washcloth was a bathing suit and use it to cover myself in the water. I started leaning my body over my legs as I did my business on the commode, not wanting to see any of my own exposed flesh. I did not look in my full-length mirror if I was naked. When I was clothed and I looked at myself, I only saw my head. I had lost my body.

...

I SPENT MUCH of that fall playing alone in my room or the backyard. I found solace in raking leaves into a pile and then letting myself fall into them, disappearing into the heap.

In bed, I spent hours listening to the last of the birds before migration. When I began to get lost in the fear of him one day picking up a knife and murdering us all, the sound of the birds acted as a touchstone. I found comfort in the repetition of their song. *Oo-wah-hooo hoo-hoo.* I tried again to figure out the expansiveness of the Universe. I concentrated on using my thought-power to move my chair in front of my door, and I decided that a couple of times, the chair had in fact moved a millimeter or so. The mind so wants to believe.

...

I VISITED TU-TU in early November. When I walked in, she had the rubber hose and warm-water bag set up for me in the bathroom. I pretended to oblige, though I really just sat on the edge of the tub and waited for a while before coming out.

The next week, on a Saturday, I was in the living room of

Martha's house watching a re-airing of the 1976 miniseries, *Sybil*. I went straight to Martha. "Mom, what is it called in the movie *Sybil* when the mother puts a tube in her bum and squirts water up there?"

"When did you see *Sybil*?" she asked, her voice a little strained.

"It's on TV right now. So, what is it called when the mother puts the tube-"

"-It's called an enema, Katie."

"Okay. Well, I don't like getting enemas at Tu-Tu's place."

There was a look of shock on her face. "She gives you enemas?"

"Well, she has me do them, but yes. I thought you knew. I thought you told her to."

"No. I wouldn't tell her that, Katie."

"Oh." I was surprised that Tu-Tu would do something like this without asking, but it was obvious to me that my mother was being truthful, and she had not condoned this activity. In fact, she seemed angry about it.

Martha's face turned red and her mouth was tight. "She and my Aunt Madeline used to give me enemas all the time when I was a kid."

I was alarmed. "Why?"

She batted her hand. "Oh, they all did that back then. I don't know why. It was sick. I think it's abuse."

I was glad to know she was on my side. "Will you tell Tu-Tu not to do it anymore?"

"Katie, you have to learn to stand up for yourself. You're eleven years old."

"But I don't want her to think I'm mad at her."

"You should be mad at her."

"Can you just tell her?"

"No. You can tell her yourself, Katie."

I once got so far as to ask Tu-Tu if she had ever seen *Sybil*, but I wasn't able to bring myself to tell her that I wanted her to stop. Tu-Tu continued to set up the enema equipment, and I continued to pretend that I was complying.

...

A WEEK BEFORE Thanksgiving, Martha gave me a book about understanding a woman's body. There were lots of pictures of naked women and breasts and pubic areas, all of which made me generally uncomfortable. But there were some interesting parts as well. I learned about Chinese foot binding, Mesolithic goddesses and the Suffragette movement. There was also a whole chapter devoted to depression and suicide. Although it surely wasn't intended for such a purpose, I read it for ideas on how I would kill myself if I could ever get up the nerve. I was most interested in how Marilyn Monroe had chosen to kill herself. At thirty-six she had apparently died of a pill overdose. The only discrepancy I found in the book was that it read that Marilyn had been a young woman when she died. But thirty-six seemed old to me and too long a time to wait before finally ending the pain I was feeling.

A week later, while I was watching Martha fix her hair in the bathroom, she inquired, "So did you look at the book?"

I rolled my eyes. "Yes, Mom."

"Well, do you have any questions?"

"No," I said blandly.

"What about menstruation? Do you have any questions about that?"

"Mom, geesh. Do we have to talk about this?"

"You're such a prude, Katie. You're just like Tu-Tu." One of Martha's thrills of parenthood had been when I was three years old and put a doll between my legs, exclaiming "I'm having a baby" to Tu-Tu. Martha had laughed hysterically. Tu-Tu had been mortified. Since that time I had not been quite so bold in displaying or discussing the wonders of being a woman.

Martha came into my room to show me aspects of the book to which she wanted me to pay special attention. As she entered, her eye caught my great-grandmother's Jesus needlepoint. She asked again, "Why don't you take that thing down?"

"Mom, can you just show me what you want to show me?"

She flipped the pages, and as she did so, I saw something on her wrist that I'd never noticed before: a horizontal scar. I had read in the book that when women try to commit suicide, they tend to do so by taking pills or slitting their wrists. "Mom," I asked cautiously. "What's that?" I touched the scar.

She brushed my fingers away and covered the scar with her other hand. "Oh, that's nothing."

"Did you try to kill yourself?"

She took a deep breath and sighed. "It was a long time ago, Katie."

"What happened?"

"When I was living in San Francisco I got very depressed and I tried to take my own life." I breathed in sharply, and she said reassuringly, "And it didn't work, because I'm still here."

I felt terrible knowing that, like me, she had once been so sad that she wanted to die. "I'm sorry, Mom."

"It's alright. The worst thing about it was that it ruined my coat."

"What do you mean?"

"I had this gorgeous Harris Tweed, herring bone wool coat. And if you know anything about Harris Tweed, Katie, you know that this was a very expensive coat. And when my friend found me naked and bleeding in the bathtub, he wrapped the coat around me and took me to the hospital. And the coat got blood all over it. It was ruined."

I was a little dumbfounded. "Oh. Sorry, I guess." I had also read in the book that if a person slits her wrists horizontally, she can often be saved, but if she slits vertically, there's usually too much blood loss. I asked Martha why she chose the horizontal method.

"Oh," she said lightly. "I wanted to be able to cover the scar with a watch."

. . .

IN SCHOOL WE had to do oral reports on topics of our choosing. I opted for the last days and hours of Adolf Hitler, creating a timeline for my listeners. "April 25th. Before dawn, Hermann Göring is arrested. ...April 27th. The Soviets bombard Hitler's Chancellery buildings with shellfire. ...April 30th, 2:30AM. Hitler comes out of his private quarters to have a formal farewell with staff members. ...April 30th, 12:00PM. Hitler is informed that the Soviets are a block away. ...April 30th, 2:00PM. Hitler sits down for his final meal, a vegetarian lunch. ...April 30th, 3:30PM. Hitler and Eva Braun return to their private quarters where Eva Braun swallows poison and Adolf Hitler shoots himself in the head with a pistol. They are both found dead moments later."

To my surprise, the report was met with rousing applause. I was excited that my classmates seemed as interested in the details of Adolf Hitler as I had been. My concern had been growing ever since I had first read Anne's diary. I was fascinated by how one man could convince an entire nation to turn on one another. The only snippets of speeches I ever saw depicted an obvious madman. In my research, however, I learned that these were often the end portions of the speeches. He always started calmly and often spoke in places where people were drinking, getting more frenzied as the patrons got more inebriated.

The German people had been on top of the world at one time, but they had fallen politically and financially. Adolf Hitler offered them a way back. All they had to do was believe what he was saying, and that would make all their actions justifiable. It turned out that if the right words were spoken at the right time and to the right people, even the most good-hearted were vulnerable to being fooled. And as long as everybody else was too afraid to speak out against it, terrible things could happen.

...

MARTHA WAS LOOKING through some old photo albums in her room, and I went downstairs to have some company and see what I could see. She spotted a picture in which she was wearing a long heavy coat and showed it to me with great enthusiasm. "That was the Harris Tweed I was telling you about. Tragic what happened to it. Just tragic." She took back the picture and stared at it for a long moment.

Then she picked up a thin, orange album and handed it to me. "Do you want this, Katie?"

"What is it?" I asked, as I took the album in my hands.

"They're pictures of your father when he was a kid. I offered it to Michael, but I think it upset him."

I started flipping through the pages. "Why?"

"Oh, there are some pictures of your Dad on his boat."

I was more than a little surprised. "He had a boat?"

"Yeah. I think Michael was upset because your Dad had a lot of advantages growing up that Michael doesn't have."

Image after image depicted a prep-school youth who wore blazers and seemed perpetually like he had just gotten a haircut. It didn't look at all like the man I called 'Dad.' And then I came upon it, the series of pictures of him in a small, sleek fishing boat. Michael and I were on Welfare at the same age that he was when had his own boat. I could barely take my eyes off of the pictures when Martha asked, "Do you want his torah?"

Peeling myself away from the album, I said, "You have his torah?"

She started digging in a drawer. "I don't know why I have it. He must have left it after the divorce. I asked Michael if he wanted it, because it was for your Dad's Bar Mitzvah, so it should really go to his son. But, Michael said he didn't want it."

I carefully held the torah in my hands. The small scroll was enclosed in rose colored silk. All I could think of was that Matthew had once held this in his hand when he was just a bit older than I was. "Yes, I definitely want it. It's wicked cool. Thank you."

Her eyes were already on another album. A photo fell out and she picked it up off the floor. "Huh," she said. She peered at it and then handed it to me. "Take a look at this."

I held the picture in my hand. In the image, Michael and I were seated on the sofa at the house my parents built in Limington, surrounded by boxes and a clear plastic clothes bag. I was wearing a green dress and floral blouse that I recognized as one Martha had made for me when she had time to do things like make clothes. Michael was wearing a shirt and tie. But what really struck me was the looks on our faces. I seemed tired and sad. My eyes had a glazed, dull appearance. Michael looked like he could reach through the camera and kill. "When did you take this?" I asked.

"Right after the divorce. I took it so you kids would always remember how painful it was and what your father had done to this family." Then she said, "You should keep it."

I handed it back to her. "I don't want it."

She held it in her hands and said, "I should send it to him with a little note: 'See? This is what happens when you abandon your kids.'" She handed it back to me. "Take it. One day you might want it."

...

IT WAS THREE weeks before Christmas, and in an effort to encourage me to be more mature, Martha suggested that I get rid of my Barbie dolls. It wasn't the first time she had posed the thought. "We can place an ad in the paper, Katie. People collect Barbies, and yours are in good shape. You can sell them and have money to spend on Christmas presents."

I knew that I was reaching an age when my few friends had put away their Barbie dolls, but I didn't feel ready yet. Still, I guessed that if I didn't sell them, Martha would not just hand over money for me to buy presents, and there were lots of things I wanted to get for people. This seemed like the only option, and I knew it would please her if I gave in. "I guess so," I said.

She placed the ad that day, and it was printed in the community marketplace circular two days later. I interviewed each potential buyer on the phone, and chose a lady who wanted the collection for her seven-year-old daughter. She brought the girl to Martha's house, and I gloomily showed them my Barbie dolls, my Barbie Hotel and my yellow battery-operated Barbie car that Matthew had given me, along with a box filled with Barbie clothes and shoes that I had amassed. "Do you really want to sell all this?" the lady asked.

I looked to Martha hoping that I would get a last minute reprieve. She nodded for me to complete the sale. I turned back to the woman. "Yes." As they drove away with my past in the backseat of their car I felt a mixture of pride and sadness.

Michael asked to borrow some of my newly gotten money. I flatly refused.

"You Jew," he retorted.

I found this to be a strange accusation since he was just

as half-Jewish as I was, but I was pleased that my rebuff had annoyed him.

Shortly after Christmas vacation, I came home from school and went into my room. Just before I turned on my radio, I had a feeling of 'knowing' that Madonna's "Material Girl" would be playing. I flicked the on-lever and there she was. My heart began beating faster and I caught my breath with the thought that I had finally gotten over the stalling of my psychic education, and my powers were growing at last.

Chapter 19
Why Their Birthdates Were So Close

I loved my mother almost as much as I feared her. Her bravery, her advice, her hugs, her humor, her intelligence; her anger, her depression, her blame, her criticisms, her spite. I never knew which mother I would get at any given time. 'Hope for the best, prepare for the worst' became a way of life. Even then, I knew it to be an important lesson, but I still wished I didn't have to learn it.

In April of 1985, I planned a surprise birthday party for Martha. Rainey moved out abruptly a few weeks before her birthday. It wasn't explained to me why, but they both assured me that they were still friends. Martha spent the afternoon studying upstairs in what had been Rainey's room, I assumed because she wanted to make sure I didn't burn down the house while baking the cake. I tacked up a sheet where the kitchen met the hallway and pretended that she couldn't tell what I was doing, even though deep down I knew she could smell the cake baking. Still, I maintained the illusion that I was "just puttering" in the kitchen, and she kindly supported it by not asking questions. "If you need me, just let me know," she called from the other room.

As soon as I tried to flip over the cake onto the cooling rack I realized that I had forgotten to grease the pan. The cake was stuck and after I shook it a bit, it came out in three large pieces. I could feel heat rising in my neck. My forehead began to sweat. I almost started to cry and then stopped myself. This was her day, and I was going to make it work. Suddenly I knew exactly what to do. I began scooping out frosting and using it to glue together the pieces. When I got the parts stuck together I used the rest of the frosting for the outside of the cake. There was just enough to cover the whole thing, albeit some areas were not as evenly frosted as others.

I posted a sign outside the house that read, "Door is unlocked. Do not ring bell. Just come in quietly." I got more and more excited as the guests began to arrive. When my Uncle Anthony came in with his wife he chuckled and whispered, "You're lucky you live in a safe neighborhood."

"What do you mean?" I whispered back.

"You just invited anyone who passes by to come into your unlocked house."

"Oh. Don't tell Mom, okay?" He nodded with a smile.

When Brian and his wife, Tu-Tu, Madeline and Rainey had arrived, I tore down the sign and threw it away. Then I said in a raised voice, "Mom, can you come in here?"

"Is everything okay?" she called back.

"Yeah. Just come in."

"What's going on?" she asked. Then she pulled back the sheet.

"Surprise," we all yelled in unison. We clapped and cheered for her.

"Uh, wow," she said.

"Are you surprised?" I asked.

She touched her hand to her head. "Um, yeah. I kind of wish I had showered."

My smile dropped a little, and Martha caught it, "But yes," she said. "This is a great surprise Katie." She gave me a big hug.

I had it in my mind that the cake wasn't going to taste as good because of having to glue it together with frosting, but as it turned out, this provided an added bonus to the people eating it. As she took a bite, Tu-Tu exclaimed, "I like how you put the frosting *in* the cake as well as outside of it, Katie. It's delicious."

I explained what had happened and Martha said, "That's my Katie. She always figures out how to make things work."

"That's called Yankee ingenuity," Brian said.

I could not have been more pleased. I didn't even mind when Martha mentioned Matthew. "You know, your Dad doesn't like cake?"

"What?" I was baffled by the concept of anyone not liking cake.

"He likes pie. Every birthday, I would make him a cherry pie with a lattice top pie crust."

"A lettuce top pie crust? That sounds gross to the max, Mom."

"A *lattice* top. It's when you weave the crust over and under so it looks like a basket."

"You did that for him?"

"I did." She seemed pleased with herself as she spoke, as if she enjoyed the memory.

"That was really nice of you, Mom. I still don't get why he doesn't like cake though. Who doesn't like cake?"

She laughed.

Martha's birthday and the willingness of all the guests to come to her house for the surprise made me want to be sure to keep track of their birthdays as well. After everyone left, I started a chart to list their special dates. Martha let me borrow her calendar so that I could transfer the information. When I got to my uncles Brian and Anthony, I became confused. Anthony's birthday was in May, and Brian's birthday was in July, but they were listed as being born in the same year. I approached Martha with my chart and her calendar in hand. "Mom, is this right? Brian and Anthony were born in the same year?"

She hesitated. "Yes, that's right."

"But they were born just a couple of months apart. Was Brian a preemie?"

"No, honey. Why don't you sit down..."

I did so, and Martha began to tell me more about our family's complicated history. "Tu-Tu was pregnant with your uncle Anthony. And when you get pregnant, a lot of times, especially early on, you don't feel well. And so she didn't want to go out at night like my father wanted to, and finally one night she said, 'Why don't you just take my sister?'"

"You mean Great-Aunt Madeline?"

"Right. Madeline had lived with your great-grandmother her whole life. She hasn't ever moved out of that house. She worked for a while, but she was really very alone there. So to Tu-Tu it was a way to get my father to stop bothering her about going out and to get Madeline to be more social." Martha took a deep breath and continued. "And one night my father and Madeline were both drunk and they had sex. And she got pregnant with Brian."

A hundred questions came to me at once. "So Brian is actually Madeline's son?...How did he come to live with Tu-Tu and your Dad?...Was it weird?...Does Brian know?"

She answered all of my queries. "Yes, Brian is actually Madeline's son...Tu-Tu adopted him...Yes, it was weird. Tu-Tu, my father, my brothers and I lived upstairs. And Madeline and your great-grandmother lived downstairs...Yes he knows. But you can't ever bring it up to him or talk about it with anyone else in the family. If you want to talk about it, you talk with me about it."

"How could Madeline do that to Tu-Tu?"

"There's always been a twisted competition between Tu-Tu and Madeline. Tu-Tu was sent to live with her father because her mother felt that she could only raise one child, and she liked Madeline better."

"But if Madeline was chosen to stay, why should she feel competitive?"

"How would you like to be expected to become a spinster and take care of your aging mother in the house where you'd lived your entire life?"

"I wouldn't like it much."

"No, you wouldn't."

"How did Brian find out?"

"When he was seven, my father got drunk and told him he was adopted, but he didn't know the details until he was in his twenties. It was the last Thanksgiving we had in the house your father and I built in Limington. Madeline had to get drunk to break the news. She told him at her place, and she was plastered by the time they both arrived. He just sat silently for the whole dinner, and we all ate while Madeline threw up in the bathroom."

What was it with this family and Thanksgiving, I wondered, thinking back on Matthew's departure on the holiday. Couldn't they find one other day of the year to break traumatic news?

Martha continued. "It was shortly after that when she stopped drinking. And a year after she stopped, I decided I needed to stop."

"So some good came out of it."

Her eyes were cheerless. "Katie, no good has ever come out of any of this. I think that's the reason Brian and my mother are so involved in religion, because they have to find some reason for what happened. They have to make it okay, and it's not ever going to be. What my father did was a huge violation, and now that he's gone, they'll never be able to say to him what they should have said to him when he was alive."

"What's that?"

"That they're angry."

"They don't seem angry."

"They hide behind their religion, Katie, but believe me, they're angry."

Chapter 20
Why She Wished Her Dead

Martha stood in my doorway and told me, "Katie, you need to clean your-" She glanced over at my dresser and interrupted herself. "-Where did you get that?" she asked.

"What?"

She walked over to the dresser and picked up my great-grandmother's sewing basket. "This."

I cocked my head in surprise. "You gave it to me."

"No I didn't." Her brows furrowed. She looked positively appalled.

My voice strained. "Mom, yes you did. You gave it to me on Valentine's Day when I was ten and a half."

"No I didn't. I can't believe you took this from me, Katie."

"Mom, you *gave* it to me. I've had it for a year and a half now. Ask Rainey. She was here the day you gave it to me."

"No. You stole it. And I'm taking it back."

She slammed the door, and I cried hot angry tears.

Rainey visited before I left for the summer to visit Matthew in North Carolina. I pulled her aside under the guise of playing Uno, but I really wanted to tell her what happened with the sewing basket. She shook her head as she shuffled the cards and assured me that I had remembered correctly, that

Martha had indeed given me the basket. "Your Mom loves you, but she's a little nuts," Rainey continued. "That's why I had to leave. When I first got here, I needed someone to tell me what to do and when to do it. But after a while I didn't need that anymore and she still wanted to control me. I couldn't take it. I want to be friends with her; that's why I keep coming by. But sometimes she makes it hard." Then she said, "Don't worry. One day you're gonna' leave here and you're gonna' be able to make your own decisions and have your own life."

Relieved to have an ally, I said, "Thanks, Mom Number Two."

"You're welcome, Twat."

Rainey stayed to watch the news with us. I was hoping she'd bring up the sewing basket to Martha, but she didn't. I guessed that she didn't want to start a confrontation when she was trying to keep their friendship intact.

A report came on about something called Acquired Immune Deficiency Syndrome, or AIDS. For the previous couple of years since discovering the syndrome, all the scientists had thought that it only infected gay men, but apparently a number of new cases were shown not to have anything to do with sexuality. It was all pretty confusing and scary; the pictures were awful, men who were too sick to eat and had purple blotches all over them. It reminded me of the images I had seen of the Holocaust, with tortured minds and bodies starved to the bone.

Scientists had figured out that AIDS was caused by a virus they called HIV, and they wanted to assure the public that the virus couldn't be spread from handling doorknobs or shaking hands with infected individuals. They were even doing testing to be sure that it couldn't be transmitted through sneezes or carried by bugs. The reassurances didn't seem to be working, though, because many people were still scared. According to the news report, people in Maine were particularly concerned about the possibility of HIV being carried by black flies and mosquitoes, which were prevalent everywhere.

There was a report about a boy from Indiana named Ryan White, a hemophiliac who contracted HIV through a blood transfusion. Many of the people on his paperboy route had canceled their subscriptions, believing that HIV could be transmitted through newsprint. He had also been expelled from school for having the virus.

"I can't imagine not being allowed to go to school," I said.

Mom called the school board and the superintendant "a bunch of fuckers."

Rainey added, "Somebody should give the superintendant AIDS and see if he still gets to keep his job." That seemed a little extreme to me, but I understood her point. It wasn't fair to deny anyone an education, especially for something that wasn't even the boy's fault.

There was a commercial break, and an advertisement came on for an upcoming sitcom called *Lime Street*, which I had not heard of before. When it was announced that the show would star Robert Wagner and Samantha Smith, I could feel the muscles of my face clench. Not only was she saving the world. Not only was she a writer of books. But now she was taking my dream of becoming a famous actress. I felt sick to my stomach. I did not believe that there could be more than one little girl from Maine to have this kind of success. I thought that her greatness meant that I could not be great.

Rainey said brightly, "Why don't you do something like she did, Katie?"

I was silent, and my whole body tensed. I closed my eyes

and focused my mind. I breathed in and out, in and out. The sounds of the room seemed to drift away as one thought formed with crystal clarity: *I wish Samantha Smith would die.*

Chapter 21
Why She Knew She Would Be Punished

I had prepared for my summer of 1985 arrival to North Carolina by packing as Matthew had instructed me multiple times over the previous couple of years, and when he opened my suitcase he congratulated me on its neatness. "Good job, Katie." We only had to take out and repack the socks so that he could show me how to roll them up and save more space.

I hoped that Matthew's magician friend Howard would be there, but when Matthew didn't mention him, I thought it best that I didn't either. Anyway, I had a more important question on my mind: Was Matthew from another planet? And all things considered, I thought I should only bring up one potentially awkward conversation. It took me some time, but I felt it was important to know if he really thought this about himself. I decided to ask him before Michael arrived for the last few weeks of the visit, so that it could be a private conversation. "Dad?" I tried to ask as casually as possible. "Are you from another planet?"

"I've told you before. We're all from the stars and we go back to them when we die."

"Yes, but does that mean you're from another planet?"

With an inquisitive tone, he asked, "What do you think?"

"I don't know."

"Well, do you need to know?"

"I would like to know."

"Well, learning needs to take place in stages. When a person is ready to hear something, that person will hear it."

I started to feel like I was getting a bit of a runaround. "That's not fair. Why do other people get to know things about you that I don't?"

He let out a sigh. "Okay. Yes, I am from another planet."

My eyes widened. I could hardly breathe with excitement. "Which one?"

"It doesn't have a name."

"Can we go to the planetarium, and you can show me where it is?"

"It's very far away from here, Katie. It's too far to see in a planetarium show. One day, maybe you'll be able to visit it in your mind." The thought was exhilarating.

When Michael arrived, we got along fairly well. Mostly I supposed that this was because Matthew's partner Elizabeth was new to Michael, and he didn't want to be his usual self around her. Or maybe he was intimidated by Matthew, whom even I thought liked me better. Whatever the reason, I was glad that he was mainly decent to me.

Before we left at the end of the summer, Matthew took us out to dinner. I asked him to tell us again how he had used his mind power to take off signs from buildings. Michael rolled his eyes. I sat in anticipation. "Well, yes, I have done that before," Matthew said. "But it was only an inch or so, and then I put it right back on. I used to do it a lot, though."

Prior to this, I had imagined him ripping off the signs with his mind and flinging them from place to place. 'An inch or so' and then back on again was a bit of a different story. "If you're just going to put them back again," I asked, "why take them off in the first place?"

Michael shook his head and sighed.

"Well, it was practice," Matthew continued. "It takes a lot of effort just to do that much."

It made sense to me. As we headed back to Maine, I felt that my faith had been restored. Matthew *was* from another planet, and this was another way in which he, and consequently I, was special.

...

AUGUST 26th, 1985 started out like any other late summer day. It had rained the night before, but there was a break in the weather by the time I awoke. I listened to the *oo-wa-hooo hoo-hoo* of the birds. I prayed for a strengthening of my psychic and magical powers. I tried to figure out the expansiveness of the Universe. When I got up, I was pleased to see that Michael had already risen and left for the day. Martha was at her summer work-study job.

I turned on the television. There was a news report on that was accompanied by a live shot of a plane crash site. It seemed to me that it was too early in the day for the news to be on. I flipped the channel. There was the same plane. I flipped again. There it was. I stopped to watch. And then...an image of Samantha Smith flooded the screen. The reporter said, "We have confirmation. Samantha Smith has died." My mouth went slack.

Samantha and her Dad had been returning the night before after filming an episode of *Lime Street*. The commuter plane they were on struck some trees short of the runway and crashed. All six passengers and the two crew members had been killed.

During the news report, Samantha's Mom, Jane, made a statement: "Samantha couldn't accept man's inhumanity to man. She stood fast in the belief that peace can be achieved and maintained by mankind." I had never seen anyone look so empty.

Her face was beautiful, like Samantha's, but hollow with grief. She was clearly in so much pain, and there was no question in my mind...it was my fault. The thought kept repeating: *I wished her dead, and now she's gone. I wished her dead, and now she's gone. I wished her dead.* My petty jealousy had left Jane Smith without a daughter and husband. I had destroyed the lives of the families of all eight people on the plane. I had killed Samantha Smith, and I knew I would be punished for it.

Chapter 22
Why He Destroyed Her Treasured Thing

I would not tell Kitty, or anyone else for that matter, that I had killed Samantha Smith. I didn't want to be thought of as the awful person I believed myself to be.

I obsessively watched Samantha's funeral on television. When Martha suggested I go outside to play, I clung to the clunky channel box that was connected with a cord to the television. "No. And no one can change the channel while I'm watching this." She left me to it.

I shot up in my seat when I heard people talking in the front yard. With heavy breaths, I pulled back the closed curtain and peered out the window, terrified that the police had somehow found out about my involvement in Samantha Smith's death and were there to arrest me. With relief, I saw that it was just Michael and his friends horsing around in the driveway. I turned back to the television.

There were over a thousand people at the funeral, which was held in Maine's capital city of Augusta. I wanted to be there but had been too ashamed to ask anyone to drive me, and I was afraid the other people there, especially Jane Smith, would know that their loss was my fault.

There were several auspicious people in attendance,

including Samantha Smith's co-star from *Lime Street*, Robert Wagner, and a man from the Soviet Embassy in Washington, who read a condolence message from Mikhail Gorbachev: "Everyone in the Soviet Union who has known Samantha Smith will forever remember the image of the American girl who, like millions of Soviet young men and women, dreamt about peace and about friendship between the peoples of the United States and the Soviet Union."

Even President Reagan had sent a message to Jane Smith to ask her to "take some measure of comfort in the knowledge that millions of Americans, indeed millions of people, share the burdens of your grief."

The most striking moment to me came when another little girl, a friend and classmate of Samantha's rose to read a poem she had written in remembrance: "Friends. She was smiling and caring. He was happy and daring. But both were so sharing. She was small but so strong. He was our own Mr. Mom. And both were so loving all along. She was cute, and we loved her. And we loved him just as much. And when they became famous we always stayed in touch. We'll always love them, and it's hard to see them go."

I began to sob silently as a sense of guilt pounded my brain. Why did I have to do it? Why couldn't I have been proud of her like everyone else? Why did I have to be so jealous? I took her from all of them.

I feared that any awful thing that happened as a result of her being gone, any war or terrible thing that could have been prevented by her continuing her mission of peace, would be my fault. If people forgot her message, and we had a World War III, it would be because of me.

I tried to *will* Samantha back to life. Then I remembered the book I had written about the pilot. She wouldn't look like herself anymore. I tried to *will* a reversal of time. I would go back and have a do-over. This time I wouldn't wish her dead, and she would live. My suicidal ideation grew to its peak. Not only did I want to die, but I felt I *should* die for what I'd done.

...

SEVENTH GRADE BEGAN and I tried to focus on my studies. During an early fall weekend, Martha came into my room and sat down on the bed. She looked at me with warmth and sensitivity. "Katie, I know you like your kitchen set, but I think it's time for you to get rid of it."

During the final Christmas that we all spent as a family before the divorce, Martha and Matthew made the most wonderful gifts two kids could have. Michael received a bookshelf, but to keep it from looking like an ordinary bookshelf, Martha had painted a big yellow sign with red trim that read "Mike's Market" and posted it on the back of the shelf. She had collected and cleaned empty Campbell's soup cans, Saltine cracker boxes and egg cartons to create a store, and Matthew had found a small, plastic cash register.

I received a storage cabinet for my toys that was designed to also function as a marvelous kitchen set. My parents had built it together, and Martha had painted it. It had a blue stove with red knobs on the front and blue knobs on top, next to the painted-on burners. My parents had cut a hole in which they placed a yellow, plastic sink and had added more knobs behind the sink to look like a faucet. Connected to the stove was a white ply-board refrigerator with red handles. Martha had appliquéd floral designs on the oven and fridge doors and had even made a little window out of a magazine picture and some homemade curtains. The final touch was a square iron sign, a little over five inches on each side that read, "No matter where I serve my guests it seems they like my kitchen best."

I had planned to keep it for my whole life. If I didn't ever have a little girl to whom I would pass it on, I wanted to have it as a reminder of something my parents had done together just for me. "No, Mom." I cried out. "I want to keep that."

Her tone was kind but firm. "Katie, it's for little kids."

"But I want to keep it."

"Your room is too small for it."

"But I store things in it. And I still use it sometimes."

"That's what I mean. You're too old for this kind of stuff. You have to grow up."

"Please Mom."

There was no winning this argument. The decision had been made. I asked if I could take off the iron sign and keep it. Martha helped me to do so. She said I could give away the kitchen set or sell it and keep the money. It was priceless to me, and I thought any other family would feel the same way, so I decided to sell it. Tears ran down my face as Martha, Michael and I lugged it onto the edge of our yard. I posted a sign on it that read, "For sale."

I watched through the living room window for an hour. Three cars had stopped, but no one had approached the house. I did not want to suffer the indignity of it not selling, so I went out to the street and added the words "50 cents" to the for-sale sign. Another half hour went by along with two more cars. I went downstairs and knocked on Martha's door.

"Come in," she said.

I lumbered into the room and slumped on her bed. "Mom, I don't think I want to sell it. I think I want to give it away."

"Okay. I'll have Michael bring it to the side of the house so no one tries to buy it."

I sat on Martha's bed idly flipping through her textbooks

and notebooks while she left the room. When she came back, I stayed and we talked about her classes. She told me that her favorite was a Sociology class for which she was preparing a paper. We talked for a few minutes, and then I glanced out her small basement window and saw Michael. He had dragged my kitchen set into the middle of the street and he and two of his friends were using it as a bike jump. I screamed.

"What, Katie?" Martha said in a panicked voice.

"Look," I yelled and pointed. She looked out the window just as a piece of the set went flying. "Stop him, Mom."

Her tone was immediate. "Don't look at it Katie. Just go to your room."

She rushed upstairs, and I heard the front door slam. In a daze I walked up the stairs and into my room. I sat on my bed. Tears rolled down my face until I didn't have any tears left. I was numb. A few minutes later, there was an abrupt knock on my door. I thought it might be Martha, but when the door opened, it was Michael. He tossed two quarters on my bed and said with a tone of indignation, "Here's your money."

Martha never spoke to me about what had happened or what she said to my brother, and I never brought it up. I feared that I wouldn't get the response of sympathy or empathy that I wanted, and it seemed better to leave it alone. Things are just things, and sometimes they get lost, or broken, or tossed aside, or destroyed by older brothers. But a treasured thing is hard to lose.

The punishment for killing Samantha Smith had just begun, and I suspected it would get worse...for Maine, for the world, and for me.

Chapter 23
Why She Gave Her the Bolt Lock

Michael was out, and Martha and I were having dinner together at the dining table. "So, how are things going?" she asked.

It was as if we were old friends catching up. I wanted Martha to know what I had done to Samantha Smith. I wanted her to know that the world's loss was my fault. I wanted her to know that I too had thought of suicide as she once had. I wanted her to know about what had happened that night with Michael in his room. All I could say was, "Okay."

"Yeah? How are things between you and Michael? Have they settled down some?"

The opportunity was right before me. I wondered if I could take it. I looked down at the plate. I opened my mouth to speak, but then closed it. I pressed my lips together. I closed and opened my eyes. I opened my mouth again. No words came out.

"Is there something you want to tell me, Katie?"

I looked up at her. Her face was soft; her eyes, serious. I couldn't speak.

"Did something happen?"

I nodded.

"What?"

More silence.

"What, Katie?"

I forced a chuckle. "I'll tell you when you're older."

We sat without talking for what seemed like a long time. And then she said, "Do you want to talk about it?"

I shook my head no. I wasn't sure that she understood what I wanted to say, but I knew that she recognized it to be something serious. "Do I have to go back to Dr. Fink?" I asked. I wasn't exactly disinclined to go, and I did like the hot chocolate I got there, but I didn't want to have to tell him what had happened either. My mind was lost in the images of that night.

"No," Martha said. "Anyway, this isn't something to really talk about, not with Dr. Fink or anyone else. You can talk to me any time you want to Katie. Any time. But this isn't something that other people need to know about. It's none of their business. And that includes your father. This is something that has to stay in this house."

I nodded; I didn't want to talk about it anyway. Before ending the conversation, though, I asked, "Why is Michael the way he is?"

With a hint of sarcasm, she said, "He had three more years with your father." Then Martha said quietly, "At the end of your sessions with Dr. Fink, he told me that you could be helped but that Michael was a 'lost cause.'"

...

MARTHA RETURNED HOME one night a couple of weeks later with a lunch-sized paper bag. "Is Michael here?" she asked.

"No."

"Good. I have a present for you." I was excited. It had been a long time since she had randomly brought home a present for either Michael or me. The bag was heavier than I imagined it would be. I reached inside and pulled out a clear plastic package with something round and brass sealed inside. "It's a bolt lock," she said in a cheery voice. "I'm going to install it today."

I felt a mixture of relief and fear as she took out the doorknob and inserted the flat round lock. Relief because it would provide some protection against my brother. Fear because he might guess why it was there. It turned out, I was right to fear.

"What's that?" he nodded his head toward the lock that night when we were all in the living room watching television.

Martha spoke with a surprising amount of lightness in her voice, "Oh, Katie's doorknob wasn't working so I replaced it."

He looked suspicious. I held my breath.

The next day was a Monday. As was typical, I got home before Michael. I never knew where he spent his afternoons, and I never asked. I assumed it was some combination of detention and trouble-making. I pulled out my new key and unlocked my door. Then I went in and shut myself inside. I turned the lock and then checked it to be sure it was closed. I was putting together a puzzle on the floor when I heard Michael enter the house a little while later. I double-checked the lock and sat back down in front of the puzzle.

He pounded on my door. "Open up," he yelled. My body froze. "I know you're fucking in there, you bitch." I heard him kneel down, and I saw a shadow under the door frame. "I can fucking see you in there." Then I heard him get up and walk back down the hallway. I moved to the door to check the lock a third time and then sat in the corner where I didn't think he'd be able to see me if he looked under the door again.

I could hear him rifling through the tool cabinet in the kitchen. "I'm gonna' kill you," he called from the kitchen. He stomped back to the door. My eyes widened at the sound of him trying to jimmy the lock with what I guessed was a screwdriver. "I am going to fucking kill you." He worked the lock for a few minutes and then stopped. I heard the television go on in the living room and then the sound of him plunking down in a chair. It seemed that Michael was going to stay just outside my room until I opened the door.

The next two hours went by slowly. I was afraid my floor might squeak if I moved, so I stayed seated in the corner. I prayed to be forgiven for what I had done to Samantha Smith as well as all the awful thoughts I had ever had so that my punishment could end. When I started to get the urge to pee, I held it. I occupied my time by mouthing the names of the Seven Dwarves: Sleepy, Sneezy, Dopey, Doc, Happy, Grumpy, Bashful. Then the names of all the characters of Scooby Doo: Scooby, Shaggy, Velma, Daphne, Fred. And finally, all the characters of *The Dukes of Hazzard*, along with their real-life counterparts: Bo, Luke, Daisy, Uncle Jesse, Boss Hogg, Cooter, Sheriff Rosco P. Coltrane; John Schneider, Tom Wopat, Catherine Bach, Denver Pyle, Sorrell Booke, Ben Jones, James Best. By the time Martha arrived home, I was bursting.

"Where's Katie?" I heard her ask Michael.

"How should I know?"

She asked him whose day it was to do the dishes and when he said it was his, she told him to start them.

I waited another few minutes until I heard him start the dishes and her go downstairs to put away her books and come back up to make dinner. It was then that I quietly exited my bedroom and went to the bathroom. After using the facilities, I entered the kitchen with a cheery face and said, "Hi Mom," as if nothing had happened.

From then on, whenever I entered the house to find it empty, Michael and I had the same routine. If it was my day to wash the dishes, I would do them as quickly as possible. I prepared for my isolation by first getting an empty Cool Whip container from the kitchen cabinets and then getting some toilet paper from the bathroom. I would unlock my door, go inside and lock myself in. As soon as I heard him enter the house, I would do a quick double-check of the lock and take the Cool Whip container and toilet paper to the corner of the room and sit there. He would rummage through the tool drawer yelling that he was going to kill me. Then he would try unsuccessfully to break the lock. Then he would watch television.

If I had to pee, I would quietly pull down my pants and hover over the Cool Whip container. I learned early on to aim for the side of the container to reduce the noise and splashing, similar to the technique of pouring beer. Then I would sit back down and wait until Martha would arrive. When she did, I would wait a few minutes and emerge as though all was right with the world. Later in the evening, I would wash out the Cool Whip container and put it in the far back of the kitchen cabinet.

I never complained to Martha. I assumed it would just make things worse, and anyway, I figured I deserved what was happening for what I had done to Jane Smith and everyone else who loved Samantha. Part of my punishment for not honorably killing myself was for me to be humiliated and terrified privately.

Chapter 24
Why it's Okay If You Do It

On October 2, 1985, Rock Hudson died of an AIDS-related illness. He had shocked the world as the most famous victim of the infamous virus. A few weeks after his death, I used some money I had saved from my twelfth birthday in June to buy a copy of *People Magazine*. It featured an article about him entitled "The Long Goodbye." I was surprised to learn that Rock Hudson was gay and had hidden it for many years. It was sad to me that even when people became grown-ups they could still be afraid of getting found out. According to the article, many people in Hollywood knew, but no one spoke of it. It was as though no one wanted to admit that this strong, swaggering man who played the 'good guy' so well could also be gay.

Also in the month of October 1985, Samantha Smith's Mom, Jane Smith, established a foundation in her daughter's name. The non-profit would foster international understanding by organizing summer visits for children, mainly between the ages of eleven and sixteen, to and from the Soviet Union. In December of 1985, the Soviet Union issued a postage stamp honoring Samantha. Each tribute reminded me that my time was running out. Kill or be killed. I believed that I should kill myself, or I would wither away anyway. I continued my routine of pulling down the Cool Whip container from the kitchen cabinet and retreating to my room each weekday with a sense of shame and obligation, penance for what I had done.

Sitting on the floor of my room, I prayed for forgiveness and wrote in my journal. I told Kitty that I wanted to write a time-travel book. I didn't tell her that I wanted to go back in time and have a do-over of my whole life.

My brother became less vocal in his attempts to infiltrate my room. He still occasionally made threats through the closed door and tried to break the lock, but mostly he just slammed his palm against the door and sat down in the living room chair outside my room to watch television.

...

SEVENTH GRADE CARRIED with it more concerns about fashion than I had experienced prior. The 'cool' boys wore corduroys and Oxford shirts. The trendy girls wore leg warmers and got spiral perms. Fall progressed, and one day at the bus stop, a neighbor boy who had started sixth grade that year commented on a video his science class had been shown. It was entitled *Masturbation: It's Okay if You do It, It's Okay if You Don't*. The other kids at the bus stop, who were all boys, laughed. So that I wouldn't look out of place, I laughed too, even though I had no idea what the word 'masturbation' meant. As soon as I got to school, I looked it up and was somewhat shocked at the definition. We didn't study *that* when I had been in sixth grade. I wondered if maybe the masturbation class was just for the boys. Then I wondered if the boys in seventh grade knew what masturbation was. The idea made me uncomfortable, and I decided not to think about it.

I asked Martha for new clothes, showing her how my long pants had become high-waters, and she balked. "I can't keep buying clothes for you, Katie. They're too expensive. Why don't you ask your father to help?"

I blurted out, "He left us. Do you really think he's going to buy me clothes?" I could risk asking Martha to buy things for me because, after all, she had stayed. Whenever Matthew said no to me, however, it felt like part of a much larger rejection.

Martha looked at me with a stone face. "And you still blame me for that, don't you?" she said crisply.

"What are you talking about?"

"I remember you stomping your foot and yelling, 'You made my Daddy go away.'"

I closed my eyes. "Mom, I apologized for that before. I was four years old. I don't even remember saying it."

"Well, I remember. And I will never forget." She slammed around the kitchen, getting dinner ready. "If your grandfathers were alive, things would be very different around here. If your father's father were alive, you kids would be taken care of, and we wouldn't have to be on Welfare. And if my father were alive, I assure you, your father wouldn't be." Martha could be at once clever and frightening.

...

I WAS TO visit Tu-Tu for the weekend. When I arrived, I was grateful to see she hadn't set up the enema equipment. "Oh, I forgot," she said. "I'll go get it ready."

Without missing a beat, the best lie I had ever told came out of my mouth. "That's okay, Tu-Tu. Um, I'm not really having a problem with that anymore."

She smiled brightly. "Oh, that's wonderful news. I guess it worked then."

"Yes, it sure did. Thank you very much, Tu-Tu. Now I know exactly what to do if I ever have a problem with it again."

She pumped her fist in an awkward 'go get em' motion. "Oh, good. I'm glad to have helped."

"You did," I affirmed. If I had known how to do a

cartwheel, and if her living room had been more than ten feet wide, I would have flipped and spun right then and there.

As was often the case, the rest of the visit was focused primarily on the Bible. Tu-Tu explained that dinosaurs didn't really exist and that, "The bones that archaeologists have found are just big people bones." This, she explained was because, "The world is just a few thousand years old, so there isn't time for there to have been dinosaurs."

We read aloud parts of the last book of the New Testament. "This book actually goes by three different names," Tu-Tu explained. "It's called the *Book of the Revelation*, and it's also called the *Book of the Revelation of Saint John the Divine*, but that's mostly what Catholics call it. And it's also called the *Apocalypse of John*."

"What's an apocalypse?"

"It's a lifting of the veil, Katie. It's the time right before the Rapture. It's designed to give everyone one last chance to see how important it is to become a Christian. And the Rapture is when Jesus will come back and take all of the Believers with him."

"What happens to the non-believers?"

"They all stay here."

"So they get to live, and the Believers all die?"

Tu-Tu chuckled. "No. Everyone's going to die. It's just whether they'll go to heaven and be with Jesus or whether they stay here."

"Then what's the difference?"

"Well, let's read about the Apocalypse and see."

Tu-Tu and I took turns reading from Revelation, chapter eight: "The first angel sounded, and there followed hail and fire mingled with blood, and they were cast upon the earth. And the third part of trees was burnt up, and all green grass was burnt up.

And the second angel sounded, and as it were a great mountain burning with fire was cast into the sea. And the third part of the sea became blood. And the third part of the creatures which were in the sea, and had life, died. And the third part of the ships were destroyed."

I started feeling more and more anxious. Revelation, chapter nine told of the earth being covered by darkness and smoke and locusts and scorpions. "And in those days shall men seek death, and shall not find it, and shall desire to die, and death shall flee from them."

My throat felt constricted, as I uttered, "This is all going to happen?"

Tu-Tu patted me on the hand. "Yes, but don't worry. It's a good thing. If you're a Christian, then you're going to be with Jesus. And the best news is that it's going to be soon."

"How soon?"

"Well, Biblical scholars believe that it will be sometime in the late 1990's. But I've been doing some figuring of my own," she continued. "And I don't think they're accounting correctly for the differences in the Jewish calendar. I think it'll be in 1992."

"But that's just seven years from now. I'll only be nineteen. I'll miss my whole life." I realized that I would still be older than when Samantha Smith died, and I felt a terrible sense of shame over my words.

"But again, Katie, you're forgetting how wonderful it's going to be when we're all with Jesus. Being with Jesus is going to give you such a good feeling you won't miss anything about your life here. And as long as you're a Christian, it won't matter when it happens."

It seemed to me that I only had one option: become a Christian, get forgiven by Jesus, and don't tell Mom.

...

SCHOOL CONTINUED TO be a social maze to try to navigate. Along with my regular classes, I worked on small carpentry projects in Shop 101. Because of my experiences working with Matthew, I was pretty handy. I knew how to hold a hammer without the teacher, a man with a thick mustache and a surly disposition, having to show me. And I regularly finished my projects before the other kids. I was pretty pleased with myself until one day the shop teacher commented on one of the other girls' projects. It was supposed to be a mirror frame, but it looked more like a crooked spice rack. "I swear," he shook his head. "I don't know why they allow girls in this class. Next quarter I'm going to get all the girls switched to home economics."

I complained to the lady who worked in the Principal's office and asked several other girls in the class to do the same.

"But I don't care about shop class," one of the girls told me.

"I'd rather be in home economics," another said.

"That's not the point," I retorted. "He shouldn't be allowed to do this. It's discrimination." Then I made sure I was signed up for his class again when the first session ended.

The shop teacher made his feelings clear by then refusing to help or instruct any of the girls when they asked for assistance. He would simply walk by them ignoring their questions. I went back to the Principal's office but the lady who worked there said that as long as the shop teacher didn't prevent the girls from being in the class, there was nothing that could be done. So, I just made sure that my projects always looked better than my classmates' projects, and I never once asked for help.

My science teacher was a favorite of mine because he was even-handed in his interactions with the boys and girls. One day when a message came over the intercom that four kids were needed to help the custodians, hands shot up all over his classroom. All the hands except for mine belonged to boys, so the science teacher chose three of the boys and me to go. When we arrived to help the two male custodians, they both looked surprised and asked why I was there. At first they tried to convince me to leave, but when I told them I wanted to help, they *instructed* me to go. I went back to the science teacher's room crestfallen and angry. He patted me on the shoulder and chose a boy to go and help. That night I decided to write a letter to the editor of the *Portland Press Herald.*

I wrote feverishly: "I am a girl at 12 years of age. I have been discriminated against because of being a girl. Sometimes it is hard to notice when you're being discriminated against because people are brought up to believe that girls are supposed to play with dolls and boys with toy trucks.

"On one occasion, my shop teacher wanted to prevent girls from going into his class. After many complaints, the Principal decided this was not a good idea. My shop teacher is a man.

"On another occasion, four people were chosen to help unload some boxes from a grocery truck. Three boys and myself were picked. There were two custodians there waiting for us. One of them said, 'Oh, you're a girl. You shouldn't do this. Why don't you go back to your classroom?' I said, 'That's OK. I don't mind doing it.' The other custodian told me, 'You'll get your clothes dirty. Girls shouldn't do this.'

"The boy next to me was wearing an Oxford shirt and corduroys. Discrimination against girls or women is illegal. I think it should be stopped."

When Martha arrived home that evening, I showed her my letter. In an enthusiastic voice, she said, "This is awesome, Katie. I'm proud of you."

My smile beamed. "Should I sign it? I don't want to get

in trouble, but I want to be able to say I wrote it."

"Katie, I think that if you're willing to stand up for something, you have to be willing to put your name on it."

I signed the letter and sent it in.

Though I didn't know it, the letter was printed in the morning paper four days later. I learned of my first ever published piece that afternoon, when I was called into the Principal's office. The Principal told me that I was "not to send any more letters to the editor" and that I had "caused the school embarrassment." He summarized by telling me, "If you ever have any other problems or issues, you need to come to my office and my office alone." I was silent the whole time, not able to bring myself to tell him that I *had* gone to his office about what happened with the shop teacher, and that I had gone back to science class and told the teacher what happened with the custodians. At the end of the Principal's lecture, all I did was nod and agree.

I left the Principal's office and walked alone to the cafeteria for lunch. I had been so proud of myself, but this response from an authority figure made me question what I had done. 'Snapping Turtle's All-Wrong *Life*,' I thought to myself. I pulled the handle of the lunch room door and stepped inside. As I walked past the popular boys' table, I heard a lone, slow clap. Then, more clapping. I turned to see each one of the boys rise from their chairs and applaud me. I smiled so hard my cheeks hurt.

That day, I confidently walked over to the popular girls' table to eat my lunch. It was a social risk to be sure, and I knew that this would be the only day I could get away with it. I second-guessed myself as I sat down, holding my breath. The girls stopped talking for a couple of seconds, but to my relief, no one questioned my presence. They continued their discussion about their favorite soap operas. I had only seen nighttime soaps when I visited my Great-Aunt Madeline, but they were talking about the daytime ones. A classmate, who was one of the pretty girls, turned to me. "Do you watch *Guiding Light?*" she asked.

I had never seen the show before. "Yes," I lied.

She tested me further. "Do you like the old Philip Spaulding or the new Philip Spaulding?"

The entire table seemed to await my answer. I was good at reading people, and I presumed the girl wouldn't be asking if she liked the new Philip Spaulding, so I glanced around and then said, "The old Philip Spaulding."

Her face softened, and she smiled. "Me too."

For that afternoon I forgot about all the bad things I had thought and done. I forgot about upsetting the Principal and my lies and even Samantha Smith. Perhaps by being good and making a difference, I thought, I could make up for all of it. Lunch tasted especially delicious that day.

Chapter 25
Why God Is a Mafia Kingpin

I spent hours reading the Bible. I liked some of the stories, especially how God used his magical powers to create the heaven and the earth. It seemed strange to me, though, that I wasn't supposed to believe in Santa anymore, but it was okay to believe in this fellow who walked on water and cured leprosy. Still, I liked the idea that I wouldn't have to give up my father's God-genie in order to become a Believer.

I enjoyed the part of the Bible where Noah gathered two of every creature in the world to save, but I didn't get what the point was of him becoming an alcoholic, or why God decided to have a second flood and destroy everything anyway. I liked Moses because he was Jewish and because he had once viewed himself as a failure but ended up saving loads of people.

But I couldn't make heads or tails of the point of all those boring "begats" in the New Testament, and the whole Adam and Eve story seemed to put a lot of unnecessary blame on Eve instead of that pesky snake. In general it seemed to me that God didn't really like most of the people he created in the Bible but wanted them to like him, and if they didn't, he would smite them with all sorts of dreadful curses.

The primary benefit of being on God's side seemed to be His willingness to punish one's enemies. I didn't know much about organized crime; there were unconfirmed family rumors that a great-uncle was involved in the Valentine's Day massacre, but other than that, I only knew the little bit I had seen in movies and on television. Still, it seemed to me that the whole God-human relationship was a lot like signing on to the mafia: 'Join me, and I'll take care of your immediate problems. I'll ask you for a favor later.'

...

A FEW DAYS before Christmas, Martha came into my room with a square box that she said was addressed to me. She set it on the bed and sat down beside it. "Your Dad sent this a couple of weeks ago. I kept hoping he'd send a present for Michael, but he didn't. Do you mind opening this in your room so that Michael doesn't see?"

I had no feelings of fondness for my brother at that point, but to not send him a gift seemed cruel, so I agreed. "Will you stay with me while I open it?" I asked.

"Sure honey. And did you notice I put up an extra stocking for you this year because you've been so good."

I smiled. "I did notice. Thank you, Mom."

The box was sealed very well, almost too well, and Martha and I both had to fiddle and tug at the tape in order to get it opened. Once we did, I could see that it was a vinyl record collection. "Neat," I said pulling out several at once. I quickly counted twenty-three albums.

Martha began flipping through them. There were albums from Jimi Hendrix and Janis Joplin and Stephen Stills. A good quarter of the lineup at Woodstock was represented. Then Martha cried out, "These are mine."

"What?"

"These are records that your father stole from me during the divorce. I can't believe that son of a bitch."

My heart sunk. "Can I keep any of them?"

"I'll look through them and give you the ones that aren't mine." Later that day she returned with the Stephen Stills album, two bluegrass records, a Tom Lehrer album, Paul Butterfield's *Put it in Your Ear* and Helen Reddy's *More than You Could Take*. She set them on the bed in a perfunctory manner. "The Helen Reddy one is actually mine, but I don't want it, so you can have it."

"Thanks," I said, though I wasn't feeling very thankful.

The Tom Lehrer record was a collection of political and religious satire songs, which I played over and over again. My favorite was 'The Vatican Rag,' with lyrics that went, "First you get down on your knees, fiddle with your rosaries, bow your head with great respect, and genuflect, genuflect, genuflect."

It opened up a benign opportunity for me to ask Martha about Catholicism. She answered questions I had about genuflection, the confessional, original sin, the wine and wafer, and transubstantiation, all in the guise of understanding the lyrics to the song. By the time we were through, Catholicism sounded like a good combination of self-punishment and magical ideas.

...

IT WAS JANUARY 28th, 1986, and I would miss the latest NASA launch because it would occur just when I had to run from my chorus class on the bottom floor to my science class on the top floor. When I got to class, however, the teacher wasn't there. He had always been there at the start of class before, and we students sat quietly waiting for his arrival. Within a few minutes, he entered the room and slammed his hand on the desk. His face was beat red. "Dammit," he said in a raised voice. All of us turned to watch him inhale and exhale loudly through his nose. Then he said quietly, "The Challenger exploded." We all sat stunned.

That night I learned from the news that although there

were no concrete findings as yet, it was thought that there might have been a problem with a rocket booster. Everyone onboard had died, including Christa McAuliffe, the first member of the Teacher in Space Project.

I prayed again for all the pain in the world. I put a special focus on Christa McAuliffe's family as well as Ryan White, whom I very much wanted to be allowed back in school. "If you won't give me the pain for a full minute, at least give it to me for a second. One second. That's all I ask. Give everyone relief from their pain for one second, and give it to me instead."

...

RYAN WHITE WAS permitted to return to school in February of 1986, but he only stayed for one day. One-hundred and fifty-one of the three-hundred and sixty students stayed home, and the school could not justify saving one over the many. It reminded me of the story of the train station manager who had allowed his son to be crushed to save the passengers on the trains. Like that boy, Ryan White had not asked for any of this. If the Jesus story was true, at least he had sacrificed himself willingly. It didn't seem fair to force a child to give up everything.

Of all the viewpoints presented to me, it seemed that Catholicism had the most to do with suffering. My belief in my culpability in Samantha Smith's death led to a desire to suffer, and I hoped that by doing so, I might be brought back into my God-genie's favor. Then I would be able to be special again.

I watched *Agnes of God* on HBO and decided that I wanted to have stigmata. I prayed for painful, bleeding sores on my wrists to correspond to the crucifixion wounds of Jesus. This, I hoped, would accomplish the dual goal of punishing me for Samantha Smith as well as bringing me worldwide attention as a phenomenon.

My Uncle Anthony and his wife had made a full

conversion to Catholicism. His wife left behind her involvement in Transcendental Meditation because she and Anthony decided it wasn't Christian enough. I talked with them about my desire to have stigmata, and they applauded me for my growing interest in Catholicism.

As I read the Bible more and more, it seemed strange to me that God was described as not being male or female but was always referred to as He. I approached Martha to ask her, "Why is it that it's *Mother* Nature, but God is a man?"

"Actually, the Old Testament was first written in Hebrew and Aramaic, and in both those languages, the word for God and Spirit are feminine. The New Testament was originally written in Greek, and low-and-behold, God became male. Then when the translations were done, everything changed to male."

I was somewhere between surprised and shocked. "What? Why didn't they change the translation of the New Testament to have God be feminine like in the Old Testament?"

"Because the people doing the translation were men. All of Christianity is patriarchal, Katie.

"Patriarchal?"

"Patriarchal is a social system ruled by men. Matriarchal is a social system ruled by women. That's why Jews believe that being Jewish passes down through the mother. It's patriarchal."

"Wouldn't it be matriarchal if it's through the mother?"

She chuckled and shook her head. "No, Katie. You see, if a woman is pregnant, you know she's the mother; but you don't necessarily know that who she says is the father really is the father. So the assumption is that women can't be trusted."

"Oh."

Then she got serious. "Katie, the Bible is allegory. It's a bunch of stories made up to teach lessons."

"That's not what Tu-Tu and Uncle Brian believe. They believe it's real."

"I know. And I get worried sometimes that you think they're right."

I feared she would be even more worried if she knew I also believed Matthew was right. I desired to switch the subject immediately. "Why do you carry a cross with your keys if you aren't a Christian?" For as long as I could remember, Martha had always had a three-inch long metal cross on her key-ring.

"I just like it," she said. "It's made of railroad nails."

I went upstairs to think. The Bible had been changed? It was one thing for a book to be translated into another language, but to be altered? I wondered if the intent had also been changed in some places. It was possible that everything it once stood for might have changed as well. That was a frightening thought.

It also bothered me on a creative level. Someone had changed the writers' words. The people who wrote the Bible did so as part of their own personal legacy. It was their contribution. The idea that anyone could come along and just *change* what someone wrote and say that it was still from the same writer was creative blasphemy to me. In all the terrible actions I had committed, stealing, lying, and even bringing on the death of Samantha Smith, the one thing I hadn't done was to plagiarize. To me, books were as sacred as people, and while it wasn't exactly plagiarism to change someone's words and still attribute them to the writer, it was pretty darn close. It may even be worse if what the writer intended had been lost.

Although it bothered me tremendously, or perhaps because of it, I had to put it out of my mind for the time being. I had bigger worries. I still had to figure out how to make up for what I had done to Samantha Smith, and now I had to combat Martha's fears that I was getting too involved with religion.

So it was that I became a Fundamentalist Christian around Tu-Tu and Uncle Brian, Catholic around Uncle Anthony, a mystic around Matthew, and non-religious around Martha. It was a balancing act, to be sure, but it seemed worth it to keep everyone satisfied and to purify myself of my awful thoughts and deeds.

Chapter 26
Why She Was a Spoiled Brat

On April 26th, 1986, America got news of the worst nuclear disaster in history. The Chernobyl meltdown dwarfed the Three Mile Island accident that had occurred in 1979. The battle to contain the contamination involved over half a million workers and crippled the Soviet economy. It caused thirty-one direct deaths and countless others from exposure.

I knew that it was in part because of what Samantha Smith had done, and all those images of Russian people that we saw when she made her trip in 1983, that Americans overall saw Chernobyl as a human tragedy instead of the just desserts of a Communist nation. It again brought home how much I had taken from the world by her death.

My social life, or lack thereof, acted as a distracter from the turmoil I felt over Samantha. In an attempt to be fashionable, I saved up enough money for a spiral perm, and Rainey and Martha went with me to the salon. When the process was finished, my hair resembled that of a poodle. Because I didn't want the hairdresser to feel bad, I gave her a large tip and told her how much I liked it. As we left the salon, Rainey asked with a hint of suspicion, "Do you really like it?"

"Oh yes," I said enthusiastically. Social death was part of the punishment.

Even kids whom I didn't know noticed my hair. Comparisons to 'Orphan Annie' and 'Alice' from *The Brady Bunch* were frequent. I didn't mind the 'Orphan Annie' association, but I would have preferred 'Jan' or 'Marsha Brady' over 'Alice.'

While trying to brush out my hair one afternoon home from school, I asked Martha, "Can we adopt?"

"What made you think of that," she asked.

"I don't know. I just feel like there should be three of us."

Martha looked at me for a long moment. It felt as though her eyes were burrowing into me. Then she offered a soft smile and said, "We hardly have enough money for us, Katie. We can't adopt someone else."

I nodded and let the matter drop.

In June of 1986, I turned thirteen, and America learned that it had been lied to by its space program. The 'Commission Report on the Challenger Disaster' indicated that as early as 1977, NASA managers had been aware of the design flaw that caused the explosion, and moreover had known that it had the potential for catastrophe. This led the Commission to conclude that the Challenger disaster was "an accident rooted in history." Why, I wondered, weren't these important organizations being held accountable so that history would not repeat itself?

I made friends with a neighbor boy named James. At five years my junior, James might have been an unusual choice for a playmate, but unlike my few girlfriends, he enjoyed some of the messier things I enjoyed, like climbing trees, playing in the field that I called the 'Dinosaur Lands,' and making forts. And unlike the boys my age, he wasn't interested in making jokes about masturbation. Like me, his parents had divorced. He had two Moms, both of whom were kind to me. Martha told me that they were a couple.

Rainey had stopped by on a Saturday while James and I

were building a fort in Martha's backyard. Martha had said that we could paint it, and James had agreed to my choice of electric blue. Before we got started, I ran inside the house with a splinter in my finger. Rainey got a set of tweezers from the bathroom. "Here you go, Twat," she said as she pulled out the splinter. She held my hand in hers. "I can't get over how much your pinkies are like Anna's." I thought about Anna's death again. That was it. That would be my punishment for Samantha Smith. I was sure I was going to get cancer like Anna did.

I was lost in thought as James and I painted, and that night, I had the recurring nightmare again of being trapped in a terror-filled version of an amusement park. The next day, however, I awoke to the most wonderful sound. The birds had returned to Maine, and I nestled in bed listening to their song: *oo-wah-hooo hoo-hoo*. I closed my eyes and prayed. "If I'm supposed to live another day, please make it a good one." When I got up, I passed Michael in the living room without saying hello and meandered into the kitchen where Martha was having a cup of coffee. "Mom, what's the name of those birds that make that wicked pretty sound."

"Which ones?"

"The ones that go, '*oo-wah-hooo hoo-hoo*.'"

"Those are mourning doves, Katie." She took a sip of her coffee.

"Is that because they come out in the morning?"

"No, it's 'mourning' as in sadness."

"But they don't sound sad. They sound so beautiful."

"Listen to them closer, Katie," she said. "They may seem like happy birds at first, but it's really a very haunting sound that they make."

Just then, Michael yelled out. "Mom, Katie took all my stuffed animals." I realized I had closed my door but had forgotten to lock it.

"What?" Martha called back.

"My stuffed animals. Katie has them all in her toy trunk."

I whispered to Martha, "Those are the ones he gave me two years ago. You remember. It was my eleventh birthday."

Martha told me to stay in the kitchen while she spoke with Michael. She went into my room, and a few minutes later, she and Michael came back out. Michael was holding his stuffed animal collection as he walked past me and into his room.

"Mom, what are you letting him do? He gave those to me. Remember? Everybody said what a great present it was?"

"I know honey, but he didn't mean to."

"What do you mean? He gave them to me; I play with them."

"He left you some. He only took the ones that are really special to him."

I stormed into my room. Michael had moved the ragdolls I had on top of trunk so that he could open the lid. My dolls were in a pile on the floor, and the lid was still open. He had taken all of the stuffed animals he had given me except one hot-pink snake, which I never really liked anyway, and I suspected he didn't either or he would have taken it with him. The other ones that remained, to which Martha had referred, were mine to begin with. I slammed down the top of the trunk. She had let him take back what had been mine; but more than that, the one nice thing he had done for me in years had just been canceled out. The punishment was getting me on all levels.

Later that day, Martha was fixing the kitchen sink again, this time from the underneath up. I heard a clank and then her voice. "Ow," she muttered. Then I heard her climb out from under the sink. After what had happened earlier in the day, I didn't want to ask if she was alright, so I stayed silent. I heard her pull out a chair and sit down. A few seconds later, she said "ow" again, only louder. I wondered what she'd do if I kept quiet. Sure enough, after a moment she said, "Darn that hurts." I listened for what would come next. Another few seconds, and "Wow, that really smarts." I bit my lip. Finally, a moment later, I heard her sigh deeply.

I went in my room, muttering to myself, "And she says *I* need to find an outlet for *my* dramatic energy. Geesh."

Martha didn't approve of my friendship with James. She said he was "too young" a person with whom to spend my time. She was right, but friend-beggars couldn't be friend-choosers, and anyway, we liked one another's company.

Michael was spending the night at a friend's house, so Martha let James and me make a pillow fort in the living room. We tried to stay up to watch *Saturday Night Live* but we both fell asleep long before it began. I woke up while "The Star-Spangled Banner" played and the American flag blew in the wind onscreen. I woke up James, and he and I stood with sleepy eyes and put our hands over our hearts. We sang quietly so as not to wake Martha, whose bedroom was directly below the living room. "And the rockets' red glare, the bombs bursting in air, gave proof through the night that our flag was still there. O! say does that star-spangled banner yet wave, o'er the land of the free and the home of the brave?" Then a long beep took over the music and the screen faded into a color bar test pattern. I turned off the television, and James and I fell asleep end-to-end in our pillow fort.

The next day, James and I planned to play outside, but I had to wash the dishes first. He went out to plan our next Dinosaur Lands adventure, and I started cleaning. After I got done I told Martha that I was heading out for the afternoon. She agreed, but then the phone rang. "Tell them I'm not here," she said.

I halted. The phone continued to ring. "Mom," I said. "Can't I just say you're not available? Do I have to lie for you?"

"Just do it, Katie."

"No," I snapped back. I was determined to be better so that God would forgive me for everything I'd done. The call went to the answering machine, and I flung open the door and ran outside. "I'm going to play." I could feel my heart beat double-time with my refusal of her instructions.

She stood in the doorway and called after me. "You know, for a kid growing up on Welfare, you're a real spoiled brat." It seemed to me that the people in my life wanted very much to teach me to stand up for myself...to everyone but them.

In late June, James and I had an argument that damaged our friendship. While studying the Bible, I had read in Matthew 18:20 that, "For where two or three are gathered together in my name, there am I in the midst of them." Since God, to me, was still a God-genie, I took this to mean that if I could focus my energy and that of another person, we could together evoke the God-genie to do our bidding. This would mean not only the material dreams of clothes and dolls and money, but it would mean that I could go back in time and have a do-over. I could fix what I had done to Samantha Smith and change all my other failures to successes.

I had an empty Tootsie Roll piggy bank, and I took it with me to James' house. In the backyard, I told him to focus all of his energy and to imagine a quarter in the piggy bank. We stood holding the bank with our eyes closed for a full minute. Then we checked inside. Much to my surprise, it was empty.

"What was supposed to be in there?" James asked.

"A quarter. I don't know why it didn't work. It's supposed to work when there are two of us."

I took the Tootsie Roll bank back home and considered

what had happened. Maybe James just didn't believe enough. I had to convince him in order for the two of us to have the mental strength to make things happen. I decided to go back to his house with the Tootsie Roll bank, only this time I would slip in a quarter when his eyes were closed. It would be a lie and a cheat, but I thought that God would be alright with it because it was such a necessity for me to get James to believe. If I could get him to believe, then two would be gathered, and everything wrong could be righted. The trouble occurred when James did not accept for one second that magic had placed the quarter inside of the bank. "You think you can fool me because you're thirteen and I'm only eight." He stormed off to his house, and I solemnly walked back to mine.

    The next day was my last in Maine before heading to Matthew's place in North Carolina. Martha was watching the news while I packed, and I overheard the reporter say Samantha Smith's name. I walked into the living room, holding some folded shirts. The newscaster announced that Jane Smith was to accompany twenty of Samantha's classmates on a trip to the Goodwill Games in Moscow, where a monument to Samantha had been built. Many people from the USSR had gone to the dedication of the monument, and images of crying Russian children were shown on the screen. I swallowed hard. Why was it that my wishes never seemed to work for any of the good things I wanted? Why had it only worked for this awful thing? I blinked away tears from my eyes and went back to packing.

Chapter 27
Why He Called Himself God

For a while, being with Matthew took my mind off of my troubles. New Coke had been introduced the year before, and Matthew set up a blind taste test for us between New Coke and Classic Coke. I didn't like drinking cola because I considered it to be 'grown-up soda,' whereas I preferred 'kid sodas' like root beer; but it was fun to put on the blindfold and guess which one was the Classic Coke. Then we made homemade ice cream. Or, rather, Matthew set me up to work an old-fashioned churn while he picked squash and okra from the garden. We made a "corn run" with Elizabeth. Matthew set a big pot of water on the stove to boil, and the three of us went out to the garden to find and pick the ripest ears of corn. To ensure that they would be cooked at their freshest, we shucked them while running at full speed back into the house and then tossed them into the boiling water.

Matthew had bought an old black pickup that he named La Bomba, Spanish for "The Bomb." We were going to paint flames on the doors, but then the engine caught fire while Matthew was driving back from the Piggly Wiggly one afternoon. He didn't like losing his vehicle, but even he saw the humor in La Bomba's engine blowing up.

One morning a bat flew out of the fireplace in the living room, and I called to Matthew for help. Although I wasn't too thrilled to see Matthew and Elizabeth running from their room wearing nothing but robes, it was pretty fun to chase the thing out of the house. Then they got dressed and we all went out to the yard for our morning Tai Chi practice. In the afternoons we all played croquet, and in the evenings I ran around catching fireflies. All in all, it was turning into a fine summer. And then the sheriff came.

Elizabeth was out, and Matthew was in the living room. I was in the kitchen when two cars arrived with their lights flashing. Three deputies stood by the open car doors, while the sheriff came up the porch. "Dad?" I called out. "There's something going on." The sheriff knocked and then walked back down the steps to wait. Matthew came out of the living room, and he and I both walked outside.

"Are you Matthew Lippa?" the sheriff asked.

"Yes."

"Is this your daughter?"

"Yes."

"Why don't you send her inside..."

Matthew did so, and I waited in the kitchen, where I could hear everything anyway. One of the deputies spat on the ground and then kicked the dirt. "So," the sheriff said. "I understand you haven't been paying child support for your kids."

"Well, as you can see, my daughter's here."

"Yep," the sheriff said with a slow drawl. "But my understandin' is that she and her brother are usually at their mother's place up north. That right?"

"Yes." Matthew's tone was getting progressively cool.

"So, why is it that you haven't been payin'?"

"I have been."

The sheriff had a tone that sounded half surprised and half mocking. "Really? Doesn't seem like it from what I heard."

"I pay child support every month for both of my kids." I gasped. He was lying. Martha might drink a lot of Diet Pepsi and smoke a lot of those discount cigarettes, but I knew there was no way our refrigerator would be empty so often if he really was paying child support. I couldn't listen anymore. I walked into the living room and sat in silence.

A few days later, Matthew asked me to mow the lawn. When I got to a particularly rough spot, he took over. After a minute or so, he suddenly stopped the mower. He screamed and shot past me like a blur. "Run," he yelled. I didn't know what was happening, so I followed him into the house. When I got there, he was soaking his hand under running water. It turned out that the mower had hit a wasp nest on the ground. Matthew had been stung multiple times, and there were red blotchy spots on his hands, arms and neck. It was a moment later when I realized that I was smiling, satisfied that God had gotten him back for lying about paying child support. Then I felt a little ashamed of myself and was glad that he hadn't looked up from the sink to see me.

To make up for my bad thoughts against Matthew, I offered to help him fold and distribute fliers he had made to advertise a new class he was organizing. The text read that he planned to charge $2,500 per student, and the header indicated that the sessions would be taught by someone named El Alim Akhbar. "Who's that?" I asked.

"That's me. It's the name I go by for classes."

"What does it mean?"

"Well, 'El' is Hebrew. It means 'God.' Alim Akhbar has an Islamic derivative."

"Derivative?"

"Derivative means that it 'derives.' It comes from."

"Oh. What does it mean?"

"It means 'the All-Knowing Greatness.'"

I was silent. I stared at the flier in my hand, unable to look at him or even move. My father was calling himself 'God, the All-Knowing Greatness.' I could accept that Matthew had magical powers. I could even accept that he was a prophet from another planet. But God Himself? This pushed a line that I did not know if I was willing to cross. A half-formed thought came to mind. I wondered if he was just calling himself God to gain more paying followers. I began to fold the flier in my hand, "Why do you teach?" I asked, still not looking him in the eye.

"To assist people, individually and collectively, toward a higher consciousness. To be a guiding light for future generations. To assess people's actions, thoughts and needs."

So it wasn't just about money. It seemed he really believed himself to be God, the All-Knowing Greatness. For the first time ever, it struck me as strange that a person who didn't take care of his kids would teach classes about enlightenment. "But how do you know you're the right person to teach?"

"In life, everyone gets what is deserved as a response to their intentions, desires, and needs, including the teacher they need."

I wasn't sure I bought that completely. I still felt I was getting what I deserved for what I had done to Samantha Smith. But the idea that innocent children were starving, or that there were qualified individuals who had been refused work because of racism, or that someone like Ryan White had endured such unnecessary suffering...well, it just didn't seem like they were getting what they deserved as a response to their intentions, desires and needs.

Chapter 28
Why She Picked Up the Hitchhiker

Matthew sent me to stay with Grandma Barbara for a while before I was to go back to Maine and start eighth grade. After the removal of her tumor, which had been benign, Grandma Barbara took Matthew up on his offer to help her out if she moved near him in North Carolina. She had rented a house in Carrboro, a woodsy town near Chapel Hill.

I put Grandma Barbara's polio sticks in the back seat of her car. One of the many puffy stickers on them was peeling off, so I pressed it back in place and climbed in the passenger seat. "I like your new stickers Grandma. Oh, and I like your bumper sticker too."

"Which one? I've got about ten."

"The 'Question Authority' one."

She laughed.

I pointed to a contraption on the floor of the car that looked like a walkie-talkie but had a spiral cord. "What's that?"

"That's my CB radio. I talk to truckers when I'm on the road. I find out if there are any cops around or accidents on the road."

"Do you do a lot of traveling, Grandma?"

"Not so much anymore. I used to drive long distances, but my legs get too tired now. Did I ever tell you about the time I picked up a hitchhiker?"

"Nope." I fiddled with the CB cord.

"Well, as a rule I never pick up hitchhikers. I don't trust them. But I was driving home one day; this was back in the mid or late 60's, and I hadn't heard from your father in months; I didn't know where the hell he was. So anyway, I pass by this dirty, scummy looking guy thumbing for a ride. And I get about a mile down the road, and something tells me to go back to him. So I turn around and pick him up. When he got in my car we introduced ourselves, and you know 'Lippa' isn't exactly a common name, so when I tell him my name is Barbara Lippa, he says, 'Lippa? I just left a guy named Matt Lippa in the woods of San Francisco. He's been there dropping acid for six months.' And that's how I found out where your father was."

"Wow. Just...wow."

"Are you hungry?"

"A little. ...Wow." I didn't know how Grandma Barbara was really related to Matthew if he was from another planet; but I found it very interesting that it seemed she, too, had an element of psychic powers.

"Let's get some food," she said.

We pulled into the parking lot of a barbeque restaurant. Grandma Barbara took the spot next to the handicap spot, which had been filled by a big pickup truck. "Look," she said, shutting off her engine. "That asshole parked in a handicap spot without a handicap license plate." She reached into her purse and dug around until she found a pad and pen. I took impish pleasure in watching her write what I hoped would be a blistering note.

"What does it say Grandma?" I asked, peering over her shoulder.

"It doesn't 'say.' It reads," she spouted. She finished writing and reviewed the note, finally reading aloud: "Dear Asshole, I hope that one day you are handicapped and cannot find a fucking parking spot, so that you know how it feels. Fuck You."

Short and sweet. Then we got out of the car and I got Grandma Barbara's sticks for her. I smiled broadly as she jammed the note under the driver side windshield wiper. Then I paused, worried for a moment that perhaps the driver was traveling with someone who was indeed handicapped. I let it pass out of my mind and enjoyed the moment as we walked into the restaurant.

When we sat down, I asked Grandma Barbara, "Why is it that the Christians in my family are really concerned about me becoming a Christian, but no one on Dad's side ever tells me I should be Jewish?"

"Because you *are* Jewish."

"What about the rule that a Jewish person is only Jewish if her mother is Jewish?"

"That's a stupid fucking rule. You're Jewish."

Her response satisfied me enough to at least drop the matter for the time being. I asked if we could order my favorite, hush puppies. Grandma Barbara never refused the request for fried cornbread spheres. When the waitress came to take our order she nodded her head toward Grandma's polio sticks. "Did your grandkids put those stickers there?"

Grandma laughed. "No. I did."

Chapter 29
Why the Hostages Really, Really Were Released

In an effort to help Michael feel more connected to a male presence, Martha gave him her father's hunting rifle. I did not think this was a particularly good idea. "Give me a large, personal break," I announced to her, quoting the Rebecca Schaeffer character from my new favorite television show of 1986, 'My Sister Sam.'

Although I never saw the gun in person again, it wasn't for lack of imagining it. I spent long nights in bed, afraid Michael would kill us all. I constructed elaborate plans in my mind as to how to escape if he ever got shells for the gun: If he uses it first on Martha, then I'll hear the shot. I'll quietly slip out of bed and place a pillow under the covers. That way, when he shoots through my bolt lock, he'll think I'm still in bed. If I'm lucky, I will have slipped out of the window and gotten away by stepping onto the roof of the shed. Thank goodness it's located just below my window. I will have to lean back and shut the window, so that he won't know I've escaped. Then I can jump from the shed onto the ground. If it's winter, I'll be able to land on a snow bank. If it's spring or summer or fall, I'll have to be steady enough not to sprain my ankle, but even then, I might be able to limp over and climb the fence in the backyard without him spotting me. It'll be okay to break the rules and climb the fence this one time. ...If he goes for my room first, there still might be enough time to get from my bed to the closet, where he might not suspect I'd be hiding. Then, Martha will come up the stairs, wondering what the noise is. I can use that distraction to get out. It will be a terrible thing for her to die, but then she was the one who gave him the gun in the first place. If we're both lucky, the gunshot won't kill her or she might have called the police before she is shot. ...Or, better yet, perhaps he won't be able to get into her room at all, and I could call the police before escaping. Then she and I will live, and he'll be taken away. That will be a best case scenario. The worst case scenario will be that we all die; he'll surely commit suicide after killing Martha and me.

...

RYAN WHITE WAS two years older than I, but because of all the school he had been forced to miss, he entered his eighth grade year in Indiana at the same time I entered eighth grade in Maine. He had few friends and was required to eat with disposable utensils and to use a separate bathroom from the rest of his classmates. He was also prohibited from enrolling in gym class. It bothered me that Ryan White wasn't fully accepted and that some people even considered him to be possessed of evil because of his illness. After all, it wasn't his fault that he had gotten HIV. He was a hemophiliac. If he had stigmata and hemophilia, he might have been considered a saint.

In November of 1986, John McKernan was elected governor of Maine. "He was my divorce lawyer," Martha told me with a chuckle. "He did the very best he could for my divorce settlement, but in the end it wasn't worth the paper it was printed on because no one could enforce it." When John McKernan took office in early 1987, he signed a bill proclaiming the first Monday in June 'Samantha Smith Day.'

As both of our birthdays fell in June, this would be a lasting reminder every year that, because of my actions, I would age, and she would not.

In December of 1986, a bronze statue of Samantha Smith was unveiled in front of the Maine State Cultural Building. It showed Samantha releasing a dove, with a bear cub at her side. The symbol of Russia was a ferocious bear, and the statue represented that this lone little girl had tamed the beast. Here she would stand, frozen in time.

Before the year was out, I heard the name "October Surprise" on the news, and it caught my attention. I recognized the name but couldn't remember from what. The report was about the journalist who had written those articles about why the American hostages had been held in Iran until the very moment Ronald Reagan took the oath of office. I understood a little better this time that some people thought that Mr. Reagan and Mr. Bush had made a deal with Iran to sell them weapons in exchange for Iran holding the hostages longer. That way, Jimmy Carter would be sure to lose the election. But the focus in the report was how the government had just raided the offices of the journalist and that he had been indicted on charges of credit card fraud. I shook my head. Clearly this fellow was dishonest in various aspects of his life. Maybe he was just a liar when it came to all that October Surprise business as well.

In newspaper articles and on television, there were reports that some people believed President Reagan had threatened to "nuke" Iran, and that was why the hostages were released when they were. But a lot of other people thought that Iran would never have taken that threat seriously and that it wouldn't make sense for the United States to start selling weapons to Iran after threatening to drop a nuclear bomb on them.

There were also some big questions as to whether or not the profits from those weapon sales were going to the Contra rebels, to support them in their efforts to overthrow their government in Nicaragua. I had never heard of the Contra rebels before, but it worried me that we might help people topple their own government. I wasn't sure we had the right to do that. And I was very certain that if people came in to topple our government we definitely wouldn't like it.

Some people said maybe Iran hated Jimmy Carter so much that they didn't want him to get elected; but apparently that didn't make sense because Iran had spent a whole year negotiating with him. A year did seem like an awfully long time to "play nice" if Iran had no intentions of working with Mr. Carter.

According to the news, the alternative, then, was that Mr. Reagan and Mr. Bush might have derailed the talks that Iran was having with Mr. Carter. I learned that Iran had been involved in a war with Iraq at the time and that the hostages had been very important to Iran. I wasn't exactly sure why they were so important, but news commentators said that Iran would not have just released the hostages without getting something in exchange from Mr. Reagan and Mr. Bush.

I figured there must be a good explanation or that there was something I just wasn't understanding. The news people said that if Mr. Reagan and Mr. Bush had interrupted Mr. Carter's negotiations for the release of the hostages that would be treason. I knew from my history class lessons on the Constitution that treason was the worst possible thing an American could do. I couldn't imagine our president and vice president doing such a thing, let alone allowing fifty-two Americans to endure an extra month of captivity just because they wanted to win the election. Then again, I had wished a girl dead just because I wanted to be seen as special.

    Still, I had to hope that the fact that weapons had been sold to Iran after the hostages were released had some other reason behind it. And certainly they wouldn't have sent the profits to Contra rebels to overthrow their leaders. That was ridiculous. The United States Government was of the people, by the people, and for the people. Surely, they would not betray us.

Chapter 30
Why She Screamed

I was just being nice. I was the eighth-grade lead in the new school musical, *Pandora*, and I could tell that one cast member, Todd, was not well liked by the others. He was overweight, taller than most of the kids, looked older, and had bad skin. We rehearsed during chorus class, and as the kids were putting away their costumes, I said to Todd, "You did a good job today."

His face lit up. "Thanks. You were good too." I smiled and thanked him and went on my way. Todd followed me out of the classroom. "Where are you going?"

"Um, just to class."

"I'll walk with you."

I didn't like the idea of walking with any boy. "No, that's okay. It's just upstairs."

He insisted. "Let me take your books."

"No thanks. I've got 'em."

He wrested my books from my hands and held them away from me. "Now you have to let me walk with you. I've got your books."

There was something in his eyes that wasn't about nicely carrying my books. It was something dark. I was silent during the rest of the walk to class. When I arrived at the door, I turned to Todd and said, "I need my books."

He held them firm in his grasp. "Say thank you. I carried them for you."

"Thank you," I said coolly.

He handed me the books and said something in French to me. I didn't know what he had said, but the sexual way in which he said it made me uncomfortable.

"What?" I asked, annoyed.

"It's French, the language of love."

It was not unusual for kids who lived on the northern border of Maine to speak fluent French, since Quebec was so close, but further south in Maine it was a bit of an anomaly. It bothered me that he was speaking to me in a language I didn't understand, and it bothered me more that he called it the language of love. "Gross," I said and walked into my classroom without looking back at him.

For the next few months, Creepy Todd followed me around the school. He walked next to me, pressing the side of his body up against mine and pinning me against the lockers if I moved away from him. He wrote notes in French to me, which I promptly threw away. He sat behind me on the bus, touching my neck and hair. Even sitting in the very front seat, near the bus driver, didn't seem to help. When I complained, the driver told him to stop bothering me, but he just pulled his hand away and began to whisper vulgar things to me. He told the other kids on the bus and in the school hallways that we had a sexual relationship. While I had a few supporters who agreed that Todd was indeed creepy, it seemed that most of the other kids either didn't believe me when I said he was lying or perhaps thought it was funnier to agree with him and watch me squirm. This included my arch-enemy, who lead the charge in supporting Todd's efforts. "What else did you guys do?" she asked with a broad smile.

Todd went into great detail about made-up sexual encounters and things that he said I did to him.

"No I didn't. I have never and will never, ever kiss or touch you," I exclaimed.

"But we *have* touched."

"You've touched me, and I've told you to stop," I retorted.

"Methinks the lady doth protest too much," he said in a slinky way.

"Who says 'methinks'? We're in the eighth grade, you asshole." The other kids laughed, and his eyes took on a kind of malevolence. That day, he began to amplify his actions.

For a while I thought that I deserved every bit of what was happening because of Samantha. Then one day I told God that if I had to hide in my room with the Cool Whip container every day after school and ultimately die of cancer, my punishment shouldn't include having to deal with Creepy Todd. When God didn't change my circumstances, I tried to tell Martha about Todd's harassment, but she didn't seem to want to hear it. "Katie, you can't come to me for every little thing. You need to start figuring out how to deal with things on your own." It seemed Martha wanted me to have life skills that she, herself did not have, or at least didn't know how to teach me. I decided to just pretend that it wasn't happening.

...

"I JUST GOT off the phone with DHHS," she said.

"What's that?"

"The Department of Health and Human Services. Your father got out of paying child support again. He convinced them he's been paying all along."

"How?" I asked.

"A few years ago, your Dad sent a hundred dollars for

Christmas presents. I didn't have a checking account, so he wrote the check out to Judy. He told DHHS that he's been sending her checks all along. Judy's furious with him."

"Oh." I thought back on our Christmases and tried to remember one when there was a particularly large number of gifts from Matthew, but all I could think of was one when there were a large number of gifts from 'Santa.'

A few days later, while I was in math class, I nicked my finger with a sharp pencil point. It was a tiny hole, but it would not stop bleeding. I went to the Principal's office, but after the blood soaked through three Band Aids, Martha was called. She was going to have to pick me up and take me to Dr. Kaz. When she walked into the school, she looked like she had just woken up. Her hair was disheveled, and she wore an ugly pale blue jacket. She looked tired and angry and poor. I felt embarrassed. On the way out, Creepy Todd was in the hallway. "That's him," I whispered to her.

"Who, Katie?" she said.

My voice was hushed. "Say something to him, Mom. Tell him to leave me alone." She kept walking. When we got outside, I pleaded, "Why didn't you say something to him, Mom?"

"That's the kid who's been bothering you?"

"Yes. Why didn't you say something?"

"He looks like the Pillsbury Doughboy. Just tell him to leave you alone."

"I have. It doesn't work."

We got to Dr. Kaz's office and he looked at my finger. "It hit a blood vessel; that's why it won't stop bleeding. I'll need to cauterize it." Dr. Kaz injected a little bit of Novocain into my finger and then took out a device that looked like a soldering iron. He plugged it in, and it made a loud humming noise. Then the phone rang. He had one hand on the cauterizing tool and one hand on the phone, as he began working on my finger. He spoke with a distressed voice into the receiver. "She wants what? ...No, she can't have it."

Whatever it was that 'she' wanted, Dr. Kaz was not pleased. Martha and I glanced at one another. He kept tapping the tool to my teensy wound. My skin sizzled and emitted a foul odor.

Dr. Kaz raised his voice into the phone, "This divorce was her idea in the first place. No, I will not give her that." He touched the tip of the cauterizing tool to my finger some more.

Martha and I kept our mouths shut for the rest of the visit. On the way out the door, she said, "I thought he was going to cauterize your whole hand." We both laughed in relief as we got in the car.

By the middle of spring, I was fed up with Creepy Todd. I walked past the chorus room one day on my way upstairs, and Todd pressed his body against mine and pushed me against the lockers. I couldn't get past him. I tried to wrestle away, but he was too strong. I glanced around for help but there was no one else in the hallway. I yelled at him, "Stay away from me." His eyes opened wide with surprise at my outburst, and he backed up a step.

Just then, the chorus teacher came out of her room. "Todd, Katie, get in here." We both walked into the classroom. "What is going on?" she demanded.

I let loose. "Todd keeps telling people we had sex, and I've never even kissed a boy. And he brushes up next to me and passes me notes and won't let me walk down the hallway."

The teacher turned to Todd and in a stern voice said, "Todd you can't do that."

Then she turned to me, and in an even sterner voice said, "But, Katie, you can't go around yelling in the hallway."

I apologized even though I didn't mean it, and we were both told to go to our classes.

When we walked outside, Todd got close again and began speaking in French. I stormed away.

That night I went to Martha again. She was lying on the sofa watching television. I leaned against the wall and said, "Please, you've got to help me, Mom. I can't get Todd to stop."

She kept her eyes on the set. "I'm tired of this, Katie. You have to handle your own problems."

In that moment, I let out a long, piercing, shrill scream. There had been times when I had raised my voice to Martha before. I had even yelled some of my complaints. But this was a formless scream directly from my throat and gut. This was new.

It lasted just a few seconds, but I had gotten her attention. When I was finished, she sat up and turned to me. Her manner was calm, cold and definite. She stared directly into my eyes. Her nostrils flared, and her eyes were piercing. Her tone was guttural, and she spoke slowly. "I only *wish* my life were as easy as yours."

Chapter 31
Why Her Body Was a Punchbowl

"I'm going to church. Do you want to come with me?" Martha's voice rang in my ears.

"You're going to church?"

"Yes. I can go to church even if I don't believe in everything. I like the ritual of it."

"Give me a large, personal break."

"I'm serious. Do you want to come with me, or not?"

"Yes."

As we drove to the Catholic Church across the bridge in Portland, I sat in the backseat, wondering if aliens had swapped out Martha's brain and thinking that she might now be a pod-person. But, with the exception of this very strange development, she seemed to be herself.

Almost as soon as we sat down on the pew, Martha began silently weeping. I wished I could soothe her pain. It was difficult to pay attention to what was happening during the service. There was a lot of rising up and sitting down and rising up again. I didn't care about all the rigmarole. I wanted to know what it all meant and why Martha was crying. I wasn't sure I should ask, though, so I kept quiet.

Her attendance lasted a few months, but she said it didn't seem to be a good fit. I was disappointed that we wouldn't be going to church together, but I was also glad to know that she seemed to be struggling with all of the choices, as I was.

...

I TOLD MARTHA that the only thing I wanted for my fourteenth birthday was for her to draw a picture for me. She balked at the idea. "Oh, Katie, I haven't drawn in years."

"I know. That's why I want you to draw something for me. Mom, you're so good at it, and you never draw anymore. Please?"

She told me she would think about it, and on my birthday she presented me with an extraordinary drawing of a ballerina. She sighed. "It isn't very good," she said.

"Mom, it's just beautiful." It was more than beautiful. It was precious.

Soon afterward, the Samantha Smith foundation brought its first group of Soviet campers to Maine. Because of threatening letters, the foundation arranged a special session, with counselors patrolling the camp's perimeter and the state police on alert. It was a relief to learn that there had been no problems, although it made me think about all the work that was still left to do in world relations, all the work that Samantha could have done.

My summer visit with Matthew was going to be at a house that he and Elizabeth had rented in Davenport, Iowa. Martha suggested to me that he had moved there to avoid paying child support, but I suspected that it had more to do with the fact that Grandma Barbara was still living in North Carolina. Whatever the reason, this would be another summer without Michael. It would also be the first summer that I had chosen to spend partly in Maine; I would only be with Matthew until late July. I had hoped that Howard, the magician, would appear again, but it seemed that as long as Matthew and Elizabeth were together, I wouldn't be seeing him.

It was a tense time, during which Matthew seemed irritable with me, Elizabeth and life in general. He hadn't been able to successfully form a spiritual group, so he took on a job as an encyclopedia salesman to make ends meet. I suspected he didn't like it much and that it contributed to his foul mood. For lack of a better option, I bonded with Elizabeth, who, as it turned out, was surprisingly likable.

While Matthew was at work one day, I walked into the bedroom where Elizabeth was sitting on the mattress sewing. I stood in the doorway watching the smooth motion of her hands and the needle. "You're good at that," I finally said.

"I've had a lot of practice," she smiled, still focused on her work. Then she put down her hands and looked up at me. "Would you like me to show you how to sew?"

"Sure," I said. I leapt onto the bed, and Elizabeth showed me how to thread a needle and tie it off. She gave me a piece of cloth on which to practice, and we sat for a while gabbing away about whatever came to mind.

We were having a good time when the front door to the house slammed. I could hear Matthew pause in the kitchen and then stomp up the stairs. He entered the room red-faced and looked directly at me. "You were supposed to do the dishes."

"I'm sorry. I forgot. I'll do them as soon as we finish up here."

"You'll do them now."

"But I'm just learning how to sew." I could feel Elizabeth's body stiffen next to mine.

"Get downstairs and wash the damn dishes, now," he said. I put down the needle and cloth and got up off the bed. As I walked past him, he said, "You may get away with everything at your mother's house, but here you'll do what you're told, when you're told."

I went downstairs to wash the dishes. Then I quietly picked up the phone extension in the kitchen and called Martha. When she picked up, I asked, "Mom, would it be okay if I come home early?"

...

PLAYING OUTSIDE MEANT possible rejection by my peers, so back home in Maine I spent the rest of the summer of 1987 watching *Stand by Me* multiple times on HBO and the Iran-Contra hearings on PBS. I clipped out pictures of River Phoenix from my *Teen Beat* magazine while watching several politicians not listen to or repeat questions that already had been asked. The hearings were fascinating, except when they were mind-numbingly boring. The only surprising thing I learned while watching the hearings was that the Contras might be drug dealers, and I only learned that because Orrin Hatch, a Republican Senator from Utah, mentioned it. My favorite part was when a retired U.S. Marine Corps officer named Oliver North testified. It amazed me how many times he repeated the phrase, "I do not recall."

When Martha got home, I said, "That guy Oliver North sure seems to have some memory problems."

Martha responded, "When they get that high up in politics, they *all* have memory problems."

We watched *The Cosby Show*, and during a commercial break I sneezed. I waited, but Martha didn't say anything. So I said, "Mom, I sneezed."

"Good for you, Katie."

"Aren't you going to bless me?" Martha rolled her eyes but didn't say anything. I followed up with, "I always bless you."

She breathed a heavy sigh. "Bless you, Katie."

I crossed my arms in annoyance, thinking to myself, 'Who doesn't say *bless you* when someone sneezes? It's like I'm not even in the room.'

JUST BEFORE HIGH school started, I heard on the news that the threats against Ryan White had continued. When a bullet was fired through his family's living room window, they decided to move. The sense of isolation I assumed Ryan White must have felt troubled me greatly. I knew what it was to desperately hope to be accepted.

To that end, I wanted some new clothes. I didn't dare ask either of my parents, and I didn't have money enough, so I thought and thought and then made a decision. I would steal them. It had been five years since I had taken anything, and two and a half years since I had been accused of taking anything; but high school was a special circumstance. For three days in a row, I rode my silver Centurion to the local shopping mall to determine the best strategy for procuring my fall wardrobe. On *Starsky & Hutch* reruns, they called this "casing the joint." I settled on a store, parked my bike outside and nervously entered with an empty backpack. I exited ten minutes later, my bag stuffed with an ankle-length skirt, pants, sweater, blouse and even a pair of socks.

To celebrate my ill-gotten plunder I rode my bike across the parking lot from the clothing store and into the McDonalds drive-thru where I ordered a lobster roll, a specialty only offered during the summer. It was more expensive than the hamburger, but then, I had just saved quite a bit of money on clothes. The fellow working the window told me, "Don't ride through on your bike again after this. It isn't safe."

I sat on my bike in front of the McDonalds and ate the lobster roll. As I finished and threw away my trash, I spotted a female clerk open the front door of the clothing store. She approached, and I considered my options. I could ride away; but if she got in a car and followed me, then my goose would be cooked, and I'd be in extra trouble for "leaving the scene." I decided to stay put and accept the consequences. She got up to the bike and said, "You need to come back in." At that moment, I changed my mind and decided to bolt; but as soon as I put my foot on the pedal she grabbed the handlebars. "I don't think so," she said. "Get off the bike." I climbed off and she led me back into the store while I shook my head to myself. I was just not cut out for a life of crime.

As we sat in the back room waiting for the police, the clerk had me fill out a form to promise that I would never set foot in the store again. She looked it over. "Your last name is Lippa?"

"Yeah."

"I know your brother. You go to school with my little sister."

Of all the stores in all of South Portland...

Martha was called to meet me at the police station, and she and I sat across from the Chief. I felt tiny, sitting in front of his looming desk. Martha began to cry and said of me, "She's always anxious when she comes back from her father's place."

He turned to me. "Your parents are divorced?" I nodded. "Why don't you go out and wait on the bench while your Mom and I talk?"

"Okay." I got up and walked out. The Chief shut the door behind me.

Eventually Martha came out of the office. Her face was red and shiny from crying. I stood up. The Chief looked at me sternly. "So, you're going to come back here for the next three days, and I'm going to put you to work cleaning."

I nodded quickly. "Okay."

Martha and I didn't speak on the way home.

For the next three days, I rode my bike back to the

police station to arrive promptly at eight o'clock in the morning. I cleaned desks and commodes and floors until four o'clock each evening. On the last afternoon, I spotted a handsome, young officer. I smiled softly at him, trying to get his attention in a flirty way. Unfortunately, it worked. He walked past me and asked one of his colleagues, "Why's the kid here?" The colleague whispered something back, and a moment later the handsome officer let out a rolling belly laugh. My face went flush with embarrassment.

Although we didn't talk about what happened, I knew Martha was sorely disappointed in me. To try to make her feel better, I filled out a 'Just Say No' contract that I found in the back of the *Parade Magazine* in the newspaper. It read, "I promise to say no to drugs. I promise this to my family and friends. I can do this by staying in a good buddy system and choosing the right friends. Also, by getting involved in school activities and community service." I signed it and brought it into the kitchen where Martha sat at the table filling out some paperwork.

"I filled out a 'Just Say No' contract, Mom."

She looked up as I taped it to the refrigerator. "That's nice, honey." She looked tired.

I sat down across from her and nodded toward the papers before her. "What's all that?"

"It's for Michael. He's going to be getting his GED."

"What's that?"

"It's a general education diploma. It's for kids who don't finish high school."

"He's dropping out of school? Why?"

She sighed. "He doesn't want to be in the same class as his little sister."

I immediately grew defensive. "It's not my fault he keeps staying back."

"No. I don't mean that, Katie. He can't get ahead in that school. Even the principal has it out for him."

I was torn between the thought that the principal probably didn't "have it out for" any student and the thought that if the principal indeed did have it out for Michael, that was a good thing because somebody ought to. I refrained from voicing either thought.

There were tears in Martha's eyes as she continued. "Katie, if he stays there he'll be twenty-two when he graduates high school." My heart hurt for her, knowing this couldn't have been what she wanted when she decided to have children.

...

RYAN WHITE ENROLLED in a new school in a new town that started a week before my school was to begin. The news reported that on August 31, 1987 he was met at his new school by the Principal, school system superintendent and a small group of students who had been educated about AIDS. Each one shook his hand. 'Maybe,' I thought, 'things are going to get better for everyone.'

High school started for me, and much to my relief, Creepy Todd wasn't there. I imagined that he might have been institutionalized, though it was more likely that he had simply moved away. My arch-enemy and I settled into a comfortable pattern of mostly ignoring one another.

The female clerk at the clothing store had told her little sister about my thievery, and the little sister told a friend. Whenever I saw them in the hallways, they made fun of me, but in this case the shame was probably for the best. My crime spree was over. Never again would I steal from a store or a person. It had been a good run, but it was over.

In the afternoons, I locked myself in my bedroom, prayed to be forgiven and added new pictures to my River Phoenix devotion wall. I decided that if I wasn't dead of cancer by the time I was of a marriageable age, I was going to become a vegetarian and marry him. While my fantasy romances could go to extremes, real romances were strictly prohibited in my mind. The hallways of high school were filled with teenage hormones, which I found increasingly intimidating and uncomfortable.

Some people experience a difficulty and can remain without bitterness or fear that it might happen again. They can experience a trauma and not be traumatized. They are still able to have trust in others and maybe even turn their pain and fears into something that changes the world for the better. Some people are Anne Frank or Samantha Smith. I was not. Even memories of playing doctor with Dominic's son, Mark, got twisted in my mind. After all, if I had willingly done that, then why shouldn't I be subjected to however anyone else wanted to use or comment on my body? Those few sexually bizarre happenings of my childhood, the obscene phone call that I assumed was from Matthew's friend Zaire, the experiences with Michael and Creepy Todd, those events affected me to my core. They informed every exchange I had with every person I knew and met, particularly boys and men. And for those first years, the information was not good. It was: Don't trust. They will hurt you. They will assault you. Want them privately, but show only purity.

My Uncle Anthony's wife took me out one weekend afternoon to have 'the talk.' It seemed to me that fourteen was a little young to be having this conversation, but I supposed the point was to catch me before I did anything untoward. She told me, "I want you to imagine your body as a crystal punchbowl with all sorts of intricate designs." As I pictured myself as a piece of glass, she continued. "Now, this is a very expensive and beautiful crystal punchbowl, and it's been made especially by God. If you're not careful, you might give this punchbowl to someone who doesn't respect it enough, and that person might drop and break it. So you wouldn't want to give it to just anyone, right?"

"Right."

"It's important to share this beautiful punchbowl only with someone who will respect it and cherish it, someone who understands how important it is. Do you understand?"

"Yes." I felt a little uncomfortable with the idea that she suspected I might have burgeoning feelings in the arena of romance, but I liked the idea that she thought of my physical self as important and beautiful and something to cherish, even if I did not.

Chapter 32
Why She Didn't Kill Herself

Early in the 1987-1988 school year my new science teacher, an older gentleman with white hair, lost his wife to cancer. He took a few days off and then returned to teaching, but he was clearly still distraught. During an afternoon when I was making up a test, he said to me that I looked like his wife when she was a teenager. I didn't know what to say, so I eked out an uncomfortable smile. Another science teacher happened to walk in the room, and my teacher turned to him and said, "You didn't know my wife when she was young, but from the pictures you've seen, doesn't Katie look like her?"

The second teacher paused for an awkward moment and then asked if I wouldn't mind leaving the room. I left with a knot in my stomach. As far as I was concerned, my fate was sealed. This was an even bigger sign than my pinkies being the same shape as Anna's pinkies. It was confirmation that I would one day get cancer as punishment for killing Samantha Smith.

I called Matthew collect. I always had to call collect because Martha wouldn't pay for the calls. Then Matthew would pick up and refuse the charges so he didn't have to pay the more exorbitant fee for a collect call; but it would be his cue to call me back. I always felt a bit embarrassed when the operators came back on the line. They had pity in their voices when they told me he had refused. But this time I thought to tell the operator ahead of time, "Don't worry. He's going to refuse the charges, but we have a system, and he's going to call right back." I wanted to hear his voice to calm me, but I couldn't bring myself to tell him that I was going to die of cancer. Instead, I told him about my plans to become a vegetarian.

"Well," he began slowly. "If you want to become a vegetarian for health reasons, then by all means. But if you want to become a vegetarian because you don't want to 'hurt the animals' then I invite you to consider the concept that plants have consciousness."

"I want to become a vegetarian for health purposes." I left out the part about marrying River Phoenix.

"Then go ahead. Just pay attention to what your body is telling you, especially early on." Within two weeks, my body was telling me to eat meat, and I decided I would wait and become a vegetarian once River Phoenix and I met and fell in love. Then he could help me through the process. I thought that I would have to meet him soon, though, so that we could marry and have a life before I died of cancer.

Arguments between Michael and Martha were becoming more volatile. One night Martha, who never believed in corporal punishment, slapped him, and he slapped back. Even Molly seemed to be picking up on the tension. She started eating the zippers out of any pants that were left around. Martha told me, "If it weren't for you, Katie, I would have killed myself." The thought was not comforting.

Chapter 33
Why Anne Frank Saved Her

In late September of 1987, I learned that there would be auditions for a fall play, and that play was going to be *The Diary of Anne Frank*. I wanted this role so badly that I could barely sleep before the auditions. I held my journal in my hands in bed and prayed to both my God-genie and to Kitty that I would get the role. "I know I've done awful things. I know that I'll still die of cancer for what I did to Samantha Smith. But please, just this once. Please give me this."

The director would be the same person who taught my freshman English class. He seemed to like me, but I had only known him a few weeks, and I wasn't sure that being a student of his would help or hinder my getting the part. Any teacher who knew me for more than a minute knew that I was a student who paid attention and did what I was told, but if he thought that his class would be relatively tough or require a lot of studying or papers, he might not want me to split my attention with the theatre.

I showed up early on the first of two days of auditions. The brother of my arch-enemy was there, and my heart sunk. Even though it had been six years since I had stolen her sticker book, I assumed that he knew all about it, and I feared that if he told the teacher, I wouldn't get the part. But the brother, while cool to me at first, warmed up as soon as we started an audition scene together. The director had him read for the part of Anne's father, Otto, the person who had presented the diary to Anne, and later the world, and the only survivor of the Frank family. We had an instant chemistry. By the end of the first day's audition period, I could tell that he had the role of Otto and that the role of Anne would go either to a pretty sophomore, who was also auditioning, or to me. We were all called back for the next day's auditions.

On the day that the cast was to be announced, I walked to school feeling a mixture of hope and dread. As I entered the school building, I spotted a boy who had auditioned and whom I assumed had gotten the role of Anne's friend Peter. He ran up to me and yelled, "Congratulations."

My eyes filled with tears. "Are you sure? You're not teasing me, are you?"

"No, I promise. You got the part." He grabbed me by the shoulder and led me down the hallway to where the casting notices were posted. We got to the board and I stood looking at the list, stunned. There it was: Katie Lippa. I touched the ink with my fingers, hardly believing it was my name I saw.

"I'm playing Peter," the boy said.

I nodded and said breathlessly. "I knew you'd get it. I just didn't know I'd..."

"But you did. I'm so glad it's not that sophomore girl. She's such a snob, and she always gets every part she tries out for."

I spent the rest of the day in a dreamy cloud. My last class was English and after the bell rang, the teacher called me over to his desk. He spoke in a serious tone. "So, I assume you saw the casting notices?"

"Yes. Thank you so much."

"Well, I want you to know that you have a lot of responsibility on your shoulders. I never cast freshmen. Never." He raised his eyebrows. "But I cast you because you were the best and, also, because you look a little like Anne." My already broad smile broadened even further. To me, Anne was beautiful.

As I walked home, I wondered, if Anne Frank had lived, and if I had lived in the same place and time, would I be as jealous of her as I had been of Samantha Smith? It was a hard pill to swallow when I realized that as much as I loved Anne, I might have been someone who wanted her to fall from her pedestal, just as I had wished for Samantha. I didn't want to be this person who wished ill will on perceived competitors. I wanted to be someone who could be happy when someone else succeeded. I wanted to be someone who valued others, who valued myself.

On the day I started rehearsals for *The Diary of Anne Frank*, I stopped calling my journal "Kitty." I felt a little embarrassed to start each entry with, "Dear Kitty." After all, I hadn't exactly gone through a holocaust in my lifetime, and I felt like that was a name that should be reserved for Anne to call *her* diary. I would be able to connect with Anne in another way, so I didn't mind letting go of Kitty. What I hadn't counted on was that by doing so, I also began to let go of the idea that I had an imaginary person in my life who had the power to turn me into a good witch.

Working on the play meant I had less and less time for James, and things hadn't been the same between us since that Tootsie Roll piggy bank argument anyway. A girl who had been a friend in middle school was on the play's crew, and because we were spending so much time together, I started to consider us best friends. Martha did not approve of her despite the fact that she was smart and good natured. Privately, Martha called her a "priss" and a "prude" and said that her parents were like the characters in the movie, *The Stepford Wives*. "They're too perfect. There's something wrong with them."

Rehearsals were after school and ran into the evenings. This meant that I would often arrive at the house after Michael and Martha got home, or that Martha would have to pick me up once she got out of school or work. After two years of locking myself in my room every day after school, my brother fell out of the habit of threatening to kill me and trying to break into my room. My dear Anne was saving me. I began to think that maybe I wasn't all bad. After all, even Anne Frank had written numerous entries about how she felt she was all wrong, and she was a hero.

As the only cast member with any Jewish background, I was tasked with all things Jewish, like looking up the history of certain customs and activities and learning the meaning behind certain words and songs. In my research, I found out that many Jews grapple with the existence and understanding of God. They don't blindly believe. That seemed to fit me more than Christianity, and I decided it was time to become Jewish.

As I learned more and more about Judaism and saw how it fit so well in my own life, I began questioning some of Matthew's beliefs. I had yet to be able to fly or move objects with my mind, and I had practiced for a very long time. I had been devoted to my psychic studies, and the only thing that had happened was the death of Samantha Smith. That was something of which to be ashamed, not to celebrate. I wondered if it was possible that a belief in Matthew's God-genie had actually evoked a kind of dark magic, and that was why only bad things had resulted.

Being Jewish also had some perks. When I got home to Martha's place one evening, she had made my least favorite food, pork chops, for dinner. It occurred to me that there might be a way out of having to eat them. "Mom," I said as she handed me the plate of meat. "I can't eat pork chops. I'm Jewish."

"Oh," she said, pulling back the plate. She paused for a moment and seemed to be considering what I said. I kept quiet, trying to make my face appear neutral. Then she set down the dish. "Okay. Just eat some mashed potatoes and green beans."

With the successful performances of *The Diary of Anne Frank*, my confidence grew in leaps and bounds. I was more proud of myself than I had ever been, and after the show closed, Martha told me that she was proud of me as well. Weeks after the play, when I was still quoting lines from it, she mentioned, "You know, you get into character really easily, but it's very hard for you to get out." Even with that accurate critique, however, she continued to tell me how well I had done. It occurred to me that my ability to "get into character" was part of why I had acted so well when it came to the religions and beliefs of the adults in my life.

It was after the play ended that I decided to start going by the name Kate because it sounded more mature than Katie. I was finally beginning to get comfortable with the idea of growing up. It wouldn't have to be that day, or even right away, but for the first time, I believed that someday I might be ready.

Chapter 34
Why He No Longer Frightened Her

When I hinted to Tu-Tu that I had become Jewish, she became very worried for my spiritual well-being. She drafted Uncle Brian to talk with me, and he did so even with the threat of Martha's wrath. He told me about the day his good friend became a Christian. "We were in our twenties, and he was going through a very difficult time in his life, so we went out for a drive, just the two of us. Of course, we're never alone when God is there. I suggested that my friend come with me to church, but he kept telling me he wasn't interested. Then, all of a sudden, Kate, we both had a spinning feeling, and the car was on a different road, facing the opposite direction. It had been transported...by God. We got out of the car, and neither of us said a word. We just walked around the car dumbfounded. And my friend decided then and there to become a Christian."

"So, the car spun, and you ended up in the opposite direction?" I asked.

"No. The car didn't spin. We just had the sensation of the car spinning. And then we were in the opposite direction on a different road."

My logic side was skeptical, but I so wanted to believe that something other worldly had taken place. Although I was starting to question Matthew's beliefs, I still wanted magic in my life, so that I could fix things with Samantha Smith and my all-wrong life. If I could have magic and still be pure and good, then that was a win-win. Perhaps I had given up on Christianity too soon.

In early winter, Martha found out that she had been nominated for a fellowship that would allow her to travel to the USSR for a semester. I encouraged her to go. "Mom, you have to. Think of the opportunity. And you can go see Samantha Smith's monument. You can't pass this up." Too wary of leaving Michael and me alone or with relatives, she opted not to go. I don't know who was more disappointed, she or I. With my newfound confidence boost from the successful run of the play, I had hoped that Martha would gain confidence as well.

With a brighter attitude toward my self-worth, I redesigned my wardrobe. I turned pants that were too short into retro kulots. I sewed colorful patches over holes and wove bright fluorescent shoelaces up the sides. One afternoon, I walked into the kitchen to look for a stronger pair of scissors and saw Michael at the table. I realized then that my fear of him had dissipated. He was just my brother, and he was just in the kitchen. As I got closer, I saw that he was sketching an image of a dragon. The detail and perspective was incredible, and the image seemed to leap off the page. I hadn't even known he could draw.

In school, I worked up the nerve to tell the boy on whom I had once had a crush in elementary school that I had always been impressed that he used to carry a pink comb.

"What's pink?" he responded.

"Huh?"

"I'm colorblind."

All those years I had assumed something entirely different. Things, I supposed, were not always what they seemed.

Martha took me to Dr. Kaz's office for my annual checkup. "Did you know Michael can draw?" I asked her on the way.

"He draws?"

"Yeah. He's really good too."

"Huh. No, I didn't know that."

Dr. Kaz told us that I was indeed a healthy fourteen-year-old and that it was perfectly fine that I had not reached certain feminine milestones.

"Are you sure? But I was twelve when I started."

"Martha, she's not you," he said with a kind but clear tone. I smiled internally with the thought that he saw me as my own person.

Martha then took me to the mall so I could buy another River Phoenix poster. On the drive home, I noticed the sun streaming through the clouds. It looked like a painting of heaven that I had seen in Tu-Tu's church. "Mom, stop the car."

"What?"

"The sun. It's coming through the clouds in silvery rays."

She pulled over and turned off the engine. "You've never seen that before?"

"No." I couldn't take my eyes off of it. "It's beautiful."

We sat for a few minutes, and then Martha said, "Ready?"

"Yes. Thanks."

We drove the rest of the way home. As we approached the local cemetery, Martha said, "My father is buried there."

"I had no idea he was buried so close to us. Do you visit him?"

"No," she said.

I held my breath as we passed the cemetery and neared the overpass. Someone had spray-painted a question on the side. I let out my breath and read the words to myself: "Do you know where your children are?"

Chapter 35
Why There Should Be Three

What's in a name? Well, if Shakespeare is to be believed, everything. The adults in my life made a concerted effort to call me by my new moniker of Kate. I considered that part of their adherence to my wishes might be because they were pleased that I was finally making some inroads toward maturity. Still, it struck me as a loving and supportive act. Whenever one would forget and call me Katie, another would step in and say, "She wants to be called Kate."

Tu-Tu was particularly good about this, as she had never cared for the name Katie. She liked Michael's name because it was a literal translation of the Latin sentence meaning, "Who is like God?" But when Martha told her that she wanted to name me Katherine so that she could nickname me Katie, Tu-Tu's response had been, "That's an Irish barmaid's name."

I was grateful that my family had so easily made the change for me. One's name is so important after all. In drama, the Capulets and the Montagues had prevented a romance over their names. In actual history, the Hatfields and McCoys had murdered over theirs. A name connects the person to the minds of others and, moreover, to oneself. A name is part of one's identity.

...

JUST BEFORE CHRISTMAS 1987, Rainey was at the house with Martha and me. Michael was out somewhere, and the three of us settled in to watch *Miracle on 34th Street* starring Maureen O'Hara and Natalie Wood.

The phone rang and Martha left the living room to answer it. After a few minutes she returned with a tear-streaked face. She looked at Rainey and said, "They found my son." Rainey immediately got up and took Martha out of the room.

As I watched the scene where 'Gailey' tells 'Doris' that "Faith is believing in things when common sense tells you not to," I periodically looked over my shoulder, wondering what was happening. Michael had become more and more of a rabble-rouser, and I thought that Martha might return to tell me that he had been found dead of a drug overdose or a street fight.

Martha entered the living room about ten minutes later and asked me to come with her. Rainey went back to watching the movie, and Martha and I sat down in a couple of chairs in the room Rainey once occupied. "Kate, I have to tell you something."

My heart was in my throat, and my whole body started to sweat. This was it. Martha was going to tell me that Michael was gone. She took a breath and spoke, "I had another child before I had you and Michael."

"What?"

"When I was twenty years old, I went out to California for a wedding. I got pregnant. ...I couldn't go home. I just couldn't face my family. That was when I joined the Holy Order of MANS and met your father."

"Wait. So, Dad's not the father?"

"No. The father was from the wedding party."

"Oh. What's his name?"

"My son?"

"Yes."

"Well, I named him Aaron, but he was renamed Ernie."

"Ernie? As in Bert and Ernie?"

She shook her head and batted her hand. "I know. Listen, Kate, he's going to call here in a little while. Would you like to talk with him?"

"Yes."

Martha spoke first with my new brother. After a half hour or so she came to get me. I excitedly picked up the receiver from the end table and spoke. "Hello?"

A warm voice responded, "Hi."

"I'm Kate. I'm your sister."

"Hi Kate. I'm Ernie. I guess this is a little strange, huh?"

That was all I needed to hear to feel comfortable. We chatted for a few minutes and then I said, "Well, I guess I'm going to hand the phone back to Mom. Martha. Well, our Mom."

As I drifted back to the living room and sat down next to Rainey all I could think about was having asked Martha if we could adopt. "I knew there should be three of us," I said to Rainey.

In the coming days I learned more about my new brother and Martha's choice to keep him a secret. "Why didn't you tell me?"

"I thought you were too young to handle it. I told Michael last year."

I was indignant. "Michael knew?"

"Kate, he's three and a half years older than you are. He could handle it."

"Well, obviously I could have handled it because I'm handling it now."

She sighed.

I switched the subject. "How did Ernie get renamed?"

"He got adopted by a family, and they changed his name to Ernest Henry. I guess they had another child, and that child got sick, and they decided they couldn't handle having an adopted kid, so they gave him back when he was four years old."

I was livid on Ernie's behalf. How dare they change his name and then put him back into the foster care system. And to Ernest Henry? That in itself seemed cruel.

Martha explained that for the first three years after he was born, she called regularly to get checkups on Aaron, or rather, Ernie. When she married Matthew, she hoped that she might be able to get her son back, but the adoption caseworker told her that, as he had been legally adopted, there was no way for her to be in his life in any way. The caseworker assured her that if anything changed, Martha would be notified. But when his first family returned him to the foster care system, Martha was not notified and, eventually, she gave up hope.

In a way, it all worked out for the best. Martha didn't have the resources to care for a third child, and Ernie ended up with a kind, well-to-do family in San Francisco. I was particularly impressed that his adoptive father was a professor at Stanford University. Both his parents had been very supportive of Ernie finding his birth mother and even paid for a private detective. These were good people, and although it pained me that I hadn't grown up with my own brother, I was pleased that he had opportunities he might not have had if he had lived with us.

That Christmas, Ernie sent me a lovely peach turtleneck, matching socks, a sweater, and a short peach skirt. They were the nicest, trendiest clothes I had ever received (legally or illegally) and although I knew I wouldn't wear the skirt because I didn't want to expose my legs to anyone, I would proudly wear everything else.

"Don't tell anyone who gave those to you," Martha said

when I opened the package. "I don't want people to know about this."

"But Mom, you were a kid when you had him. And you tried to get him back."

"Kate, I'm already judged for being a single mother. I don't want to be judged for this too."

I didn't see why we should have to keep quiet about it, but at least it was a good secret, not like the awful ones about having caused the death of Samantha Smith or being brought to Michael's room that night. I abided by Martha's wishes and kept quiet.

Chapter 36
Why They Shouldn't Die Alone

On the day I turned fifteen, an article about the Samantha Smith Foundation came out in the newspaper indicating that the foundation had fallen on hard times. In some ways it had become a victim of improved relations between the superpowers. The work that Samantha Smith had put into motion had been continued. Although I didn't like hearing that the foundation wasn't doing well, it was somewhat of a relief to know that her death would not be the cause of World War III.

On the night of my birthday, I got to choose what television programs we watched. I opted for a re-run of the movie *Mommie Dearest*, a movie about the abuses Joan Crawford hurled onto her daughter Christina. After a particularly brutal scene in which Joan Crawford, as played by Faye Dunaway, beats Christina with a coat hanger, Martha commented, "See? I'm not *that* bad."

...

MARTHA GRADUATED FROM college Suma Cum Laude and got us off of Welfare. I wanted to attend her graduation, but she said she was just going to pick up her diploma and leave. I thought perhaps it was something she needed to do on her own. It was her success, having nothing to do with kids or an ex-husband.

Michael and I were in the living room when she arrived back at the house. We were having a conversation about nothing in particular when I heard Martha open the front door. Michael and I continued talking for a minute or so longer and then he said, "Didn't Ma come in?"

"Yeah. I thought she did too."

"Ma?" Michael called to her.

Martha entered the living room slowly, with wide eyes and mouth agape. "What's the matter," Michael asked.

"That's the first time I've ever heard the two of you talking. Just...talking. Not fighting."

"Oh, Mommie Dearest," I exclaimed. "You're so silly." Michael and I laughed. Martha looked like she had just walked into the wrong house.

The girl who had been on the crew for *The Diary of Anne Frank* went through my revolving door of friendship once the yearbook came out. In the Drama Club group photo my friend was giving me a piggy-back and both of us were smiling into the camera. When a fellow student said of the two of us, "You look gay," my friend stopped talking to me. It didn't matter that neither of us were gay. Just the appearance of it caused her to back off of our friendship. Martha said I was better off without her and told me again that she was a "priss" and a "prude."

It did open the door for another friendship with a girl named Sonja, of whom Martha completely approved. I considered that Martha's respect might be in part because Sonja had overcome several struggles, including the loss of a parent and a transcontinental move from Germany to America, as well as having to learn a whole new language. Ours was a relationship built on mutual respect that also included a healthy dose of teasing.

Martha seemed to like the idea that I might be a bit

toughened up by having a friend with whom I bantered back and forth, rather than pussyfooted around. She didn't even seem to mind when Sonja and I spent countless hours on the phone together. She would only shake her head and say, "Don't the two of you get enough of each other in school?"

"No, Mommie Dearest."

"You've got to stop calling me that," Martha said with a half-smile.

More than opening up a new friendship, however, the experience of being judged for being gay without actually being gay made me realize that women and gays had something in common. In some ways, we were both second class citizens.

I began volunteering at Peabody House in Portland, Maine. Frannie Peabody began her activism work at the age of eighty, when her grandson Peter was diagnosed with AIDS. She helped to establish The AIDS Project in Maine and co-founded Peabody House, an all-male assisted-living facility. All of the men at Peabody House were out as gay or bi-sexual. Therefore, they didn't pose the same emotional threat to me as heterosexual men did.

It did take me a while to get used to their appearance. Their gaunt figures still reminded me of images from the Holocaust. The men who were closer to dying were often covered with Kaposi's sarcoma, reddish-purple lesions on their skin. Once I got used to that, though, I found that they were just people. Some were angry. Some were funny. Some were distant. Some were kind. Some were all of those traits and more.

I decided not to visit Matthew for the summer, so that I could spend time with Sonja and be at Peabody House more often. It turned out that while the religions and beliefs of my family had many differences, the one thing they had in common was the value of being of service. Volunteering got me out of my head for those few hours a day. I wanted to love as much as I wanted to be loved. Here were vulnerable people who wanted love, and I could give it to them. I spent many afternoons there visiting with the men, entertaining them as much as I could, holding their hands, and listening to their stories. I knew that it might not change the world, but it would help these few men to have some dignity and companionship before they died.

Chapter 37
Why Permanent Marker Is Not for Declarations

I took a weekend off from my volunteering commitment to go with Rainey to a campground outing with her family. I was to stay in the cabin with Rainey's granddaughter, who was about my age. We stayed up late, looking at magazine pictures of the actress Alyssa Milano, who played 'Samantha' on *Who's the Boss?*. That night, I prayed to my God-genie to make my nose and chin look like hers.

On the second day we were there, Rainey's granddaughter ran to me out of breath, "My grandmother and some other people are smoking pot in the cabin." I was surprised but not overly-concerned. "You don't understand," she said. "My little cousin is in there. He's just a baby. I don't want him to breath in that stuff."

That did seem to be worthy of more concern. "What do you want to do?" I asked.

"I want to tell my Mom. Will you come with me?"

I agreed, but when we got to her mother's cabin, Rainey's granddaughter said, "I can't tell her. I don't want to get in trouble. Will you tell her?"

"Why would you get in trouble?"

"You don't know my Mom. She'll get mad at me. Just tell

her, please." I was sympathetic, so I relayed the information as Rainey's granddaughter had told it to me.

The next day, we were walking along when Rainey called after us. We turned, and Rainey stormed over. She bent down to my height and stuck her finger in my face. "What are you telling my daughter that I'm smoking pot for? What business is it of yours?" Rainey had never yelled at me before, and I burst into tears. "Don't you cry," she said. I feared our relationship was over.

I turned to where her granddaughter had been standing next to me and saw that the girl was no longer there. I watched as she strolled away. I would not break her confidence by telling Rainey it was her idea to rat on her, but at the first opportunity I approached her with great indignation. "Why did you walk away? Why didn't you say something?"

"I just thought she was talking to you. I didn't know what it was about."

"Yeah, right. Give me a large, personal break."

The ride home with Rainey was very quiet. A few days later, she stopped by the house and handed me a note. She told me not to read it until after she left. I waited, and when I unfolded it, I saw that her handwriting was childlike. It occurred to me that I'd never seen her handwriting before. The note read that she was sorry that she had yelled at me and she hoped we could still be friends. 'Friends,' I read several times. Sonja and I were friends, but I had thought Rainey and I were more than friends. I thought we were family. She was 'Mom Number Two.' I was 'Twat.' It was difficult to accept that Rainey thought of us as friends, but I was glad that she wanted to remain in my life. I had thought that this one quarrel meant that our relationship was spoiled; but relationships, it seemed, were like people. They had many layers.

...

IN THE LATE summer of 1988, Vice President George H.W. Bush became the Republican nominee for president, and Michael Dukakis became the Democratic nominee. It seemed like the most important issues fell by the wayside during the debates. Michael Dukakis never once brought up the potential fixing of the 1980 election, the would-be treasonous act of getting the Iranians to withhold the hostages, or the weapons sent to the Contra rebels so that they could overthrow their government. In my mind Iran-Contra made Watergate look like a mosquito bite. It seemed, however, that no one, not even the Democratic nominee, cared. George H.W. Bush easily won the election, and when Michael Dukakis's wife was caught drinking rubbing alcohol, it seemed most people figured they'd made the right decision.

Matthew came to Maine for a brief visit. I felt embarrassed to introduce Matthew to Sonja, so I kept my distance from her while he was around. While he was there, I pushed my boundaries with him in small ways. Knowing full well that Matthew's magician friend Howard had left his house because Elizabeth moved in, I asked him, "Whatever happened to Howard?"

"Oh, I think he's out in Los Angeles these days, working as a magician."

I asked Matthew for new clothes, daring him in my mind to say no. I wanted him to give me an opportunity to let loose on him for his lack of financial responsibility with his children. I wanted to tell him that although he may not have wanted to have kids, he had them, and he had the duty to care for them, whether he felt they were "worthy" or not. I wanted to tell him that any person should be very careful before having children, because they were bringing someone into the world who would feel pain. Yes, one hoped that children would feel joy, and love, and success; but anyone born into this world would experience loss and tragedy as well. Having children willy-nilly, or making the decision that one could control his sperm emissions with mind control, was irresponsible. I wanted to tell him *all* of this, and then he said, "Okay, let's get you some new clothes."

I was finally starting to develop, and I was acutely uncomfortable with the idea of any boy or man identifying my shape as that of a girl. Without telling him my reasoning, I asked Matthew if I could get some men's clothes. He bought me two pinstriped button-down shirts, two men's sweaters, and a tie.

Michael had opted not to see Matthew during the visit, focusing instead on a girl that he liked. After Matthew left, I walked by Michael's open door and saw that he was writing "Mike + Michelle" on his wall. I stopped short.

"What?" he asked, looking up at me with a marker in his hand.

"Nothing. I just hope that your relationship is permanent, because that ink is." He laughed.

...

I WENT TO the football coach and told him I wanted to join the team. I was ninety pounds soaking wet and was only asking him as a test to see what he'd say. He responded in a friendly, matter-of-fact tone, "Great. If you're good enough to make the team, you'll be on it." That was not the response I was expecting. He encouraged me to try out, and although I considered it, I figured it was better not to get squashed by football players.

Instead, I focused on the theatre. The Drama Club went to a one-act competition, during which I won an acting award. I was flying high when one of the boys tossed me in a snow bank, soaking me through to my skin. I was wearing the peach socks Ernie had sent me the Christmas before, and when I saw that the color from my jeans had stained them, I started to cry. I smacked the boy on his arm, infuriated.

"They're just socks, Kate," he said.

"You don't understand. My brother gave them to me." Per Martha's instructions, I couldn't explain further. I ignored the strange looks from the other kids and blotted my tears with my cold, wet glove.

...

ERNIE HAD JOINED the Marine Corps, and was to spend his brief winter leave with us. I hid the socks in my drawer so he wouldn't see that they were stained, but other than that I was very excited for the visit.

I adored my new brother the first moment I met him. He was tall and funny and smart, with movie star good looks. He sat with me for hours, pouring over photo albums. I pointed out who everyone was, so he could get to know them before he met them in person. Michael, who had been working at a seafood restaurant, brought home some lobsters and scallops for a special dinner.

I wanted Sonja to meet Ernie, but Martha was explicit in her instructions not to tell friends about him. We did bring Ernie around to meet members of the family, who were all very welcoming. My Uncle Anthony gave him such a huge hug that I thought he might have bruised his ribs. Ernie seemed to take it all in stride and spoke of even possibly going to college in Maine. I hoped he would.

After he left, Martha told me that she had discouraged him from applying to any nearby schools. I was crestfallen.

"But why, Mom?"

She was crisp in her tone. "I'm not his mother anymore. His parents are his parents."

"I hope you didn't say it like that when you told him not to look at schools here."

"I told him that I didn't want to disrespect his parents by having him here."

I closed my eyes. That wasn't what I would have wanted to hear in his place, and I hoped he hadn't been hurt by it. "Mom," I asked in earnest. "How could you give him up in the first place?"

"It was those people who ran the Holy Order of MANS. Earl and 'Mother' Blighton." She said their names with disgust.

"What did they do, Mom?" I asked quietly.

"They knew I was pregnant. I told them when I got there. They said it was alright, but then two weeks after I had the baby, they came to me and told me I had to give him up. They let me keep that boy for two weeks before they told me. I was exhausted already. Having a baby takes a lot of energy, and afterwards you're emotional and not really thinking straight. And I didn't have any family to support me. The Blightons locked me in a room with them for eight hours, telling me that everybody in the Order was complaining about noise from the baby crying. Finally 'Mother' Blighton told me in this sickly sweet voice, 'Dear, if you keep the baby, you'll both have to leave, and you have nowhere else to go.' I hated her for that. But by the end, I decided I had to give him up."

"Why didn't you leave and go home to Maine?"

"I couldn't go home. I couldn't face them. And you don't understand the power that this man had. That night was eight hours of brainwashing. Earl Blighton had us all convinced he was psychic. He could read people. Somebody would walk into a room, and Earl Blighton could tell by the way the person was holding himself that he had back problems. So when Blighton said it, the person would get all excited, thinking Blighton must have some great power. It was all a sham. It was a cult, and we all bought into it. And your father learned from him."

This was new information. If Matthew learned from Earl Blighton, did he really have powers or was he just good at reading people? And if he didn't have powers, did I? Then, it occurred to me, "Wait. You knew Dad when you had Ernie, and he didn't offer to help?"

"I barely knew your father then. The Blightons put us together after I gave up the baby because they wanted all the people who had been ordained to mastery to be in a mother-father partnership."

It seemed my parents' relationship was doomed before it even began. "Did anyone offer to help you?"

"One friend of mine did. He was this really nice, gay man, and he offered to marry me. But, I couldn't do that to him. He wouldn't have been happy."

"They accepted gay people in the organization?"

"It was a cult. Cults accept everybody who's willing to join, especially if you're considered an outcast. That's what they're banking on to get you to stay."

"What's the difference between a cult and a religion?"

Martha chortled. "Tax status."

"Huh?"

"If you ask me, they're all the same, but once a cult gets tax status it gets to call itself a religion."

It was all a lot to consider.

...

MICHAEL WAS FINALLY moving out. Martha had allowed him to stay while he got his GED, but now that he was making enough money to pay rent, she wanted him to get his own place. I was thrilled. I had the local radio station play a song that I dedicated to him, Steam's 'Na Na Hey Hey Kiss Him Goodbye.'

Martha was gone when Michael gathered up the last of his belongings. I went into the kitchen and leaned against the counter. I opened my mouth a couple of times to speak and then stopped myself. Then, once I worked up the nerve, I said, "Michael, we've spent the first part of our lives learning how to manipulate. Now we have to spend the next part learning how not to manipulate."

He looked at the floor and nodded. Then he looked back up at me and offered a half, crooked-smile. "See ya' 'round, Kate." He patted me on the shoulder, and then he was gone.

Once Michael had moved out, I thought everything would settle down at home. I would be able to have Sonja over without concern over anything he might say to her or me. Moreover, Martha and I would be a Mom-and-daughter team, supporting one another and laughing and telling jokes. At the very least, I expected an ease to the tension. Within days, though, I noticed that Martha started using the same curt tone with me that she had used with Michael for so long. Everything she said was spoken in a way that felt like I had become an inconvenience. I had a sinking feeling as I suspected that Martha might *need* someone at whom to be angry.

Chapter 38
Why She Was Braver

I kept up a pen pal relationship with Ernie and told him about my first audition for a professional play. It was called *A Day in the Death of Joe Egg*, and it would be produced at Portland Stage Company, Maine's largest fully-professional theatre. The story centered on a British couple struggling to save their marriage while trying to raise their only child, Joe, a girl with cerebral palsy. I auditioned for the title role, and after the callback the casting director told me the producer and director were going to decide between one other girl and me.

The casting director phoned at the end of the weekend. "I'm sorry," she said.

"I guess I didn't get it, huh."

"No. I fought for you because you were the better actress. But they went with the pretty one."

"Oh."

"She's blonde and cute, and they think that'll make the character more sympathetic."

I left out the details when I wrote to Ernie, just telling him that it had been a good experience to audition for my first professional play.

...

ON JULY 18TH, 1989 Rebecca Schaeffer, the actress from 'My

Sister Sam,' was killed. She had been stalked and gunned down by a young man named Robert John Bardo. The name sounded familiar, and I caught my breath when I heard on the news that this was the same person who had come to Maine those years before to see Samantha Smith. I recalled at the time not knowing the word 'stalker' but wanting someone in my life who wanted me. I had gotten Creepy Todd.

My heart beat fast and my palms sweat. And then, in that moment, I made a choice. Though I had spent years believing there was no such thing as coincidence, I decided that maybe I was wrong. Creepy Todd had been a dreadful part of my school life, but I hadn't asked for him. I liked to quote the character played by an actress, and that actress had been shot and killed, but I hadn't wished it. It was all just an unfortunate twist of fate. It was tragic and awful, but I was not responsible. I had not conjured a stalker in my own life, and I had not conjured one in Rebecca Schaeffer's life.

I might have been responsible for the death of Samantha Smith, although I was starting to have some questions about that too. And I could not take on the burden of my own harasser or this new death. I could no longer believe that every connection meant something.

...

MATTHEW CALLED TO tell me that he was going to marry Elizabeth on the banks of the Mississippi, and that they would be wearing red fedoras and matching red velvet pants that she had made. "When?" I asked with some excitement.

"In two weeks."

"Oh," I said. That seemed very soon. He had always prepared travel plans for me at least a month in advance because of the cost. Then it occurred to me that this might just be an informational call. After a pause, I asked, "Can I come?"

"No. It's not a big deal. It isn't worth the expense of the plane ticket for you to come out. I wasn't even going to mention it, but your Grandma Barbara said I should."

When I told Martha about it, I assumed she would sympathize with my sadness over being excluded. To my surprise, she instead suggested with great sarcasm that she send him the ring he had purchased for their engagement, which happened to be inscribed with the name Elizabeth. I understood that she had some unresolved feelings about the divorce, but I didn't feel like I could take on her disappointment while dealing with my own as well. So, I decided to pretend I hadn't noticed the sarcasm and instead told her that it was a nice gesture but I didn't think it was necessary.

Matthew sent me an invitation as a keepsake after the event. It was, in my mind, such a distancing action, that it gave me the opportunity I needed to pull away from him further. I considered what Martha had told me about Matthew being a student of Earl Blighton. It did seem that much of what Matthew had claimed just wasn't true. What if what I had thought was psychic or magical powers was nothing more than intuition? Even scientists said there was such a thing as intuition. They had even figured out which part of the brain was the intuitive side. The left hemisphere is logic-based, and the right hemisphere is based more in subconscious or unconscious associations. If Matthew wasn't psychic or magical, and if he hadn't passed down these traits to me, was I really at fault for all the things I thought I had brought to bear? Could I really be that powerful? I was coming to believe that I was not.

...

TU-TU HAD STARTED going to a Baptist church because her previous church had started to take a metaphorical approach to the Bible, rather than a literal one. She still considered herself

Fundamentalist, but she liked the applications her new Baptist preacher ascribed to the Bible. She urged me attend church with her, and even though I didn't want to, she was so nice about it that I decided not to turn her down. Also, Sonja was a Christian, so I figured it would be nice to have some common ground there.

When I went to the church, I found the preacher quite amiable. He was a roly-poly man with a shiny, bald head and a funny sense of humor. He did not, however, take lightly the state of women in the church. As I sat in my best pair of pants, the preacher spoke of how "girls and women should not wear slacks or have short hair." I worried he was speaking directly to me.

I was determined to return to the church wearing a skirt, so that the preacher would be pleased. I had one long jumper, which I dug out of the closet. I wasn't exactly comfortable in it, but I was glad to have made up for my previous error. When he didn't notice me, I decided to go back again and introduce myself. By the time I turned sixteen, going to church started becoming a habit.

...

IN THE FALL of 1989, several weeks of civil unrest took place in Germany. On November 9th, the East German government announced that German citizens could visit West Germany and West Berlin. Crowds of East Germans crossed and climbed onto the Berlin wall, which had separated the two parts of Germany since 1961. I was pleased for Sonja that her birth-country was gaining some peace; but most of my thoughts were about Otto and Anne Frank. As celebrations took place and the wall was destroyed, I imagined father and daughter looking on. So much of history, it seemed, happened after those who got the ball rolling were gone.

On March 29th, 1990, Ryan White entered Riley Hospital for Children in Indiana with a respiratory infection. The hospital received hundreds of calls from well-wishers. He died on April 8th, 1990. Over fifteen hundred people, including Elton John and Phil Donohue, attended the funeral for the boy who had once been ostracized. On the day of the service, former President Ronald Reagan wrote a tribute to Ryan White that appeared in *The Washington Post*. Mr. Reagan told of how Ryan White had helped change social perceptions of people with HIV and AIDS.

In the summer of 1990, the Samantha Smith Foundation brought to Maine its first group of children from the Chernobyl fallout zone, many of whom suffered radiation-induced health problems. There were no letters of protest to the foundation this time.

...

AS CHANGES IN the world rolled slowly along, I pushed my boundaries with Martha. My anger with her curtness toward me grew. I played John Lennon's song 'Mother' over and over in my room, singing along at full voice. "Mother, you had me; but I never had you. I wanted you; but you didn't want me." One afternoon, there was a soft knock on my door. I opened it to see Martha there with a concerned look on her face.

"Yes?" I asked in a cool tone.

She was calm and straightforward. "Uh, Kate, I used to play that song a lot when I was younger, and I know why I was playing it, and I was just wondering...is there something you'd like to talk about?"

Something that I'd *like* to talk about? No. Something that I probably should talk about? Yes. My eyes widened. "No."

She seemed suspicious. "Okay. Well, if there's anything you ever do want to talk about, you can come to me."

"Okay, thanks. I'm going to close the door now."

"Okay."

I still couldn't articulate myself in ways I wanted to, but it did occur to me then that it would probably be a good idea to learn.

...

THE CASTING DIRECTOR for *A Day in the Death of Joe Egg* called me. She was directing her first show with Portland Stage Company, and she wanted me to be a part of it. It was a reader's theatre project called *Maine Lives on Stage*, and I would be playing a young Frannie Peabody, another coincidence. The idea of there being such things as coincidences was turning out to be a much more pleasant way for me to look at life.

When I told Martha that I would be performing at a dinner where Governor McKernan would be, she reminded me that he had been her divorce lawyer. After the show, I went up to him and mentioned it. "Who's your mother?" he asked.

"Martha Lippa."

He remembered the name and smiled. I decided not to mention that the settlement hadn't worked out the way he had planned it.

I was becoming a big fish in the small theatre pond of Maine, and I began practicing what I would say when I won my first Academy Award. Instead of the recurring nightmare I had for so long, I started having dreams featuring David Letterman, where he would visit me during family barbeques and give me advice on how to navigate Hollywood. I asked Martha if we could move to Los Angeles. She came back to me the next day and said no, but she encouraged me to move there after high school or college. Most importantly, she had considered it. "You're braver than I ever was, Kate. You do something I wasn't able to do. You go for your dreams."

Chapter 39
Why It Pays to Be Poor

As a gift, when I turned seventeen, Martha bought me a tank shark. Tank sharks, I learned, are really part of the catfish family, but they look like miniature sharks and that's where they get their name. I would watch him for hours. Since it was a shark, I decided it must be a boy, because in my mind, boys were still dangerous. I decided to name him Norman, after 'Norman Bates' from *Psycho*.

When my senior year of high school began, the football coach asked, "So, are you going to try out for the team this year? It's your last chance." I smiled. It was men like this, who believed in the abilities of girls and women, who gave me a bit of hope that not every boy or man was unsafe.

My English teacher, Mr. Furbush, helped to solidify the hope. Mr. Furbush liked to talk a lot, and sometimes it felt like he was talking "at" us instead of to us, but what he had to say was vastly interesting to me. I especially liked it when he posed moral questions or asked us to think about things in ways we wouldn't ordinarily. "Of all these musicians you like," he said one day, "most of them will be one-hit wonders. When you get to be my age, you won't even remember their names."

His statement was met with a chorus of nos and "You just don't get it." I was fairly certain he did get it.

One day he asked us, "If you were alone in a car, driving on a flat section of the road, where you could see way out ahead of you, and you came to a stop sign at an intersection, would you stop?"

"Of course," so many of the students responded. Mr. Furbush shook his head and sighed.

It reminded me of what my father had said, "You can do whatever you want to, Katie. You don't have to follow every one of society's rules just because they're rules." Only it wasn't accompanied by someone telling me that he was a prophet from another planet.

Mr. Furbush was very vocal when he was disappointed with members of the class. Because I never thought of myself as part of any group, I had it in my mind that, of course, he couldn't be talking about me when he said things like, "I wish we were still allowed to smack students, because so many people aren't getting this, and I just want to smack you guys." I was thrilled when I understood something that others in the class didn't, and he said, "Well I don't know how else I can teach you this stuff. It's so easy for me that I just don't know how you cannot get it." The best was when he proclaimed, "If you don't understand this now, then there's no hope for you."

The fact that I thought myself above his condescension likely had to do with my own version of internal-condescension toward my peers. They were willing to *tell* me how much they didn't like me, but if they knew how little I had come to think of so many of their opinions about politics and feminism and the world in general, things might have been worse for me. Or, maybe they had a sense of my view of them, and that was *why* they weren't very nice. Either way, it was glorious to start the day with a bit of Furbush fury. He was my knight in shining armor, bullying the bullies.

I felt like a lot of these kids, particularly the boys, had been pretty hard on me over the years. It had been a long time since they stood up and clapped for me in the seventh grade cafeteria, and since then it felt like I had perpetually crossed their boundaries of what was socially allowable by a girl. For that reason, I very much enjoyed seeing them receive a measure of disdain from Mr. Furbush. It wasn't so awful that they would be irretrievably destroyed by it; it was sort of like when Molly had chosen to protect Michael over me in our childhood kicking fights; just a little nip at their egos. I enjoyed it immensely.

In early November, 1990, Maine voted to repeal the Blue Laws to allow for Sunday shopping. Maine was the last part of New England to repeal the laws, and Tu-Tu remarked to me, "We're becoming a Godless state." It was strange to think that Maine would likely continue to change after I left for college.

Like many high school seniors, college had become the preeminent thought on my mind. Tu-Tu and Uncle Brian wanted me to go to a Christian College. Uncle Anthony suggested I consider going to seminary to become a nun. Matthew said I should travel around for several years before going to college at all. Martha cried when I told her I wanted to go to a school out of state. "You can go wherever you want to, but can't you at least look at the local universities?" I applied to several schools, none of which were in Maine. "Not even one?" Martha said with tears in her eyes. "There are so many good schools around here. I just don't want you to go." It was painful to see Martha sad again.

I considered Sarah Lawrence College because I saw Alyssa Milano on *The Arsenio Hall Show* mention that she was going there. I barely noticed her nose and chin as she spoke of this incredible school in a small village in Westchester County, New York. When I looked it up in a college directory I found it to be a perfect fit. Seminars were limited to fifteen students per class, lectures were capped at fifty students, and once every two weeks each student met with his or her faculty advisor. There was also some freedom in what were called 'Conference Courses,' which were designed by each student in conjunction with each class's professor. This was the school for me, and I was suddenly grateful to have had an inferiority complex about my looks. Otherwise, I might never have known about Sarah Lawrence College. I considered it a happy coincidence.

After I submitted my college applications, all to out-of-state schools, Martha told me crisply, "Just so you know, I won't be helping you pay for college."

"What do you mean?"

"I don't have the money to help you. I had a college fund for you at one time, but when your father left, I had to use that money for the house. If you want help with college, you should ask him."

I did. His response was, "You should pay for college on your own, like I did."

I knew that I had found the right school; but I didn't know how I was ever going to get there. During a phone conversation with Grandma Barbara, she asked me how things were going in the college search. I had no intention of asking her for help; I knew she was on a fixed income and couldn't contribute. But she was also a good sounding board, and I felt comfortable telling her what both Martha and Matthew had said.

"What?" she exclaimed.

"What's the matter?"

"Your father didn't pay a dime for college. We paid for it. And he dropped out of school a semester before he was going to graduate. He got pissed off that the teachers thought he should actually attend his classes. He figured, as long as he aced the tests, he shouldn't have to go. And he certainly never paid us back for it. The prick."

That night, I went to bed, praying yet again for a smaller nose and a bigger chin. Suddenly, in the midst of my request, I stopped. I began to cry, and I said aloud, "I don't want to live this way anymore."

I had caught Matthew in so many lies. How many hadn't I caught? What if everything he had told me was a lie? In that moment, that simple moment, I knew the truth. I had not killed Samantha Smith. I had not killed her because I never had that much power. I wasn't evil, just flawed, like everyone. While those flaws might be difficult to face because I so wanted to be perfect, the fact that I was simply flawed and not evil meant that I could stop punishing myself.

It was a relief. ...But then I had to wonder: 'What will I believe in now?' And if I hadn't killed Samantha Smith, what did that mean for all those afternoons spent with the Cool Whip container in my room? What did it mean for not having a father in my life? What did it mean for all the teasing by classmates? Maybe I hadn't deserved any of that. But then, why? Why had it happened? The questions were maddening, and I was desperate for an answer.

I became more devoted to attending church with Tu-Tu. The desire to be a part of something grew to its peak one day when I got so excited by the people heading up for the altar call, that I followed them. Without considering the ramifications or whether I even believed in what I was doing, I had just made a public commitment to Jesus Christ. The preacher told me that I would be baptized the following week, and when he showed me the tank where the baptisms took place, I immediately regretted my decision. I also had to fess up to Martha, who would likely not be very pleased about the whole thing. I asked her if she would attend the baptism, and she said flatly, "No. That's your thing."

When I realized I was far more concerned about the idea of being dunked in a tank of water than I was with the peace of my eternal soul, it occurred to me that my heart might not be fully vested in being a Christian. But I didn't want to disappoint Tu-Tu, who had been so happy and relieved to know that I would not be burning in hell. I knew that Christianity would be a placeholder until I found something that fit better, but it would be alright for a while. I needed to believe in something, and I would give myself this.

As winter lingered on, it seemed that Martha was crying all the time. She spoke often of how I was "abandoning" her for college. I began avoiding home and spending more and more time after school with Mr. Furbush.

One on one, Mr. Furbush was my own personal Alan Alda, witty, tall, kind, and fatherly. I spent countless hours talking with him about books and news reports and life in general. Soon, I felt comfortable enough to share more personal troubles, and I was grateful for his kind ear. I was able to talk about things with him that I hadn't told anyone, not even Sonja. When I told Mr. Furbush what happened with Michael, for instance, he let me cry in his classroom and closed the doors for privacy. Because it wasn't still going on and because Michael had moved out, I knew that Mr. Furbush wouldn't have to report it. Instead, he just listened, keeping a respectful desk-long distance, handing me tissues, and telling me he was sorry I had gone through that.

Over the course of the next few weeks, when I had what could best be described as a nervous breakdown, Mr. Furbush was my best source of comfort. It couldn't have been easy for him. I tested him a great deal, sharing darker and darker thoughts to see if he would accept them without judgment. I wouldn't tell him about my father's psychic teachings or Samantha Smith, but it was of such help to have someone to listen. Certain images had been in my mind for so long, and it was such a relief to get them out.

What had been real was no longer so. The things that had kept me from ending my life, my belief that I had powers beyond a normal person and my fear that my mother would suffer in my absence, were tested. I didn't have magical powers. Yes, it meant that I hadn't killed Samantha Smith, but it also meant I wasn't special in the way I had hoped and believed for so long. And as far as my mother was concerned, I was only going to college, and she was already devastated. It hardly seemed she could be more devastated if I ended my life. And ending it seemed like it might provide some much needed relief.

We read Hamlet in class. The "To be or not to be" speech became not just literature, but a question for me personally. Do I do it? Do I finally end it? Do I admit that I can't handle divorced parents and an angry brother and an angry self and crazy thoughts and being ugly and not being good enough? Is it really nobler in the mind to suffer? Or do I take arms or pills or bullets against a sea of troubles and by opposing end them? I equally wanted someone to convince me that my life was worth living and someone to convince me that I had permission to end it.

I went to Mr. Furbush after school. "To be or not to be. That *is* the question," I said. He seemed to know that I meant something more than analyzing Shakespeare. Over the course of the next hour, I finally got the words out, "I want to end my life."

I explained that I hadn't done it because I didn't want to hurt my mother. "I guess I just want to either not feel this way anymore or for someone to tell me it's okay to do it."

"To kill yourself?" he asked quietly.

"Yes."

"No, it's not okay."

There was a small part of me that was resentful that he hadn't given me permission. He hadn't given me any particular reason not to kill myself; he just told me it wasn't alright. Generally speaking, in my limited experience with suicide, I had found that people who were going to kill themselves just kill themselves. They didn't have prolonged inner-dialogues about it for ten years. I wanted someone to tell me that it was my decision or to show me how to get those dark thoughts out of my head.

When it was obvious that Mr. Furbush wasn't going to be able to do either, I decided to act as if I no longer wanted to end my life. I didn't want to give him the impression that his efforts with me hadn't worked. I had felt like I was drowning, and while he hadn't exactly saved me, he had certainly encouraged me from the shore.

Surprisingly, acting as if I were happier actually made me happier. I wasn't leaping for joy, but I was in far better spirits than I had been at my lowest. Just getting out the thoughts had been a great help, and it seemed my fake-out wasn't a fake-out at all. For instance, the simple action of lifting the muscles in my face to smile softly lightened my emotions. What started as a mask for someone else's benefit was actually working for mine.

...

IN JANUARY OF 1991, the country was on edge, wondering if President George H.W. Bush was going to lead us to war with Iraq's Saddam Hussein over its invasion and annexation of Kuwait. I was very worried about my brother Ernie, since he was still in the Marine Corps. Mr. Furbush was the first person I had ever told about Ernie, and he listened to my fears about Ernie going to war and tried to assure me that things would be alright. Mid-month, he invited me to dinner with his wife, and Martha reluctantly agreed. "Why do you like him so much?" she asked me circumspectly.

"He's nice. And he's happy."

"Kate, nice people are boring, and happy people are stupid."

On the way to his house, I imagined Mr. Furbush and his wife adopting me. When we walked through the front door, I was struck by how *normal* their interaction was. It occurred to me that I had never been with a married couple who weren't trying to convince me to switch over to their religion. They were just two nice people who had invited me to dinner. They did everything to make me feel welcome, even sending their three young boys to be watched by a sitter, so that there wouldn't be any distractions for the evening. I answered Mrs. Furbush's questions about my plans after high school and felt like I was, for a brief time, part of an ordinary family.

After dinner, Mr. Furbush and his wife went to the kitchen to wash the dishes. I asked if I could help, but they both said I should relax and watch television. They seemed a little tired from the company, and I knew I would be going home soon. As I sat in their den watching the news, a special report broke in. I watched for a minute or so and then walked into the kitchen. "You might want to come back in," I said glumly. "The war just started."

We watched as images of guided missiles took over the screen. I thought about Ernie and worried about his imminent future.

When I got back to Martha's house later that evening, I rushed into the house. "Mom, the war started," I called out.

"I know. I've been watching it on TV." She was in the living room, and I walked in to sit by her. We watched the coverage for a couple of minutes in silence, and then she said, "I don't want you going over to Mr. Furbush's house again."

"Why not?"

"It's not appropriate. He's your teacher."

"His wife was there, and I don't think they're going to invite me again anyway. It was a one-time thing."

"Good."

Desert Storm lasted just over five weeks, and, much to my relief, Ernie did not have to go.

After the fighting in Iraq ended, a young soldier who was also an alumnus from our high school came to talk with our senior-year history class. He had been on the cover of *Time Magazine*, and the teacher showed us a copy. When I left class that day, I realized that I was pleased about, rather than envious of, his notoriety. I wondered to myself, was it possible that I was becoming a person who could be happy for the success of others? I hoped so.

I got home to find that Martha had bought a new mattress for my bed. "But, Mom, I won't have much time to use it. I'm going away to college."

"You might decide to stay."

"Mom..."

"You can't go. You'll be leaving Norman."

I realized she was pretty desperate if she was bringing my tank shark into it. Over the years, I had tried so hard to make her happy, to please her. Now she was miserable, and it was because of me. It was unbearable.

...

IN MARCH OF 1991 the Iran-Contra Prosecutor reported that George H.W. Bush and Ronald Reagan had indeed sent arms to Iran and they had been aware that profits from those weapons sales went to the drug-dealing Contra rebels. Much of those drugs had flooded the streets of America. While Nancy Reagan promoted her 'Just Say No' campaign, crack cocaine created a permanent, drugged-out underclass in America's biggest cities.

Drug addicts were too otherwise occupied to do things like vote, and it seemed that now the American public was going to be made aware of it. I felt confident that some big changes were coming.

We, as a nation, would surely rally to keep our officials accountable. We would recognize that a government without accountability can torture, condemn, cheat, kill, destroy and steal without fear. We would know that this could happen with any government, whether Republican, Democrat or other. We would understand that people with the best of intentions sometimes behave badly when faced with the choice of personal and professional gain versus what is right. Even those who are good at heart can fall. We would know this, and something would be done about it. Our news writers, I believed, would lead the charge, for it is the responsibility of our writers and reporters to tell the truth in untruthful times. Samantha Smith, who had dreamt of being a journalist, would not die in vain.

...

MARTHA'S DEPRESSION OVER my impending departure to college grew. She often refused to come out of her room, even when Michael stopped by. In fact, Michael had been at the house a lot. He had seen a man die in a bar fight, thrown through a plate of glass, and he had walked into a friend's hotel room and found him dead, hanging from the ceiling.

One afternoon, while Michael fried bologna on the stove and I sat on the counter, I told him, "I was thinking of staying in Maine after graduation. Mom seems really upset by the idea of me leaving."

Michael stopped flipping the bologna and looked up at me. "You have to go, Kate. Don't let her do to you what she did to me." He hesitated for a moment and then looked back at the pan.

What did he mean? Had Martha clipped his wings so that he would never leave or try to become anything great? I realized in that moment that although we had shared the same house for so many years, my brother had his own life and his own experiences, many of which were completely separate from mine. Whatever had happened, it had caused damage, and he was doing his best to repair himself. It made me determined to go.

In March, Sarah Lawrence College approved my admission with an eighty percent scholarship. When it was announced to Martha's family, my Uncle Anthony said, "Wow. It pays to be poor."

Martha corrected him. "It pays to be poor and smart."

Chapter 40
Why She Let Him Go

Mr. Furbush's English class went on a field trip to see *Macbeth* at the University of New Hampshire. Macbeth was the bloodiest of Shakespeare's plays that I had read. As I sat in the audience, I recognized something familiar in the face of one of the actors. When I looked at the playbill, I saw that it was Dominic's son, Mark, the boy who I had liked but from whom I was told to stay away. It had been nine years since I had seen him. Half of our lives had gone by.

The first experience I had ever had with a boy had been so positive, but I was told he was dangerous and that I shouldn't like him, so I forced myself to shut off my feelings. Then some of the people I was supposed to trust had turned out to be untrustworthy, and that had changed me in a way I didn't like.

And now here was Mark, a young man, performing on a stage, just like the stages on which I had performed. I wondered if he was an actor in his own life as I had been in mine. My mind swirled and spun. The blood on the stage spilled. I suddenly felt very overwhelmed, and I had to get away. The easiest escape was to simply fall asleep, which I did. When I woke up, the first act was over, the character Mark had played was dead, and I knew that there were some things I was going to have to start to face about myself as a young woman if I was going to have a full life.

It wouldn't be that day, but I knew I would have to eventually deal with my fear of men and boys and my belief that they would hurt me. After the show ended, I looked for Mark, but I didn't see him, and we were escorted on the bus to head back to Maine.

...

DURING ONE OF the final sessions, Mr. Furbush's class got onto the topic of intuition and knowing. Mr. Furbush, who often spoke of his wife and three young boys, told us a funny story about making out with his wife when she was still his girlfriend, then falling off the sofa onto the floor and announcing, "I'm going to marry you." I wanted to be healthy enough to have that. I wanted someone 'normal' to be so passionate about me that he would fall off a sofa and tell me, "I'm going to marry you."

In fact, a part of me wanted Mr. Furbush to be so passionate about me. However, I was infinitely more comfortable with him safely ensconced in his marriage and family. This was part of his appeal. He would never be like Matthew's friend Zaire, who I still believed had made that obscene phone call to me in San Francisco, because Mr. Furbush was devoted to his wife and children. As much as I wanted a relationship, I was hardly ready for one, and Mr. Furbush was safe. I could begin to learn 'normal' from a distance.

...

IN APRIL, I sat at the kitchen table, preparing the invitations for my graduation from high school. "Is your father getting one?" Martha asked.

"Yes," I said warily.

"Don't worry. I'm just asking. I just want to be prepared to see him there."

I was relieved.

She sat down in the chair next to mine and inspected some of the envelopes. "Maybe it'll be good to have you gone.

I've never been able to have a relationship because of you kids."

I didn't think I'd ever get used to the blunt way she could say things.

...

SONJA, WHO WAS Lutheran, took me to an overnight event at her church, during which we watched a video of the movie *Flatliners*, starring Julia Roberts and Kiefer Sutherland. In the movie, five medical students bring themselves near death to learn more about the afterlife. The film's premise is that death is not a pleasant experience if there are sins in our lives for which we haven't been forgiven; but, in *Flatliners*, the forgiveness comes in human form, not by God. That, to me, seemed like a controversial idea for a church youth group to present. Not to mention the film overflows with profanities, sexual innuendo, and a few gross scenes with cadavers. "Do they always play movies like this?" I asked Sonja.

"Yeah. They won't go too far, but they try to play movies that will make us ask questions about the Bible and what we believe."

"You mean they *want* you to question them?"

"Sure. That's the whole point. They don't want us to believe something just because our parents believe it. They want us to think about it."

That was a foreign concept to me. While my family had always given me permission to think for myself, I was keenly aware that there was always a right or wrong answer. Even with Mr. Furbush, when he posited his moral questions or asked us about literature, there was an answer he wanted, and if we didn't have it, we simply weren't correct. Much of the anxiety I felt had developed because those right answers the adults in my life offered had been so different. Sonja was at ease with her opinions, and I realized that's why we could banter back and forth as we did. She didn't mind me having different views because she was secure in hers. It strengthened my already high regard for her.

...

MARTHA HAD BOUGHT me a pair of leather dockside shoes. They looked quite trendy, and I was very pleased with them. It was the 'cool' style to let them get scuffed and holey, but I kept mine in pristine condition. In Mr. Furbush's classroom after school one day, I sat shining them. He watched me for a moment and then asked, "Why don't you let your shoes get roughed up like the other kids do?"

I wasn't sure if it was a question or a fashion suggestion. I said flatly, "Because I like them, and I want them to last. And, anyway, they're the only shoes I have that fit."

"But you can buy another pair when they wear out."

"But they'll last longer if I take care of them."

He shrugged. "Suit yourself."

I left shaking my head to myself and wondering why anyone would suggest I purposely wear out my shoes. Sometimes I just didn't get people. Under my breath, I muttered, "What am I? From another planet?" I stopped in my tracks realizing what an absurd thing I had just said. According to my father's claims, he *was* from another planet. *My* father said he was from another planet. My *father* said he was from another planet. My father said he was from another *planet*.

I let out a huge guffaw, one that was straight from my gut. For over a minute, I laughed so hard that tears rolled down my cheeks. My sides felt like they would burst. I doubled over with laughter. Finally, I got myself together and resumed walking. I imagined myself at my high school graduation, making introductions. *Please meet my father. He's from another planet. ...Nice to meet you, sir; what's your name? ...My name is God, the All-Knowing*

Greatness. ...Really? And what do you do? ...I'm a prophet. I levitate.
I smiled and said aloud, "What a world."

That day, I uninvited Matthew to my high school graduation. I didn't do it to punish him, and I'd frankly wished I hadn't invited him in the first place, so his feelings wouldn't be hurt. It's just that I realized that most of the good things that had happened in my life occurred in spite of him, not because of him. My graduation from high school was a good thing for me, and I didn't see how he should share in that when it wasn't his work or support that got me there. When it came down to it, Matthew was just a deadbeat dad with a God-complex. I would not let the damage he had done become permanent; I would let him go. It was somehow fitting that he was the one who had taught me that just because there is a familial tie, doesn't mean that one has to maintain the connection.

It was a bonus that Martha would not have to deal with him during graduation. After all, at least she stayed.

Chapter 41
Why the Water Was Invisible

Just before school ended, Mr. Furbush conducted an experiment. Many of the girls in class had complained that the boys talked over them and didn't let them express their views, so he held one class where the boys were not allowed to speak. As a response to being temporarily silenced, a boy in the class with whom I'd had a particularly acrimonious relationship, put up a sign that read "Lippa: Shut up." At first, I felt embarrassed, but then it occurred to me that I must have made some impact on him to have chosen me as a target. 'That's right,' I thought. 'Put up your sign. You may not like what I have to say, but I will never shut up.'

Sonja and I visited Mr. Furbush after school that day, mainly because I wanted to, as she was not such a big fan. As she and I stood before his desk, we playfully insulted one another.

Mr. Furbush looked at us with raised eyebrows. "You two must either love each other or hate each other."

Without missing a beat, Sonja and I glanced at one another and then turned back to Mr. Furbush. "We hate each other," we said in unison. Then we laughed as Mr. Furbush looked at us with a crooked smile.

One of the pretty girls asked me what I was going to do when I graduated. I told her that I was going to go to Sarah

Lawrence College and then head out to Los Angeles to be an actress. With palpable jealousy in her voice, she said, "You're probably gonna' end up like Meryl freakin' Streep." I was flabbergasted. It went to show that there's always something that someone else might envy in us, even as we're envying them.

I received a small leadership scholarship and a theatre scholarship from the local community playhouse. At graduation, Martha told me how proud she was of all I'd accomplished. She didn't have enough money for an expensive gift, so she had her old gold jewelry melted down into an ingot. I suspected, but did not ask, if the wedding ring Matthew had given her was in there. I hoped it was, as I liked the symbolism behind it; we were moving on. Whatever the case, the ingot was lovely.

...

IN THE SUMMER, the Samantha Smith foundation started a business internship program in the U.S. for young adults from the USSR. The Soviet Union was dissolving; the Cold War was over. I wished that Samantha could have seen it. And with that, I recognized the first non-jealous and non-guilty thought I had about her. It was a shame that she hadn't lived to see this just as it was a shame that Anne Frank hadn't lived to see how her words affected so many.

I had learned from my selfishness toward Samantha that there was room for the success and accomplishments of everyone. To be great, one doesn't have to make someone else small.

...

AS I NO longer had sticky fingers, I worked during the summer months at the same pharmacy from which I had once shoplifted. When the bill for the remainder of my college tuition came due, my earnings and scholarships weren't quite enough, so I cashed in a few fifty-dollar bonds I had received over the years. The teller told me, "You're not going to get as much as you would if you waited the whole twenty years."

"I need it now."

I pawned some jewelry. The only piece I cared about was the ingot, so that was something with which I would not part. Instead, I got rid of some rings and earrings. After all was said and done, I covered the bill with enough left over for a few books. I packed my well-worn script for *The Diary of Anne Frank* in my bag and then waited out the last week before college.

...

MARTHA WAS IN the kitchen washing dishes. She called to me, "What happened to the dirty dishes in the living room?"

I entered the kitchen and, despite the fact that her back was to me, I took a dramatic pose and exclaimed, "What happened in the green kitchen Sybil?"

"What?"

I relaxed my pose. "It's from the movie. Joanne Woodward's character says it when she sees Sybil cowering in the corner."

"I know what it's from. I don't want to hear it. I used to get enemas when I was a kid. It was awful."

I stood silently watching her for a moment, wondering if her tendency toward revising history had caused her to forget about my experiences with Tu-Tu. My heart and face softened. I walked across the kitchen and put my hand on her shoulder. "I know Mom. I'm sorry that happened to you."

"Thanks. What happened to the dirty dishes in the living room?"

I removed my hand from her shoulder and more lightheartedly said, "I brought them in already and put them in the sink. Do you want some help?"

"Sure."

After the dishes were done, and we were sitting at the kitchen table, I asked Martha "Is it okay if I leave my things here while I go off to college?"

She looked at me with concern. "Of course you can. You know, I've never felt like you thought of this as your home, Kate. I want you to know, you always have a place here."

We exchanged hugs, and then she said, "I have something for you." She stood up and took her keys off of the hook where they hung next to the front door. She fiddled with them for a moment and eventually was able to pull off the large cross made of railroad nails. "You know how you've always thought this was a cross?"

"Yes...," I said, a little confused.

"Well, it's really for self-defense. A friend of mine made it for me when I was eighteen." She then took it between her fingers like a mini-dagger. "If anyone tries to attack you, you just jam it up into the soft part of their throat, like this." She made an upswing motion with the cross. Then she handed it to me, and I sat there stunned. Yet again, something had not been as it appeared.

...

I ASKED TO borrow Martha's car for a while, and she obliged. "Be careful," she said.

"I will."

Although I had told her I would be running errands, I was in actuality making a mini-farewell tour of the places that had meant something to me over the years. The first stop was right up the street to Helena H. Dyer Elementary School. Decades before, the school had burned to the ground and been rebuilt. I wondered if the former students had the same feeling I had as I looked at brand new jungle gyms and a full wing expansion that had been constructed. The only thing constant is change.

Next up was the middle school, which I sat in front of for a few minutes. That place already felt like a world away, and I didn't see much point in prolonging the visit. On the way back, I decided to make my first ever trip to the cemetery where Martha's father was buried. As soon as I entered the gates, I realized how massive the place was. I figured I'd drive around for a while, and if I found his site so be it. I drove up three cemetery blocks and then turned left and stopped. I got out of the car, and before me was his grave. It was a peculiar feeling to realize I'd driven directly to the exact site. But then, coincidences are like that.

I sat for a while before his stone, plucking out weeds and telling him about myself. Tears filled my eyes and started running down my face. "I'm scared about going to college," I said aloud. "I feel like I'm a combination of an eight-year-old and an eighty-year-old, and I don't know if I'm going to fit in there any better than I do here." Then, a breeze swept by. The cool wind felt so good against my face. It felt like an answer, that everything was going to be okay. I looked up, and the sunrays were streaming down through the clouds.

I made a stop to see the Furbushes. Their three young sons played in the front yard, while I said my thank-yous and exchanged hugs. Martha was wrong about this one. Nice people didn't have to be boring, and happy people didn't have to be stupid.

Last on the tour was the high school, where I had gotten the part of Anne, where I had tried to stand up for the rights of women, and where I had learned that I had something to offer despite not having magical powers. I parked the car and got out, but when I checked the school's doors, they were locked. I was about to get back in the car when a teacher I recognized pulled up. It was one of the science teachers, not one of mine, but one

I'd seen around. I figured he must be going in to prepare for the new school year.

"What are you doing here?" he asked as he opened the back door of his car.

"Just saying 'see you' to the place before I head off to college."

"Where are you going?"

"Sarah Lawrence."

His eyes lit up. "Congratulations."

"Thanks."

He leaned into his backseat and struggled with some bankers boxes.

"Can I help you?" I asked.

"Sure."

As we entered the school, I noticed that there was an area where new construction had occurred over the summer.

"Changes," I said under my breath.

He had heard me. "Yep. Everything rolls along."

Soon, the imprint of my class would be gone, and there would be a whole new crop of students. As he pulled out his keys to open his classroom door, I asked, "Do you get sad when students graduate?"

"I used to. You get close to kids and then they're gone. But not anymore. We just do our best to teach them and send them off."

The teacher and I set down the boxes next to an empty fish tank on one of the counters.

"Huh," I said.

"What's that?"

"Nothing. I was just remembering this trick I saw when I was little. A magician put a tinfoil boat in a fish tank and it looked like it was floating, but there was no water inside."

"Sulfur hexafluoride."

"What?"

"It's a vapor. It behaves like water because it's heavier and denser than air."

"Oh."

"Most magic tricks are really science."

"I guess they are. Well, I suppose I'd better get going."

"Okay, thanks for your help. What was your name again?"

"Kate Lippa."

"Well, good luck Kate."

"Thank you."

I let myself out and drove back to Martha's house. As I hung up her keys, I said, "Thanks for letting me use the car."

"You're welcome. Did you get what you needed?"

"Yeah. I think so."

...

I HAD NEVER seen the Sarah Lawrence College campus before, never interviewed, never taken a tour. I was nervous the whole six-hour drive there. When we pulled into the tree-lined drive my eyes widened. It was beautiful and lush. I watched as students and parents unpacked cars and hugged and smiled and cried. There were lots of kids who looked awkward and gangly and lots of other kids who looked comfortable and eager and smart. There were a couple of Goths and a few handsome and pretty people. I smiled to myself with the thought that surely there was room for the likes of me there.

I glanced over at my mother. She was clearly impressed as well. "Look at that sculpture, Kate," she said pointing to the middle of the courtyard. "I wonder if a student did that. It's awesome." Her newfound excitement for me was a huge relief.

I could see a whole new world before me. I had no idea what it would turn out like, but it was mine. I would make my own decisions from now on. I would choose my own classes. I would choose my friends. I would choose my beliefs. I would make my life the best it could possibly be. It was a fresh start, a new beginning. It was better than a do-over because I didn't have to live my whole life again. I had allowed myself another chance. After so many years of feeling like I had done everything wrong, I had, in the end, done something right.

Acknowledgements

This book would not have been possible without the daily encouragement of Andrew Tavoni; I am ever grateful for his compassion and friendship. I would also like to express my appreciation to Rhona Berens, who helped me turn the dream of writing a book into a tangible goal, and to Patricia Sutherland, who supported me the whole way through and who offered precious feedback on the manuscript in multiple stages. Special thanks to the magnificent editor Jen Howard for her critique of the first draft. Thank you also to Craig Furbush and Ernie Geballe for reviewing various drafts. Thank you to Harvey Wasserman, Sonja Starins and Steven Rowley for their comments and recommendations. Thank you to my friend, the wonderful writer Mike Meredith, whose support and creativity has influenced this and so many other projects. Thank you to Andrew Wallace for his kindness and invaluable participation in this process. To the numerous peers, friends and family members who cheered me on throughout, I cannot thank you enough. And, last but never least, to my mother, the person who first suggested I write this book and a true source of inspiration.

About the Author

Katherine Lippa is the author of several short stories, scripts and essays. *Hiding in Water* is her first full-length book. She is a graduate of Sarah Lawrence College, where her focus was on Writing as well as Science, Technology & Society (a field of study that grew out of the Cold War and the need to understand the cyclical effect of science and technology on society). In addition to her work as a writer, she is an accomplished public speaker. Her website is www.lippalogic.com.

CPSIA information can be obtained at www.ICGtesting.com
Printed in the USA
LVOW05s0100040114

368032LV00018B/666/P